SAGE was founded in 1965 by Sara Miller McCune to support the dissemination of usable knowledge by publishing innovative and high-quality research and teaching content. Today, we publish over 900 journals, including those of more than 400 learned societies, more than 800 new books per year, and a growing range of library products including archives, data, case studies, reports, and video. SAGE remains majority-owned by our founder, and after Sara's lifetime will become owned by a charitable trust that secures our continued independence.

Los Angeles | London | New Delhi | Singapore | Washington DC | Melbourne

AGRICULTURAL FACTOR MARKETS AND INDIA'S SMALL FARMERS

AGRICULTURAL FACTOR MARKETS AND INDIA'S SMALL FARMERS

EDITED BY

ANUP KUMAR DAS | BINOY GOSWAMI
MADHURJYA PRASAD BEZBARUAH

SAGE

Los Angeles | London | New Delhi
Singapore | Washington DC | Melbourne

First published in 2022 by

SAGE Publications India Pvt Ltd
B1/I-1 Mohan Cooperative Industrial Area
Mathura Road, New Delhi 110 044, India
www.sagepub.in

SAGE Publications Inc
2455 Teller Road
Thousand Oaks, California 91320, USA

SAGE Publications Ltd
1 Oliver's Yard, 55 City Road
London EC1Y 1SP, United Kingdom

SAGE Publications Asia-Pacific Pte Ltd
18 Cross Street #10-10/11/12
China Square Central
Singapore 048423

Published by Vivek Mehra for SAGE Publications India Pvt Ltd and typeset in 10.5/13 pt Bembo by AG Infographics, Delhi.

Library of Congress Control Number: 2022937675

ISBN: 978-93-5479-233-5 (HB)

SAGE Team: Amrita Dutta, Syed Husain Naqvi and Rajinder Kaur

Contents

List of Illustrations

FIGURES

TABLES

List of Abbreviations

AMC	ATMA management committee
APMA	Agricultural Produce Marketing Act
APMCs	Agricultural Produce Market Committees
APMR	Agricultural Produce Markets Regulation
ATMA	Agricultural Technology Management Agency
ATS	Agricultural technology system
BTT	Block technology teams
CBOs	Community-based organizations
CBVZ	Central Brahmaputra Valley Zone
CCIS	Comprehensive Crop Insurance Scheme
CGWB	Central Groundwater Board
CHSCs	Custom hiring service centres
COVID-19	Coronavirus disease 2019
CWC	Central Warehousing Corporation
FAC	Farmer Advisory Committee
FCI	Food Corporation of India
FFI	Formal financial institutions
FIAC	Farm Information and Advisory Centre
FIGs	Farmers' Interest Groups
GATT	General Agreement on Tariffs and Trade
GDP	Gross domestic product
GIC	General Insurance Company
GoI	Government of India
HYVs	High-yielding varieties
ICAR	Indian Council of Agricultural Research
ICTs	Information and communication technologies
ITD	Innovation in Technology Dissemination
KVC	Krishi Vigyan Kendra
LARR Act	Land Acquisition, Rehabilitation and Resettlement Act

MFIs	Microfinance institutions
MGNREGA	Mahatma Gandhi National Rural Employment Guarantee Act
MLAIS	Modified National Agricultural Insurance Scheme
MSP	Minimum support price
NABARD	National Bank for Agriculture and Rural Development
NAIS	National Agricultural Insurance Scheme
NATP	National Agricultural Technology Project
NCIP	National Crop Insurance Programme
NFBCs	Non-banking finance companies
NFHS	National Family Health Survey
NFSA	National Food Security Act
NGOs	Non-governmental organizations
NITI	National Institution for Transforming India
NSS	National Sample Survey
NSSO	National Sample Survey Office
PCIS	Pilot Crop Insurance Scheme
PMFBY	Pradhan Mantri Fasal Bima Yojana
RBI	Reserve Bank of India
RRBs	Regional Rural Banks
RWS	Reference weather station
SAUs	State agricultural universities
SBLP	SHG Bank Linage Programme
SGA	State government agencies
SHG	Self-help groups
SIA	Social impact assessment
SIDBI	Small Industries Development Bank of India
SKDRDP	Shri Kshetra Dharmastala Rural Development Project
SREP	Strategic research and extension plan
STW	Shallow tube wells
SWCs	State Warehousing Corporations
TE	Technical efficiency
TV	Television
UP	Uttar Pradesh
WBCIS	Weather-Based Crop Insurance Scheme
WEDs	Water extracting devices
ZRS	Zonal research station

Preface

It is well known that in the structural transformation that accompanies the development process of an economy, the share of agriculture in the country's gross domestic product (GDP) steadily declines. The diminishing share, however, if anything, only understates the importance of the sector in a country. Countries, both developing and developed, are rather sensitive about their farming and farmers. Even highly developed countries such as the United States, Japan and South Korea are steadfast on protecting their farmers and farming by even giving economically unjustifiable subsidies and/or protecting the sector from external competition. By doing so, countries intend to maintain some degree of self-sufficiency in food production; as such, self-sufficiency is considered to be strategically important. It is, therefore, no surprise that international trade on agriculture could be introduced under General Agreement on Tariffs and Trade (GATT) negotiations only in the Uruguay Round. The world trade talks have since had several deadlocks as countries stuck to their respective stances while negotiating over the implementation of the Agreement on Agriculture.

Given the high importance assigned by countries to their agriculture, despite the sector's declining share in GDP and workforce, it is not surprising that agriculture continues to claim a fair share of coverage in economic literature. However, it seems that production- and marketing-related issues have drawn much more attention from agricultural economists than those concerning factor markets. Notwithstanding some age-old and often reopened debates on topics such as inefficiency of sharecropping, farm size and productivity, treatment of agricultural factor markets in the literature remains thin in several areas. For instance, working and implications of relatively new markets such as the water market and markets for rental services of farm capital goods have not yet been adequately and extensively explored. Incompleteness and imperfections of the factor markets can seriously limit the economic outcomes of individual farmers and, in the aggregate, the performance of the entire agricultural sector. Furthermore, though intersectionality among the different factor markets, especially in the agricultures of developing and less developed countries, is well recognized, their full implications can easily escape attention of a reader when different factor markets are discussed in isolation. The need for bringing together the discussions on the different factor markets in one place was thus felt, and this volume was planned.

However, it would have been an unwieldy attempt to combine factor markets in agriculture all over the world, for the simple reason that socio-economic, physiographic and climatic set-ups in which farmers of different countries/regions operate widely differ from one another. It was accordingly decided to limit the geographical scope of the book to India only.

Preparing the manuscript was relatively easy, as the contributors are known to each other and have been working on different aspects of agricultural economies in India. Reviewer(s) engaged by the publisher to comment on the first draft gave very useful suggestions, all of which have been incorporated in the finally submitted manuscript. We place on record our gratitude to the anonymous reviewer(s) for comments and suggestions. We are greatly thankful to SAGE for accepting the manuscript for publication. We specially acknowledge Amrita Dutta from the SAGE family who has been invariably congenial, cooperative and understanding in our journey together in creating the volume.

Editors

Chapter 1

Introduction

Binoy Goswami, Anup Kumar Das and
Madhurjya Prasad Bezbaruah

Agriculture in India, as in most developing countries, is organized with farm households as the basic production units. But farm households rarely possess different factors of production in the optimal proportions. While only a small proportion of rural households own large plots of farmland, landless, marginal and smallholders constitute the majority of the rural population. When it comes to labour, small and marginal farmers usually have more manpower in their possession relative to the land that they own. The pattern of transactions in the markets for leasing of land (land rental markets) and the rural labour markets has been traditionally playing the role of optimizing the land–labour ratios across larger and smaller farm households. As agriculture in the country has modernized with the adoption of newer technologies and progressive mechanization of farming operations, factor markets in agriculture have also expanded in numbers and transaction volumes.

Take the case of farm machineries and equipment, such as tractors, power tillers, irrigation pump sets and harvesters. As acquiring such machines requires lumpy investments, only farmers with access to the necessary financial resources, owned or borrowed, can afford to procure them. Small and marginal farmers rarely have access to enough resources to be able to own such capital equipment. Moreover, given the small scale of their operations, it does not make sense for the small farmers to procure machineries such as a tractor, which require a certain minimum scale for their proper utilization (Sharma and Goswami 2020). But rental markets of farm machineries and equipment have now emerged to enable even the small and marginal farmers to mechanize their operations. Farmers who do not possess these machineries can now hire them from those who invest in these machines and are willing to give them on rent when the same are not in use in their own farms (Ray 2011).

Another form of factor markets found in contemporary Indian agriculture is the water markets, where farmers with access to irrigation water source sell their spare irrigation water to those who are in short supply of water. Although water markets have also been playing a useful role, their possible adverse environmental impacts in the form of depletion of groundwater resource have attracted close scrutiny of researchers.

In short, without the factor markets, rural households will have to work with unbalanced input ratios, resulting in suboptimal farming outcomes. Effective factor markets can ensure more efficient utilization of farm resources by optimizing factor ratios across farm households. By the same token, incompleteness and imperfections of the factor markets can inhibit farmers from optimal utilization of resources, which in the aggregate can limit performance of the whole agriculture sector.

It is further worth noting that market for one input can also act as a means of adjustment for other input(s). For example, land lease market can not only adjust the ratio of land to family labour, but it can also adjust the landholding size that suits the bullock power possessed (Kuri 2003). Birthal and Singh (1991) also reiterate that a temporary transfer of farmland through the land tenancy system is a useful adjustment mechanism that corrects imbalances in the endowments of various resources. As long as there is a variation in the marginal products of land, labour and other factors of production, factor market transactions can be mutually beneficial (Lin 1995).

Agricultural factor markets may also help in reducing income inequality in rural societies. Benjamin and Brandt (1997) provide historical evidence from rural China that suggests that wherever the land lease markets were active, excess return to land was reduced, which in turn reduced income inequality.

By allowing adjustment in factor endowments, factor markets can promote occupational mobility as well (NITI Aayog 2016). For instance, there may be some households that own some lands but are not interested or do not possess the skills required for farm activities. In the presence of land lease markets, such households can lease out the lands and use their other resources in the non-farm activities. This in turn can bring about overall rural and economic development.

It is interesting to note that agricultural factor markets in India (and perhaps elsewhere too) have often emerged, evolved and developed spontaneously, responding to the need of the situations. Lin (1995) views the emergence of rental markets in response to unequal factor endowment across production entities as an illustration of induced innovation in the institution. According to the induced institutional innovation hypothesis, suitable institutions are innovated in order to organize economic agents efficiently for realizing untapped profitable opportunities. Imbalance in factor endowments across households presents such opportunities. For illustration, let us take the cases of the following rental markets in India. The Indian State attempted to address issues related to imbalances in ownership and user rights over agricultural land through elaborate respective land reform programmes. This approach has been one of the notable and disruptive direct interventions aimed at achieving efficiency and equity in the use of agricultural lands. Land reforms are of course often politically and legally difficult to enforce and, hence, land reform programmes have been rarely implemented in totality. Moreover, such institutional interventions cannot be resorted to frequently, which render this form of interventions somewhat inflexible. However, while formal institutional changes occur infrequently and in a disruptive manner, markets often emerge gradually and organically in response to the need of the economy, and adapt continuously to changing conditions, performing roles that formal institutions have failed to fulfil. Notwithstanding the official ban on leasing of land in many states in India, the land rental markets have been active all along throughout the country. The second illustration is related to the use of machineries and equipment in farms. While the owner of a tractor can lease out its unutilized capacity and earn some income, a small farmer can rent the service of the tractor without having to own it. Consequently, the rental market of tractors and other farm machineries emerged. In this context, it may be mentioned that these markets, by facilitating the hiring of services of agricultural capital goods, can eliminate the constraints that farm size imposes on productivity and income generation. Goswami (2016) shows this by using field survey data from Assam in eastern India. Rental markets of farm machineries and equipment, despite being a late addition to agricultural factor markets, have a significant presence now in different parts of India. Thus, the above-mentioned two examples of rental markets show how market institutions emerge on their own to harness profitable opportunities.

Similar to the markets for primary farm inputs, markets for various agricultural support services play a significant role in augmenting performance of farms through the adoption of production and productivity-enhancing practices and the realization of a good value for farmers' efforts and enterprise. The enabling role that credit, insurance, extension services, post-harvest management and marketing opportunities play in agriculture is well documented (Boss and Pradhan 2020; NITI Aayog 2017; Samah et al. 2009; Swain 2013; Swamy 1980). While short-term credit is of use for meeting farmers' working capital needs, medium- and long-term credit is virtually essential for farmers to invest in capital goods, land improvement, irrigation systems and storage structures. Insurance can play a major role in stabilizing farmers' income, which is subject to nature-induced volatilities. Climate change is likely to aggravate farmers' exposure to such uncertainties in the future (Goswami 2018). Extension services enable the adoption of better farm practices and diffusion of new technology. On the other hand, the presence of effective post-harvest value chains can reduce crop losses due to rotting and mishandling. Besides directly contributing to farmers' incomes, the existence of a strong post-harvest management system can incentivize farmers to diversify to high-value horticultural and livestock products. Incompleteness or thinness of markets for related services of credit, insurance and marketing also deserves more incisive examination, especially in the context of small farm agriculture, which is often constrained by insufficiency of access to such services. The sociopolitical hierarchies of India's rural set-up that interfere with the functioning of these economic institutions also deserve cognizance in the analysis of efficacy and adequacy of the agricultural factor markets in the country.

Discussion on different agricultural factor markets in the existing literature is uneven in coverage and depth. The literature on the markets for farmland and labour is voluminous. The water markets and their environmental implications have also received fairly elaborate attention of researchers. Being a relatively new addition to agricultural factor markets, the rental markets for farm machineries and equipment are yet to be explored in detail. On the other hand, the literature has fairly extensively dealt with the evolution in the supporting services of rural credit, agricultural insurance, extension services and post-harvest management of farm products. However, more often than not, each of these markets are discussed in isolation, thereby missing the complementarity and intersectionality that exist among the different factor markets. The interconnectedness of these markets implies that imperfection in one market can easily spill over to another market. Hence, a comprehensive perspective of all these markets is called for. The present volume aspires to bring together the currently dispersed analyses and discourses on the different factor markets related to agriculture for exploring the interconnectedness of these markets and developing a comprehensive perspective on the agricultural factor market system, including the markets for the supporting services.

Several of the emerging factor markets such as water markets and rental markets for farm machineries have a special significance for smaller farmers. Had it not been for the emergence of these markets, small farmers all over India would be using key inputs today, like water and farm machineries, less extensively. Because of this, the book has a ready relevance to agriculture in India's small farms. That does not, however, limit the relevance of the book for Indian agriculture as a whole. Indeed, none of the chapters have been written specifically for the small farmers, and most of the contentions of the book are relevant for farmers of all size classes. Yet the fact remains that the average size of operational landholdings of farms in India has been steadily declining over time to the extent that, today, an overwhelming majority of Indian farmers falls in the small and marginal farm size category.[1] As per *All India Report on Agriculture Census 2015–2016* (Government of India 2020), marginal and smallholdings together accounted for 86 per cent of the total number of operational holdings. Further, the holdings, big or small, are often fragmented. While the average size of holding in 2016–2017 was recorded as 1.08 hectares, the average area of parcels was only 0.54 hectare (Government of India 2021). The falling average size of agricultural holdings and growing number of farm households slipping into the category of marginal farmers is often cited in the literature as an indicator of agrarian crisis that afflicted rural India in the 1990s (Reddy and Mishra 2010). However, a more recent turn of events indicates that the outlook need not necessarily be bleak for the multitudes of India's small farmers. The structural transformation of the Indian economy in terms of occupational shift of its workforce from agriculture to non-agricultural occupations has quickened since around the turn of the century (from the 20th to the 21st). The report of the National Family Health Survey 5, 2021, shows that fertility rates in both rural and urban India have declined discernibly in recent times, giving credence to the forecast that India's population is headed towards stabilization in the next quarter of a century. Both these developments are expected to substantially reduce the pressure of population on agricultural land and thereby put a break on the process of progressive fragmentation of farm holdings. The emergence of new factor markets has now broken down some of the rigidities and indivisibilities of agriculture, which kept smallholders

[1] As per the Reserve Bank of India's Circular No. RBI/2007–2008/330 (RPCD.No.PLFS.BC.72/05.04.02/2007-08) dated 23 May 2008, a farmer cultivating agricultural land up to 1 hectare is classified as a marginal farmer, and the one cultivating more than 1 hectare but not more than 2 hectares is counted in the category of small farmers.

away from using superior inputs and techniques earlier. The National Institution for Transforming India (NITI) Aayog, the official think tank of the Government in India, is now calling for reforms of tenancy laws, which will allow the land rental markets operate more freely, enabling unviable farms to exit the sector and remaining farms to upscale their operations (NITI Aayog 2016). Thus, both demographic trends and factor market evolutions have brightened up the scenario somewhat for India's small farmers. The readers will find this perspective running through several chapters of this book.

This book is a collection of 11 chapters. Chapters 2–6 discuss various dimensions of the markets of primary factors of agricultural production. Chapters 2 and 3 deal with issues related to the most important factor of agricultural production, that is, land. Chapter 2 explores some emerging issues of agricultural land rental markets in India. Using data from two relevant recent rounds of the National Sample Survey, the chapter discusses the trends and patterns of rental arrangements of agricultural land at the national level and across states and reports two interesting facts. First, the extent of tenancy has increased in almost all states. Second, fixed rent is now the dominant form of tenancy contract at the national level and in many states. The chapter discusses the tenancy reform measures adopted in the country and evaluates their impact. In view of the changing agro-economic realities of the countryside and the undesired outcomes that have resulted from the existing tenancy laws, the chapter suggests a reform in tenancy laws in terms of separation of use and ownership rights of land.

Being completely inelastic in total supply, land may become increasingly scarce with the progress of development, as demand for non-agricultural use of land is expected to expand rapidly in the process. Although the share of agriculture in India's gross domestic product (GDP) has declined to a fairly low level, agriculture retains its importance in the Indian economy from the consideration of food security and its various other roles. Against this background, Chapter 3 examines the possibility of transfer of agricultural land for non-agricultural use. The chapter looks into the nature of the land sale market in rural India and its implications for deciding on compensations for acquired land with reference to market-determined prices of land. Finally, the attempts and suggestions for reforming the framework of land acquisition and transfer in the country are discussed.

Agricultural labour market facilitates the transfer of manpower from labour-surplus households to farm labour-deficient households. Manpower scarcity adversely impacts many dimensions of cultivation such as crop establishment, growth of the crops, use of fertilizers, weeding and irrigation (Gunabhagya et al. 2017; Satishkumar and Umesh 2018). Further, a scarcity of manpower has negative effects on crop yield and cropping intensity that result in the loss of production and productivity in the agricultural sector (Prabakar et al. 2011). By making available the required manpower to labour-scarce farm households, agricultural labour market can raise agricultural production and productivity. Chapter 4 discusses the structure and functioning of the agricultural labour market in India with due considerations of the recent changes that have unfolded in the farm and non-farm sectors. Analysis in the chapter shows that agricultural labour constitutes a significant proportion of agricultural workforce, and its share is increasing over the years. Agricultural labour markets in India are largely casual and fragmented in nature. Further, such markets are segmented and localized. Interlocking with other factor markets like the land-lease market and credit market is another important characteristic of agricultural labour market in India. The chapter also examines the impact of Mahatma Gandhi National Rural Employment Guarantee Act (MGNREGA) on the labour market and finds that the programme has had some impact on the functioning of the agricultural labour market in terms of labour force participation, scarcity of labour and wages.

The role that irrigation plays in agricultural development does not require any explanation. Irrigation raises cropping intensity (Dhawan and Datta 1992; Karunakaran and Palanisami 1998) and productivity (Dayal 1984) and facilitates the cultivation of a diversified crop portfolio (Goswami 2012). However, provisioning of controlled water supply confronts several challenges. Dutta (2007) identifies that small and fragmentized landholdings constrain fuller utilization of potential created through the installation of shallow tube wells (STWs) in Assam.

Farmers' investment in the irrigation machinery is also adversely affected by small and fragmented holdings (Dobbs and Foster 1972; Shah and Ballabh 1997). Water market can play a useful role in providing irrigation in agrarian economies, characterized by the preponderance of small and fragmented landholdings, where government's initiatives in this regard are inadequate. Chapter 5 discusses some pressing issues concerning the groundwater markets in India. Based on the available literature, secondary data and a case study in Assam, the study finds that water markets are quite active and extensive in Indian agriculture. Although the nature and functioning of the water market are found to be similar across different regions in the country, there are some variations in its mode of operation, depending on geo-climatic, economic and social conditions.

As discussed earlier, small and fragmented landholdings cause a serious constraint on the use of non-divisible farm machinery such as tractor, power tiller and pump set. However, the presence of rental markets eliminates the constraint by separating the flow of services from ownership and thereby allows the farmers with poor economic condition and/or landholdings of small and marginal size to use such machineries as per their requirement (Das and Bezbaruah 2017). Additionally, through better capacity utilization, rental markets of farm capital goods encourage their ownership and use as well. Chapter 6 analyses the extent and nature of functioning of rental markets of farm machinery and equipment, their contribution to farm production and the limitations of these markets. Analysis, based on secondary data, reveals that the rental markets of farm capital goods are in operation in different parts of India and have expanded over time. These markets have facilitated farm mechanization and contributed to agricultural production and productivity. However, these markets are not free from imperfections. Further, the functioning of these markets depends on the presence of markets for other factors of production like credit.

Chapters 7–10 examine the issues of the markets for supporting services in agriculture, namely extension, credit, insurance, and post-harvest management and marketing. Extension service is an important supporting service for farm operation, and its significance can be understood from the contribution that it made towards the success of the Green Revolution in India. Chapter 7 analyses the status of and challenges confronting the agricultural extension in India. Analysis, based on data from the 77th round of the National Sample Survey and the Situation Assessment Survey, 2013, shows that notwithstanding regional variations, a substantial proportion of farm households, especially marginal and small, does not access extension services mainly due to non-availability and lack of awareness about extension facilities available. Further, public extension is the least preferred source of extension. Through econometric analysis, the chapter identifies the factors that affect the decision of farm households regarding accessing extension as well as their choice of the source of extension service. The chapter provides an important suggestion that the provisioning of public extension must be improved in terms of inclusiveness and quantity, as well as quality of manpower.

The choice of the source of extension services and the use of inputs depend on the financial conditions of the farmers. Poor economic conditions force many farmers to depend on borrowed money for farming activities. Swamy (1980) suggests that access to credit is an essential prerequisite, especially for the small farmers, to realize the potential of modern technologies. The credit market also plays an important role in the functioning and spread of various agricultural input markets. For instance, participation in the rental market of farm capital goods is encouraged by the access to credit (Das 2016). Various issues concerning agricultural credit in India are discussed in Chapter 8. This chapter, based on secondary data and review of existing literature, analyses the extent of penetration of agricultural credit in India over the years and the shares of different sources in agricultural credit. The discussion in the chapter suggests that due to information asymmetry and inflexibility, the formal financial institutions cannot efficiently work in the rural credit market. On the other hand, perfect information regarding their clients and flexibility is the main cause behind the dominance of informal sources in the rural credit market. Further, the chapter discusses different government policies and programmes that have been adopted to promote financial inclusion.

Access to credit alone is not sufficient to promote investment in agricultural activities. Farmers in India face risk and uncertainty on a regular basis due to susceptibility of agriculture to various risks. Instability of farm output and income often affects a farmer's well-being. From the perspective of long-term well-being of the farmers, it is therefore desirable that formal insurance coverage is made available to them. Despite government's various policy initiatives over the past four decades, the market for crop and other agricultural insurance has remained scanty all over the country. Chapter 9 discusses the issues related to the crop insurance market with the goal of finding a way for better insulation of farmers' well-being from shocks and uncertainties. The discussion at the national level is supplemented with the findings from a field survey in two pockets of the Brahmaputra Valley of Assam. The analysis of field survey data reveals that none of the farmers are aware of the various crop insurance schemes promoted by the government, though there is no dearth of demand for crop insurance among farmers.

Post-harvest management plays an important role in determining farmers' income. By giving better control over products in terms of the time and place of selling, product differentiation, etc., post-harvest management contributes to both value generation and value distribution (Boss and Pradhan 2020). Chapter 10 discusses different steps involved in the post-harvest management of farm products and the status of such a system in Indian agriculture. The chapter also points out to the areas where reforms are due, particularly in the marketing of farm products of the country.

Based on the discussions on various issues concerning the factor markets of primary inputs and supporting services, the final chapter (Chapter 11) provides a comprehensive discussion on essential and probable policy interventions that are required to ensure efficient functioning of the factor markets. It highlights the imperfections that plague the functioning of these markets and also suggests the policy interventions required to overcome those challenges. The chapter stresses on the point that these markets are interconnected, and hence, policy interventions should be undertaken in a holistic manner. In this context, some of the important policy recommendations made are as follows: subsidization of premium for crop insurance, innovation in mechanism for delivery of the insurance service at the grassroots, strengthening of the extension service network, strengthening the post-harvest value chain and keeping these markets free from politically motivated distortions.

The book provides a comprehensive discussion on issues related to markets of prime factors and those for the major supporting services, and thereby fills a big gap that currently exists in the literature. Besides gathering insights from the available data and literature, the authors of this volume supplement their analysis, wherever possible, with field-based work also. Thus, the analysis in the book reflects the agro-economic realities of the countryside. Anyone with interest in Indian agriculture may find the book useful.

REFERENCES

Benjamin, Dwayne, and L. Brantd. 1997. 'Land, Factor Markets, and Inequality in Rural China: Historical Evidence'. *Explorations in Economic History* 34, no. 4: 460–494.

Birthal, Pratap Singh, and R. P. Singh. 1991. 'Land-Lease Market, Resource Adjustment and Agricultural Development'. *Indian Journal of Agricultural Economics* 46, no. 3: 361–368.

Boss, Ruchira, and M. Pradhan. 2020. 'Post-harvest Management and Farm Outcomes'. *Economic & Political Weekly* 55, no. 16. https://www.epw.in/journal/2020/16/commentary/post-harvest-management-and-farm-outcomes.html (accessed on 21 February 2022).

Das, Anup Kumar 2016. 'Impact of Access to Credit on Rental Markets of Agricultural Capital Goods: Evidence from Assam of North-East India'. *Bangladesh Development Studies* 39, no. 1–2: 83–101.

Das, Anup Kumar, and M. P. Bezbaruah. 2017. 'Rental Markets of Agricultural Capital Goods as Substitute of Consolidation of Holdings: An Investigation in the Brahmaputra Valley of Assam'. *Journal of Land and Rural Studies* 5, no. 2: 120–139.

Dayal, Edison. 1984. 'Agricultural Productivity in India: A Spatial Analysis'. *Annals of the Association of American Geographers* 74, no. 1: 98–123.

Dobbs, T., and P. Foster. 1972. 'Incentives to Invest in New Agricultural Inputs in North India'. *Economic Development and Cultural Change* 21, no. 1: 101–117.

Dhawan, B. D., and Harsharan Singh Datta. 1992. 'Impact of Irrigation on Multiple Cropping'. *Economic & Political Weekly* 27, no. 13: A15–A18.

Dutta, Mrinal Kanti. 2007. 'Management of Groundwater Irrigation in Assam through Water Markets'. *The ICFAI Journal of Environmental Economics* 5, no. 4: 28–43.

Goswami, Binoy. 2012. *Economic Implications of Tenancy: A Study in Assam's Agrarian Set-up*. Unpublished Thesis. Guwahati, India: Gauhati University.

———. 2016. 'Overcoming Farm Size Induced Constraints through Endogenous Institutional Innovations: Findings from a Field Study in Assam plains, India'. *Economics Bulletin* 36, no. 1: 411–428.

———. 2018. 'Introduction'. In *Indian Agriculture after the Green Revolution: Changes and Challenges*, edited by B. Goswami, M. P. Bezbaruah, and R. Mandal, 1–7. New York, NY: Routledge.

Government of India. 2020. *All India Report on Agriculture Census 2015–16*. Department of Agriculture, Cooperation and Farmers Welfare. https://agcensus.nic.in/document/agcen1516/ac_1516_report_final-220221.pdf (accessed on 1 September 2021).

———. 2021. *All India Report on Input Survey 2016–17*. http://agcensus.nic.in/document/is2016/air_is_16-17_210121-final_220221.pdf (accessed on 23 June 2021).

Gunabhagya, A. T. Joshi, S. S. Patil, and G. N. Maraddi. 2017. 'Agricultural Labour Shortage: An Abysmal to Agriculture in North Eastern Karnataka'. *Economic Affairs* 62, no. 4: 589–594.

Karunakaran, K. R., and K. Palanisami. 1998. 'An Analysis of Impact of Irrigation on Cropping Intensity in Tamil Nadu'. *Indian Economic Review* 33, no. 2: 207–220.

Kuri, Pravat Kumar. 2003. 'Factor Market Imperfections and Explanations of Tenancy: Testing of an Econometric Model Using Evidence from Assam of Northeast India'. *Indian Journal of Agricultural Economics* 58, no. 2: 234–245.

Lin, Justin Yifu. 1995. 'Endowments, Technology, and Factor Markets: A Natural Experiment of Induced Institutional Innovation from China's Rural Reform'. *American Journal of Agricultural Economics* 77, no. 2: 231–242.

NITI Aayog. 2016. *Report of the Expert Committee on Land Leasing*. New Delhi, India: NITI Aayog.

———. 2017. *India: Three Year Action Agenda 2017–18 to 2019–20*. New Delhi: NITI Aayog.

Prabakar, C., K. S. Devi, and S. Selvam. 2011. 'Labour Scarcity: Its Immensity and Impact on Agriculture'. *Agricultural Economics Research Review* 24: 373–380.

Ray, Debraj. 2011. *Development Economics*. New Delhi: Oxford University Press.

Reddy N., and Srijit Mishra. 2010. *Agrarian Crisis in India*. New Delhi: Oxford University Press.

Samah, B. A., H. A. M. Shaffril, M. S. Hassan, M. A. Hassan, and N. Ismail. 2009. 'Contribution of Information and Communication Technology in Increasing Agro-based Entrepreneurs Productivity in Malaysia'. *Journal of Agriculture and Social Sciences* 5, no. 3: 93–98.

Satishkumar, M., and K. B. Umesh. 2018. 'Farmers Strategies to Cope Labour Shortage inNorthern and Southern Dry Zones of Karnataka, India'. *Current Agriculture Research Journal* 6, no. 2: 206–212.

Shah, Tushaar, and Vishwa Ballabh. 1997. 'Water Markets in North Bihar Six Village Studies in Muzaffarpur District'. *Economic & Political Weekly* 32, no. 52: A183–A190.

Sharma, Krishna, and B. Goswami. 2020. 'Rental Market of Pump-sets in the Central and Western Parts of Nepal Plains'. *Asia Pacific Journal of Rural Development* 30, no. 1–2: 226–243.

Swain, M. 2013. 'Agricultural Risk and Efficiency of Crop Insurance Schemes in Odisha'. In *Agrarian Crisis in India: The Way Forward,* edited by Suman Chandra, K. V. Suresh Babu, and P. K. Nath. New Delhi: Academic Foundation.

Swamy, Dilip S. 1980. 'Land and Credit Reforms in India: Part One'. *Social Scientist* 8, no. 11: 3–13.

Chapter 2

Land Market I

Realities and Suggested Reforms in Rental Arrangement

Binoy Goswami and Maheshwar Giri

2.1. INTRODUCTION

As discussed in Chapter 1, rural households rarely possess land and labour in right proportions (Goswami 2018a). While some households may have more farm workers than that can be gainfully accommodated on their owned land, the opposite may be the case for some other households. Land rental markets through tenancy contracts can facilitate better matching of the factors of production. Thus, the rental markets of land have important implications for the efficient and equitable use of land and other resources. In the absence of rental markets, households with excess labour may not find additional land to work on, or households with excess land may not be able to lease out land. Consequently, land, labour and other resources will remain underutilized. Well-functioning land rental markets can bring about equilibrium in resource endowments across households and thereby ensure efficient utilization of the means of production. Besides, by providing access to land, the rental markets can potentially deliver an egalitarian distribution of cultivable land in terms of its use.

Land rental markets also have implications for occupational mobility and, overall, rural and economic development (NITI Aayog 2016). There may be some households that primarily earn livelihood in the non-farm sector and also own some agricultural land at the same time. Rental markets allow such households to lease out the agricultural land, if they wish to do so, and devote entire resources to non-farm activity. In the absence of the rental markets, such households will either keep the land idle or cling on to it, resulting in the inefficient use of land. Occupational mobility that the rental markets can bring about in turn contributes to rural economic transformation.

In addition to the issues discussed earlier, the agricultural land rental market in India has assumed greater importance now than before for another reason. Fragmentation of landholdings has been on the rise in India. In 2012–2013, about 85 per cent of landholdings were of marginal and small sizes(Goswami 2018b). Consequently, Indian agriculture, today, confronts a viability crisis (Sharma and Malik 2021). The continuous fall in the average size of landholdings across size classes in different states is a testimony to this crisis. The preponderance of small and marginal holdings also implies that there is very little scope for land reforms through redistribution of ownership of land. Instead, improving access to land for the purpose of cultivation through tenancy arrangements seems more practical now. Improved access to land will help in increasing the scale of operation and thereby in overcoming the viability crisis. It is in this context that the functioning of land rental markets can contribute to better utilization of agricultural lands and hence assume larger significance today than before. In view of this, the chapter explores the issues related to agricultural land rental markets in India.

There exist a large number of studies on land rental markets in India that have been discussed in section 2.2. The present chapter, however, throws light on some recent developments that have occurred in the land rental market in India. The implications of these developments have been discussed as well.

The rest of the chapter is organized as follows. Section 2.2 critically discusses the relevant existing literature. Section 2.3 analyses the trends and patterns of tenancy arrangements at the national level and across states. Analysis in section 2.3 shows that fixed rent tenancy is now the dominant contract in India and also in many states. Section 2.4 provides a discussion on the reasons for this development based on the existing literature. Section 2.5 evaluates the existing tenancy laws and their impacts, and discusses the reforms required in this regard. Section 2.6 concludes this chapter.

2.2. IMPLICATIONS OF THE FORMS OF LEASING ARRANGEMENT: A DISCUSSION OF THE EXISTING ISSUES

Land occupies a key role in agriculture, in the absence of which agricultural production can hardly take place (Rawal 2008). The buying and selling of land for agricultural purposes among members of a predominantly agricultural community is rare. The transfer of ownership right usually takes place through gifts and inheritance (Bliss and Stern 1982; Himanshu et al. 2018). The market for land for agricultural purposes, in such circumstances, is in terms of the use-right that extends for a limited time period.

Existing literature shows that various forms of the land tenancy (or leasing) arrangements have emerged as a means to trade the use-right (Goswami 2018a; Sharma and Dréze 1996). Such arrangements match the non-uniform distribution of inputs of agricultural production—land, labour and capital goods—among rural households. Through tenancy, households that do not own sufficient labour and capital relative to their land are likely to lease out land, whereas households with sufficient labour and capital but lacking sufficient land lease in lands (Goswami 2018a). According to Binswanger and Rosenzweig (1986, 524–525), tenancy is a profitable venture for both landlord and tenant households, whereby the former avoids the scale diseconomies arising from the cultivation of large ownership holding through hired workers. Similarly, the tenant households that possess some managerial skill and abundant labour find it more profitable to lease in land than hiring out its labour and other endowments separately. Overall, tenancy helps to make the operational landholding size closer to the optimal size relative to household's ownership of other endowments (Binswanger and Rosenzweig 1986).

In a model of land leasing by Bliss and Stern (1982, 125), tenancy is explained as a mechanism to achieve 'desired cultivated area' by a household in circumstances where there exists a 'less-than-perfectly-marketable' factors under the ownership of the households. According to them, in a perfectly competitive market with identical farmers having the same production function with constant returns to scale technology, a household can adjust the use of their labour and capital to the size of their land ownership holding one way or the other. Hence, there is no need for a tenancy arrangement. Bell (1990, 159) shares a similar line of the argument and goes ahead to explain the emergence of tenancy as 'natural', given that the land market as an asset is not well developed, and that the capital and other complementary factors market function imperfectly. In addition, he has linked the emergence of the tenancy as a result of the incomplete or absent markets, particularly the market for insurance. Likewise, Binswanger and Rosenzweig (1986) also view tenancy arising because of the absence of poorly developed capital and land sale market. The issues of tenancy have been a central part of the agrarian question and have engaged scholars from across disciplines exploring and analysing the complex historical, political, social, cultural, economic and environmental dimensions of the tenancy and tenancy relations (Bardhan and Srinivasan 1971; Goswami 2018a).

2.2.1. Efficiency of Tenancy Contracts: Sharecropping vs Fixed Rent

Sharecropping and fixed-rent tenancy[1] are the two major prevalent forms of land tenancy. Investigation into the efficiency aspect of tenancy contracts, particularly that of sharecropping, dates back to the works of Smith (1776) and Mill (1885). Both discussed about the relative merit of the fixed-rent tenancy, prevalent at that time in

[1] Sharecropping and fixed-rent tenancy are alike, except that, in the former, the rent paid by the tenant to the landlord is the contracted share of the agricultural output per period, whereas, in the latter, payment is a pre-agreed fixed amount of cash, kind or both. In sharecropping, the cost of inputs, other than labour, may be shared by both or either of the parties.

England, over *metayage* or sharecropping arrangement that was more prevalent in France during their time. Smith (1776, 515–516) wrote about the lack of interest on the part of *metayer* or sharecropper to invest for further improvement of the land with his share of the output, as the landlord who paid nothing was to get half of whatever was produced. In contrast, upon payment of certain rent, a fixed-renter tenant invests further for the improvement of the farm, because he expects to recover it with a larger profit within the lease period. Mill (1885, 304) provided an analogous argument in line with Smith and went on to portray *metayers* as having less motivation for the improvement of the farm. Though other classical thinkers like Arthur Young (discussed in Betham-Edwards, 1909) and Richard Jones (1831) also expressed their distaste for sharecropping tenancy, it was Alfred Marshall (1920) who provided a rigorous explanation on how sharecropping tends to be an inefficient form of tenancy, unlike the fixed-rent contract.

According to Marshall (1920, 535–536), it would not be in the interest of the sharecropper to apply any additional doses of his capital and labour beyond the point where marginal returns are not enough to reward for his inputs. Out of Marshall's graphical explanation, economists have developed a mathematical model in which they have shown that a farmer, in his optimization exercises, will equate half the marginal product of his effort with his marginal cost of effort, and stops supplying inputs even when the marginal product of his effort exceeds his marginal cost (Bell 1977, 318–320; Bliss and Stern 1982, 54–55; Cheung 1989, 42–44; Quibria and Rashid 1984, 104–105). This view of sharecropping as an inefficient form of tenancy is popularly known in the literature as the 'Marshallian view' or 'Marshallian inefficiency hypothesis' or 'Marshallian approach'[2] (Bell 1990; Bliss and Stern 1982; Goswami 2018a; Otsuka and Hayami 1988; Quibria and Rashid 1984). This view on sharecropping was founded on the premise that it is difficult for the landlord to observe the tenant's inputs, particularly labour, and it involves huge cost in monitoring

[2] Although Alfred Marshall (1920, 535–536) viewed sharecropping as an inefficient form of tenancy arrangement, he talked about ways through which the disadvantages related to sharecropping could be avoided and efficiency in agricultural operation could be attained, as it would be under fixed-rent tenure.

and enforcing labour and other input contracts (Goswami 2018a). Some of the supporters of the Marshallian approach are Adams and Rask (1968), Bliss and Stern (1982), Georgescu-Roegen (1960), Schickele (1941) and Sen (1966).

Johnson (1950) proposed a major departure from the Marshallian line of thought by laying out conditions that would result in no resource inefficiency under sharecropping. According to Johnson (1950, 118–119), a landlord can achieve efficiency in sharecropping if he is able to (a) stipulate the details about what his tenant is required to do, (b) share the factor expenses with the tenant and (c) lease the land for a short period of time. Specifying the method of cultivation and the amount of the tenant's labour, fertilizers and other inputs would provide a reasonable assurance that land will be cultivated with appropriate intensities. Similarly, by sharing certain expenses on certain inputs like seeds and fertilizer, he can induce a more rational allocation of these inputs. Finally, a short-term lease contract allows the landlord for a periodic review of the performance of his tenants and, hence, adds pressure on the part of the tenant to apply more labour per acre. Although Johnson (1950) was among the first group of scholars to acknowledge sharecropping as an equally efficient form of tenancy as the fixed-rent tenancy, it was Cheung (1969) who provided a theoretical foundation to this contrasting view on sharecropping. In Cheung's (1969) model, a landlord maximizes his share of output through adjustment in the number of land parcels, rental share and the quantity of labour input put on by the tenant under a perfectly competitive labour market conditions and hence achieve efficiency across all forms of tenancy, including sharecropping. However, Cheung's work also attracted a lot of criticism. The use of partial equilibrium framework featuring the maximization exercise from the perspective of landlord alone has been criticized by Bardhan and Rudra (1980); Bardhan and Srinivasan (1971); Bell (1977); Bell and Zusman (1976); and Stiglitz (1974). Using a general equilibrium framework, Bardhan and Srinivasan (1971) show that a sharecropper still falls short in supplying labour, even when the marginal product of his labour exceeds wage rate, resulting in inefficiency. Bardhan and Srinivasan (1971) criticizes the assumption of a perfectly elastic labour supply curve also in Cheung's model. Further, Cheung (1969) has been criticized for the unrealistic assumption of costless monitoring and enforcement costs (Bardhan and Srinivasan 1971; Bell 1977; Bell and Zusman 1976; Bliss and Stern 1982; Stiglitz 1974).

Although the Marshallian approach and monitoring approach dominate the theoretical discourse on land tenancy, both lines of argument have attracted criticism mainly because of their neoclassical foundation that fails to acknowledge the possibility of interlocked market. They have also been criticized for their ahistorical nature(Bardhan and Rudra 1980; Bell 1977; Bell and Zusman 1976; Bharadwaj and Das 1975). Further, Bardhan and Rudra (1980) and Bharadwaj and Das (1975) highlight the limitations of the competitive land and labour market framework of the Marshallian and monitoring approaches to acknowledge the influences of interlocked market situation on the functioning of the tenancy market. They discuss the complication that arises in disentangling the outcome of the tenancy contract when the landlord and tenants are simultaneously engaged in land, labour, credit and other market contracts.

A recent addition to this efficiency debate is the work by Goswami and Bezbaruah (2018) that reports the incentive problem of a different nature in the case of fixed-rent tenancy, particularly when it comes to the use of production-enhancing inputs like chemical fertilizer and pesticides. In a time-bound (or short-duration) fixed-rent tenancy contract, it might be in the interest of the profit-maximizing tenant to excessively use the production-enhancing inputs, during the contract duration, without considering the implication of her action on soil health in the long term, that is, after the tenancy contract expires. Using an inter-temporal optimization framework wherein the sharecroppers and fixed-rent tenants hold land for one period and the owner–operators hold it for two periods, Goswami and Bezbaruah (2018) have shown that the input intensity is the highest under fixed rent than those under sharecropping and owner operation. The model by Goswami and Bezbaruah (2018) shows a trade-off between the current input intensity and future land productivity. Besides the theoretical model, the authors empirically examine the use of inputs across different tenancy forms in the state of Assam in India and confirm the results of the theoretical model. In fact, they find a perverse incentive on the part of fixed-rent tenants for using chemical fertilizers excessively higher than even the recommended level. Several studies have shown that the excess use of production-enhancing inputs often results in the degradation of soil fertility, leading to a decline in productivity in the long term (Goswami 2018a; Goswami and Bezbaruah 2013, 2018). If this is the case, the fixed-rent tenancy can no longer be viewed efficient from the perspective of sustainability.

2.2.2. Sharecropping, Technological Adoption and Agricultural Growth

Bhaduri (1973) initiated a discussion on whether sharecropping disincentivizes technology adoption and thereby constrains agricultural growth. According to Bhaduri (1973), using his power derived from the traditional property right to land and a role in usury, a landlord creates obstacles in procuring and adopting improved technology in agriculture in order to continue his domination over the tenant and keep him indebted towards him. Bhaduri's proposition has, however, been contested. In a study on the Green Revolution in India, Byres (1972) found that the reasons that sharecroppers and other small farmers did not adopt new technology were the lack of resources and acceptable collateral to get loans from formal financial institutions. Referring to this finding by Byres (1972) and Newbery (1975) provides an counterargument to Bhaduri's (1973) claim. Newbery (1975) argues that a landlord who wants to make his tenants indebted would rather see it as a possibility to lend out more and make him more indebted. In his alternative explanation to non-innovation, Newbery (1975, 266–267) suggests that a farmer may avoid the adoption of new technology, if innovation replaces the old technique with a more complex one, resulting in moral hazard on the part of the tenants. Further, he goes on to argue that an innovation might not be feasible for those farmers either because the complementary other inputs are not available or too costly or because the existing social and institutional constraints may be overshadowing the economic feasibility of innovation.

2.2.3. Prevalence of Sharecropping Despite Perceived Inefficiency

Sharecropping is predominant despite the perceived inefficiency associated with it. The prominent explanation for this phenomenon is that sharecropping is not only a contract to share output, but it is also an insurance contract (Stiglitz 1974). Under sharecropping, the tenant and the landlord share the risk associated with production. Contrary to this, the entire risk falls on the tenant in the case of fixed-rent contract. A risk-averse farmer, therefore, prefers sharecropping, especially when cultivation involves the risk from weather. Stiglitz (2004, 34–35) further shows that even a landlord, particularly an absentee one, would prefer sharecropping to avoid the moral hazard problem that arises due to information asymmetry regarding the tenant's skill. Further, when both the tenant and the landlord need to apply effort, sharecropping appears to be the compromised solution. Under such circumstances, a wage-labour contract and a fixed-rent contract involve the incentive problem on the part of the tenant and the landlord, respectively (Ray 1998). Sharecropping may also be preferred when the tenant and the landlord share costs of production. In fact, a sharecropping contract with cost-sharing arrangement can be as efficient as a fixed-rent contract (Ray 1998).[3]

2.3. TRENDS AND PATTERNS OF TENANCY IN INDIA

2.3.1. Incidence of Tenancy

Figure 2.1 presents the extent of tenancy in terms of the percentage of tenant holdings in the total operational holdings and that of the leased-in area in the total operated area over time in India.[4] The percentage of

[3] Basu (2005) explains the existence of sharecropping through the limited liability argument. Hayami and Otsuka (1993) discuss how inefficiency associated with sharecropping is avoided within a cooperative relationship between the tenant and the landlord. For a detailed discussion on these issues, see Goswami (2018a).

[4] A tenant holding is an operational holding, which is either a pure tenant or an owner-cum-tenant holding. As per the National Sample Survey report no. 587 (77th round, Table 39, p. A-3418), while only 1.9 per cent of tenant holdings were pure tenant holdings, 15.4 per cent tenant holdings were owner-cum-tenant holdings.

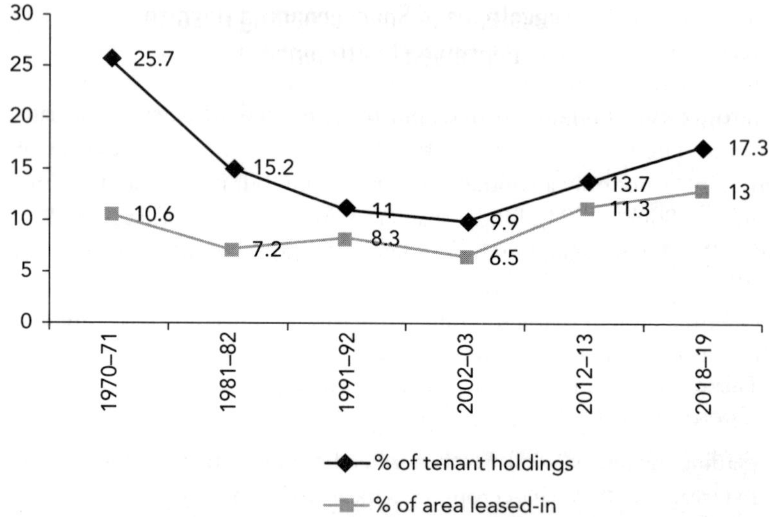

Figure 2.1 *Share of Tenant Holdings in Total Operational Holdings and That of the Area Leased-in in the Total Operated Area (%)*

Source: National Sample Survey report nos. 571 (p. 43) and 587 (p. 59).

tenant holdings shows a declining trend during the 1970–1971 (25.7%) and 2002–2003 periods (9.9%), and, thereafter, it increased to 13.7 per cent in 2012–2013 and then further to 17.3 per cent in 2018–2019.[5] The percentage of the area leased-in in total operated area also, notwithstanding some fluctuation, shows a declining trend during the 1970–1971 and 2002–2003 periods. Leased-in area as a percentage of overall operated area declined from 10.6 per cent in 1970–1971 to 6.5 per cent in 2002–2003, and, thereafter, it increased to 11.3 per cent and 13 per cent in 2012–2013 and 2018–2019, respectively.

[5] The decline in the extent of tenancy during the 1970–1971 and 2002–2003 periods can be explained in terms of reduction in both supply of and demand for land under lease. Implementation of tenancy reforms that resulted in the eviction of tenants and resumption of land for self-cultivation might have made lands less available for lease. On the other hand, declining unemployment and poverty and rising wages reduced the demand for land during the 1980s (Bansal et al. 2018).

Thus, Figure 2.1 suggests that the incidence of tenancy has increased in recent times. In fact, as Goswami (2018a) points out, the incidence of tenancy is expected to increase further going forward with the increase in the level of education among the rural population.[6]

Table 2.1 presents the percentage shares of tenant holdings within a size class of operational holdings across all size classes over time.[7] As at the aggregate level, while the shares of tenant holdings within small, semi-medium and medium-sized classes declined during the 1970–1971 and 2002–2003 periods, they increased in the subsequent

Table 2.1 *Percentage of Tenant Holdings across Size Classes of Operational Holdings*

Year (1)	Marginal (2)	Small (3)	Semi-medium (4)	Medium (5)	Large (6)
1970–1971	27.0	27.8	24.8	20	15.9
1981–1982	14.4	17.9	15.9	14.5	11.5
1991–1992	9.3	14.9	12.2	13.1	16.7
2002–2003	9.8	10.7	10.3	7.8	13.8
2012–2013	13.2	13.6	18	14.8	21.8
2018–2019	11.8	17.1	18	25.7	34.8

Source: 1970–1971 to 2012–2013: National Sample Survey report no. 571 (p. 43); 2018–2019: computed from Table 39 (p. A-3418) of National Sample Survey report no. 587.

[6] Goswami (2018a) finds that people with higher level of education tend to look for employment in the non-farm sector. As a result, more land becomes available in the land-lease market.

[7] A sizable portion of lessee households does not own land, that is, these households are landless. However, these households may not necessarily be resource-poor (Bansal et al. 2018). The study by Bansal et al. (2018) further shows that the Scheduled Caste, Scheduled Tribe and Muslim households have disproportionately less access to land in the lease market. Further, Dalit households in many states have very low access to land through tenancy arrangements.

periods. The percentage of tenant holdings within the marginal size class declined throughout the 1970–1971 to 1990–1991 periods. Thereafter, it increased to 9.8 per cent and 13.2 per cent in 2002–2003 and 2012–2013, respectively, and then declined to 11.8 per cent in 2018–2019. On the other hand, the share of tenant holdings within the large category shows fluctuations over time, although the figures for the last two periods show a continuous increase in it. Based on the figures in Table 2.1, it can be inferred that farmers belonging to all the land size classes participate in the land-lease market.[8]

Table 2.2 presents the extent of tenancy across 19 major Indian states at two recent points of time, that is, 2012–2013 and 2018–2019. We use three indicators, namely percentage of households leasing in land, percentage of tenant holdings and area leased in as a percentage of total operated area to analyse the extent of tenancy at the state level.[9]

Among the southern states, all the indicators show an increase in the incidence of tenancy in Kerala and a decline in Karnataka, Tamil Nadu and Telangana between 2012–2013 and 2018–2019. On the

[8] The fact that farmers belonging to all land size classes lease in land, and there is not much difference in the proportions of tenants within different size classes, suggests that the the incidence of reverse tenancy in India may be minimal. (Although the shares of tenant holdings within medium- and large-sized classes in 2018–2019 are relatively higher, one can ignore this fact, given that shares of these two categories in total operational holdings are only 2.7 per cent and 0.3 per cent, respectively, in the same year [p. 58, National Sample Survey report no. 587]). With the information presented here, we cannot definitely comment on it. However, the existing literature also suggests that much of the tenancy is among the lessors and tenants belonging to a similar socio-economic status (Bansal et al. 2018). In fact, with overwhelming proportions of landholdings being marginal and small, the scope of reverse tenancy is limited. Of course, reverse tenancy may be present in some specific states, which can be ascertained only through state-level studies.

[9] We consider only those indicators that are associated with leasing in of land. The proportion of households that report leasing out of land is substantially less as compared to the households reporting leasing in of land in all the relevant rounds of the National Sample Survey. This could be due to under-reporting by the lessor households. The fact that the National Sample Survey data underestimate the incidence of tenancy has been shown by many studies, such as Ramakumar (2000) and Sharma and Dreze (1998).

Table 2.2 *Extent of Tenancy across Major States of India*

State/Union Territory	% of Households Leasing In land		% of tenant Holdings		% of Area Leased In to Total Operated Area	
	2012–2013*	2018–2019@	2012–2013#	2018–2019^	2012–2013#	2018–2019^
(1)	(2)	(3)	(4)	(5)	(6)	(7)
Andhra Pradesh	37.2	31.6	42.3	42.4	34.2	36.4
Karnataka	8.6	3.6	5.1	4.3	6.7	5.0
Kerala	14.3	15.9	10.6	14.7	8.3	13.8
Tamil Nadu	13.2	6.8	13.0	9.3	14.3	10.9
Telangana	16.5	11.3	18.4	17.5	13.7	11.9
Gujarat	6.2	6.6	6.1	4.1	5.6	3.3
Maharashtra	8.4	4.3	4.4	5.6	3.4	4.3
Rajasthan	7.6	5.9	7.6	7.9	7.8	6.1
Bihar	18.7	15.8	28.0	28.2	21.6	25.1
Haryana	12.9	15.0	15.1	21.3	15.0	34.7
Himachal Pradesh	21.2	13.2	10.5	9.6	5.2	4.6
Jharkhand	5.9	7.6	4.4	13.3	1.9	7.8

(Table 2.2 Continued)

(Table 2.2 Continued)

State/Union Territory	% of Households Leasing In land		% of tenant Holdings		% of Area Leased In to Total Operated Area	
	2012–2013*	2018–2019@	2012–2013#	2018–2019^	2012–2013#	2018–2019^
(1)	(2)	(3)	(4)	(5)	(6)	(7)
Punjab	15.8	10.6	19.0	21.1	24.8	27.8
Uttar Pradesh	10.6	15.1	10.6	17.9	7.6	13.8
Assam	7.0	14.4	8.0	16.4	4.3	13.1
Odisha	19.3	25.9	20.6	39	16.7	31.3
West Bengal	17.8	21.4	21.7	29.5	14.6	22.3
Madhya Pradesh	5.6	7.7	6.4	10.9	5.0	8.6
Chhattisgarh	13.7	10.8	12.0	11.4	9.5	7.5
India	**13.7**	**13.3**	**13.7**	**17.3**	**10.2**	**13.0**

Source: 2012–2013: Statements S4.7 (p. 30) and S5.6 (p. 42) of the National Sample Survey report no. 571; 2018–2019: Statements 2.5.1 (p. 115) and 2.10.1 (p. 121) of the National Sample Survey report no. 587.

Notes: *Corresponds to the period January–June 2013; #corresponds to the period July–December 2012; ^corresponds to the period July 2018 to June 2019; and @corresponds to the period January–June 2019.

other hand, while the percentage of households leasing in land declined and that of leased-in area increased, the percentage of tenant holdings remained the same between the two time periods under consideration in Andhra Pradesh. Furthermore, all the three indicators suggest that the incidence of tenancy is the highest in Andhra Pradesh and the lowest in Karnataka among the southern states.

In the western part of India, the percentage of households leasing in land increased marginally in Gujarat and declined in Rajasthan and Maharashtra between 2012–2013 and 2018–2019. However, in terms of the percentage of tenant holdings, while Rajasthan and Maharashtra show an improvement, Gujarat shows a decline. On the other hand, the percentage of leased-in land in the area operated declined in Gujarat and Rajasthan, and it increased marginally in Maharashtra. The impression that one gets from the values of all the indicators is that the incidence of tenancy in the western states is less relative to many states in other regions of the country.

In the north of India, the extent of tenancy is not very high in Jharkhand. While Himachal Pradesh shows a decline, Uttar Pradesh and Haryana show an increase in the extent of tenancy in terms of all the indicators. On the other hand, though the percentage of households leasing in land declined in both Bihar and Punjab, the percentages of tenant holdings and area leased in increased in these two states between 2012–2013 and 2018–2019. Among the states in North India, Bihar, Haryana and Punjab show a higher incidence of tenancy, especially in terms of the percentage of tenant holdings and that of the leased-in area in the total operated area.

All the three states in eastern India, namely Assam, Odisha and West Bengal, show an increase in the extent of tenancy in terms of all the indicators between 2012–2013 and 2018–2019. The incidence of tenancy is relatively high in Odisha and West Bengal.

Finally, in the central part of India, while Madhya Pradesh shows an increase in the extent of tenancy, Chhattisgarh shows a decline between 2012–2013 and 2018–2019. The incidence of tenancy in these states, however, is relatively less as in the case of the states in the western part of India.

2.3.2. Terms of Tenancy

Figure 2.2 shows the distribution of leased-in area in terms of forms of tenancy contract. Until 1981–1982, sharecropping was the dominant form of tenancy contract prevailing in India. However, the area under sharecropping had been declining continuously. In 1991–1992, areas under sharecropping and fixed rent were almost similar. Thereafter, however, areas under fixed rent started increasing. As per the latest round of the National Sample Survey, fixed-rent contract had 56.1 per cent of the total leased-in area under it. In other words, fixed rent is the predominant form of tenancy contracts in India now.

Table 2.3 presents the distribution of the area under lease by the terms of lease across major Indian states. As per the latest National Sample Survey report (77th round), fixed rent in cash is the dominant form of tenancy in all the states in southern India. The area under fixed rent (cash and kind) is more than 90 per cent of the total leased-in area in Andhra Pradesh and Tamil Nadu in 2019. Though sharecropping accounted for 50.3 per cent of the leased in area in 2013 in Karnataka, the area under this form of tenancy declined to 19.1 per cent in 2019. A similar pattern can be observed in the case of Telangana as well.

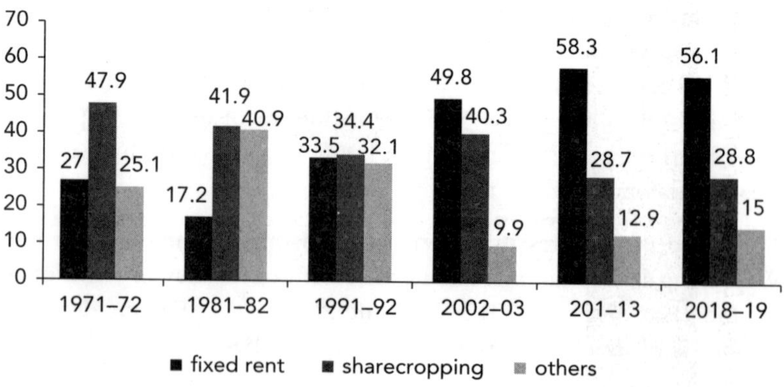

Figure 2.2 *Percentage Distribution of Leased-in Area in Terms of Form of Tenancy*

Source: 1971–1972 to 2012–2013: adapted from the National Sample Survey 2012–2013, statement S5.9 (p. 44), report no. 571; 2018–2019: Table 41 (p. A-3480) of the National Sample Survey report no. 587.

Table 2.3 *Percentage Distribution of Area under Lease by the Terms of Lease across Major States*

	January–June 2013				January–June 2019			
States (1)	SC (2)	FR (Cash) (3)	FR (Kind) (4)	Others (5)	SC (6)	FR (Cash) (7)	FR (Kind) (8)	Others (9)
Andhra Pradesh	21.2	51.9	20.9	5.8	3.9	54.1	37.7	4.3
Karnataka	50.3	34.4	8.4	6.6	19.1	41.9	3.0	36.0
Kerala	8.7	39.4	9.7	36.2	5.1	43.6	2.9	48.5
Tamil Nadu	5.7	72.3	6.6	15.4	0.6	60.4	30.0	9.1
Telangana	35.1	55.8	5.9	1.4	8.5	67.8	15.8	7.9
Gujarat	57.6	12.0	0.0	30.3	27.1	23.4	16.4	33.1
Maharashtra	29.0	43.6	3.5	12.6	19.6	51.5	1.6	27.3
Rajasthan	25.0	52.8	5.9	13.6	20.5	24.1	11.5	42.0
Bihar	35.6	24.6	27.5	3.4	49.3	22.7	22.2	5.8
Haryana	1.9	75.8	8.7	11.9	8.6	89.4	1.2	0.8
Himachal Pradesh	7.0	31.4	1.0	58.6	5.7	35.7	0.0	58.5
Jharkhand	72.2	17.4	7.0	0.0	58.5	4.0	2.5	34.9

(Table 2.3 Continued)

(Table 2.3 Continued)

States	January–June 2013				January–June 2019			
	SC (2)	FR (Cash) (3)	FR (Kind) (4)	Others (5)	SC (6)	FR (Cash) (7)	FR (Kind) (8)	Others (9)
(1)								
Punjab	1.9	93.7	1.4	2.5	2.1	92.1	5	0.8
Uttar Pradesh	35.6	24.2	9.5	26.4	44.5	30.1	7.3	18.0
Assam	55.8	17.3	10.9	8.6	78.8	7.0	11.5	2.8
Odisha	58.3	9.5	27.6	4.0	54.8	12.4	10.4	22.4
West Bengal	34.6	39.3	15.8	7.7	23.5	43.1	21.0	12.4
Madhya Pradesh	35.8	16.8	10.4	35.7	51.4	19.9	3.4	25.4
Chhattisgarh	21.3	5.3	61.6	8.6	49.0	0.5	0.3	50.2
India	**28.4**	**41.9**	**15.1**	**11.7**	**28.8**	**41.7**	**14.4**	**15.0**

Source: 2013: statement S5.9 (p. 46) of National Sample Survey report no. 571; 2019: Table 41 of National Sample Survey report no. 587.

Further, the area under 'other terms' accounts for as high as 36 per cent and 48.5 per cent in Karnataka and Kerala, respectively, in 2019.[10]

As in the southern region, fixed rent has become dominant in all the states in the western part of the country in recent times. Sharecropping, despite a fall in its share over time, however, still accounts for a sizeable portion of the leased-in area in these states. Besides, as per the recent data, a substantial portion of the leased-in area is under no specific terms in these states.

Among the North Indian states, sharecropping continues to be the dominant form of tenancy contracts in Uttar Pradesh and Jharkhand. Though the area under sharecropping in Jharkhand declined in 2019 as compared to that in 2013, it still accounted for 58.5 per cent of the leased-in area in that year. The area under sharecropping increased substantially in Uttar Pradesh between 2013 and 2019. In Bihar, though the difference between the area under sharecropping and the area under fixed rent is not high as per the recent data, the area under the former increased and the area under the latter declined over time. On the other hand, fixed rent in cash is the most dominant form of tenancy contracts in Punjab (92.1%) and Haryana (89.4%). In Himachal Pradesh, 58.5 per cent of leased-in area is under unspecified form followed by 35.7 per cent under fixed rent in cash. Among the eastern states, the leased-in area under sharecropping is the highest in Assam and Odisha. The area under sharecropping has increased in Assam over time. In West Bengal, however, fixed rent is predominant as per the latest available data. In central India, sharecropping was the major form of tenancy in Madhya Pradesh and Chhattisgarh in 2019.[11]

[10] The term 'Others' comprises two elements, namely (a) relatives under no specific terms and (b) unspecified or others. Out of these two terms, the area under the first one is much higher in almost all the states. For example, out of 48.5 per cent of the area reported under 'others' in Table 2.3, 39.8 per cent of the leased-in area is under 'relative under no specific term' in Kerala in 2019.

[11] The data with respect to terms of lease in Chhattisgarh show some drastic changes between 2013 and 2019. In 2013, the area under fixed rent in kind was 61.6 per cent, which declined to only 0.3 per cent in 2019. On the other hand, the area under 'others' increased from 8.6 per cent in 2013 to 50.2 per cent in

2.3.3. Informality of Tenancy Arrangements

Figure 2.3 presents the incidence of concealed tenancy in India. As per the 77th round of National Sample Survey data, 76.3 per cent of those households that possesses land through lease arrangement does not record lease. In other words, these lease arrangements are informal. Such a high proportion of informal lease establishes the fact that concealed tenancy is rampant. Except for some states, namely Karnataka, Tamil Nadu, Maharashtra and Punjab, the incidence of concealed tenancy is very high in all other states. It is interesting to note that the incidence of concealed tenancy is as high as 88.1 per cent and 63.0 per cent in West Bengal and Kerala, respectively. Tenancy reform programmes implemented in these two states during the 1960s and 1970s are often cited as successful cases of tenancy reforms. However, the prevalence of widespread informal tenancy in these states indicates the inadequacy of such reform measures to address manifold issues related to land-lease market in the Indian context. This has been discussed in a greater detail in section 2.5.

What transpires from the aforementioned discussion is that, notwithstanding the considerable variations across states, the extent of tenancy increased in recent times. Andhra Pradesh, Bihar, Haryana, Punjab, West Bengal and Odisha have a relatively higher incidence of tenancy with substantial portions of operated area under tenancy and higher percentages of tenant holdings in these states. On the other hand, the extent of tenancy is moderate in Tamil Nadu, Telangana, Kerala and Assam. In terms of the form of tenancy, fixed rent in cash has emerged as the major form of tenancy. This is an important development that we discuss in the next section in some more detail. As in the case of the extent of tenancy, there are variations in terms of the major form of tenancy prevailing in the states. Goswami (2018b) explains the variations in the magnitude of tenancy across states in terms of the average size of the area owned. The states with a higher average size of land ownership (relative to the national average) also have lower incidence

2019. Such dramatic changes within a short span of time raise the suspicion that there may be some problems either in recording of the terms of tenancy contracts or in sample selection.

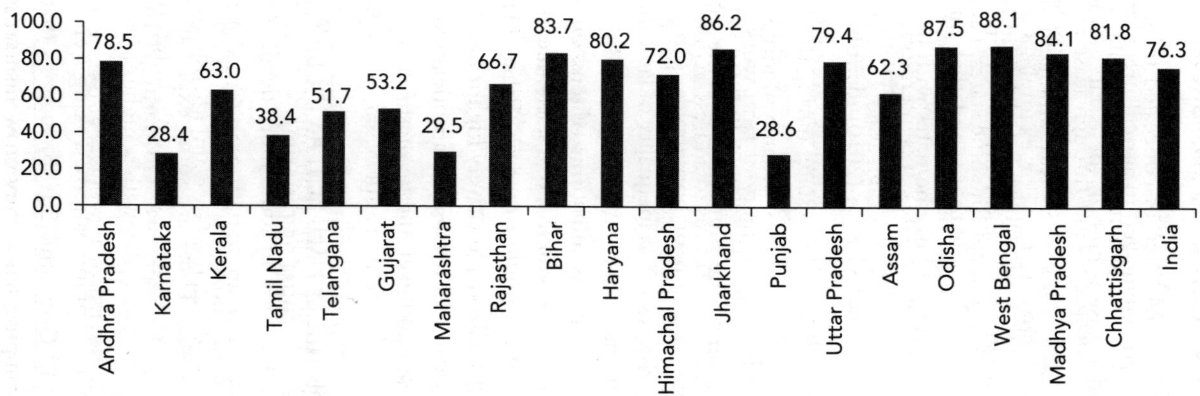

Figure 2.3 *Incidence of Concealed Tenancy: Percentage of Not-recorded Lease*

Source: Table 40 of National Sample Survey report no. 587.
Note: Data relate to January–June 2019.

of tenancy and vice versa. This explanation, however, does not apply in the case of Punjab and Haryana. These two states have relatively higher proportions of rural people engaged in agriculture. Consequently, the demand for land under lease is high in these states (Goswami 2018b). There may be many other factors that may be responsible for the varied incidence of tenancy across states. For example, Goswami (2012), Goswami and Bezbaruah (2013) and Kuri (2003) find that education creates an aversion towards agriculture, and that makes more land available in the lease market. Thus, the states with higher educational attainment may have a higher incidence of tenancy. Furthermore, Goswami (2018a) and Laha and Kuri (2010) identify access to credit, ownership of bullock and tilling machinery, access to irrigation and other household-level characteristics such as age, education and sex of the head of the household; availability of farm workers; caste profile; and primary occupation of the household as some important factors that affect the leasing decision of households. On the other hand, village-level characteristics such as inequality of landholdings, access to input and output markets and prevailing rent are also important factors that may affect the magnitude and forms of tenancy. Depending on the variations in these variables across states, the magnitude of tenancy may vary. However, the influence of these factors can be deciphered only through a field-based study. Thus, for further exploration into the variations across states in the extent and forms of tenancy, more granular studies at the state level will be required.

2.4. EMERGENCE OF FIXED RENT AS THE DOMINANT FORM OF TENANCY

Analysis in section 2.3.2 shows that fixed rent is now the dominant form of tenancy in India. There are some explanations of this phenomenon available in the literature. Goswami (2018b) explains the emergence of fixed rent as the major form of tenancy contract in terms of the change in cropping pattern. Taking a cue from Goswami and Bezbaruah (2013), Goswami (2018b) suggests that farmers prefer fixed rent to sharecropping when they grow cash crops such as fruits, vegetables and oil seeds. These crops usually involve less weather risk that incentivizes them to use production-enhancing inputs and cultivate the crops on a commercial basis. Under such circumstances, the famers like to pay the rent upfront and retain the entire returns. Consequently, fixed rent becomes the preferred choice of tenancy contract. In the Indian context, a shift in the overall cropping pattern from coarse cereals to oil seeds and fruits and vegetables can be observed around the same time when areas under sharecropping fell and that under fixed rent increased. The shift in the cropping pattern became more visible around 1991–1992, which is also the time when areas under sharecropping and fixed rent were almost equal, and since then, the area under the latter form of tenancy has been increasing.

Shergill (2019) and Reddy and Murty (2021) provide an explanation for the dominance of cash rent tenancy in the context of Punjab, Andhra Pradesh and Telangana, respectively. Among the states in India, Punjab stands out with only 2 per cent of the leased-in area under sharecropping and fixed-rent tenancy as an almost universal form of tenancy in 2018–2019. Shergill (2019) identifies five factors that led to this drastic change in the land rental market in Punjab. The first factor relates to yield stability of the most prevalent crops—paddy and wheat. He points out that the current-year yields of these two crops never fell below the mean yield of the preceding five years. The stability in production is the result of the universal adoption of high-yielding varieties (HYVs) of paddy and wheat seeds and the availability of irrigation (primarily through controlled tube well water) on the areas under paddy and wheat. These two factors virtually eliminated the production risk associated with rice–wheat cultivation making fixed rent as the favoured form of tenancy contract. This explanation resonates with that of Goswami and Bezbaruah (2013) in the context of Assam. Second, the author points out that the well-functioning minimum support price and assured purchase programme in Punjab have created a price and marketing certainty for the tenants of the state. The certainty in price and procurement coupled with the elimination of the risk of crop failure has encouraged the tenants to opt for cash rent tenancy. The third and fourth factors relate to the changing profile of the land lessors and the tenant households, respectively, over time in Punjab. More than half of the landowning households reside in the urban sector or abroad, which prevented the regular monitoring of the farm practices by their tenants. As for the tenants, they are big entrepreneurial farmers with modern machinery, modern input and better farming experiences than the lessors. Under such circumstances, the lessors find themselves in a difficult situation to monitor and control the farming practices and inputs used by tenants. Since monitoring and supervision is not required under fixed rent, the lessors, therefore, prefer this tenancy contract to sharecropping. Finally, the presence of commission agents as credit providers has also contributed to the emergence of fixed-rent tenancy. Often, tenants opt for sharecropping because of the severe liquidity constraint created by the requirement of advance payment of cash rent in the cash rent tenancy. The wider involvement of commission agents in marketing in Punjab agriculture has provided an opportunity to the farmers to obtain credit from these agents and removed the liquidity constraint.

Reddy and Murty (2021) argue that ownership of land is getting passed into the hands of those, especially urban dwellers, who lack skills and interest in farming in the field study locations of Andhra Pradesh and Telangana. This has resulted in an increase in the supply of land in the lease market. The increase in the supply of land for lease may have improved the bargaining power of the tenants. Thus, the tenants have been able to lease in land for a rent under cash rent tenancy that is lower than the rents under other forms of tenancy, although, under cash rent tenancy, they have to bear the entire risk associated with cultivation. As for the absentee landowners who wish to lease out, they prefer to receive the rental income with certainty and without having to get involved in the risk-sharing and monitoring of cultivation. Cash rent tenancy satisfies all these conditions. In other words, cash rent tenancy appears to be beneficial to both tenants and the lessors, and that explains the dominance of this form of tenancy arrangement.

2.5. TENANCY REFORMS: HISTORY, REALITY AND THE NEED FOR FRESH REFORMS

During the 1960s and 1970s, Indian states passed tenancy legislations with the objective of promoting an egalitarian land distribution. An egalitarian land distribution was expected to incentivize farmers to supply sufficient efforts that in turn would increase productivity and infuse efficiency in agricultural production. While there were variations in the exact provisions in the tenancy laws across states, three main components of these laws included (a) providing ownership right to tenants, given certain conditions, (b) ensuring security of tenure and (c) regulation of rent at a level around 20–25 per cent of the gross produce. Some states even banned tenancy, and some others introduced restrictive provisions to regulate tenancy. Given that the landlords of that time did not invest in agriculture, providing incentives to tenants through these measures was perceived to be the need of the hour. It was expected that security of tenure, ownership rights and regulation of rent would encourage investments in agriculture by tenants. Though the laws were enacted by all the states, barring a few states like Kerala and West Bengal, no state implemented them properly. It soon became evident that there was a lack of political will to implement them.

Meanwhile, banning tenancy and other restrictive provisions in the tenancy laws resulted in some unwarranted outcomes. These adverse outcomes could be observed not only in the states where tenancy reforms were implemented but also in the states where the provisions of the laws remained largely on paper. The two main undesired outcomes are (a) concealed tenancy and (b) shortening of duration of tenancy contracts. Acknowledgement of these adverse effects of tenancy laws can be found even in the Eighth and the Tenth Five-Year Plan documents.

Following the enactment of the tenancy laws, concealed tenancy became rampant. Tenancy laws in many states had the provision of conferring ownership rights on the tenants if they tilled the land continuously for certain years. For example, the tenancy law in Assam has the provision that if a tenant cultivates the land consciously for three years, he/she can put claim for ownership. Consequently, the lessors do not want to record tenancy contracts, and they do not want to lease out land beyond two years to the same tenant (Goswami 2012). Tenancy being a natural outcome of the mismatch in factor endowments (especially land and labour) across households, banning or restriction would result in only concealed tenancy. Concealed tenancy hurts the tenants even more as they cannot use the laws in case of any dispute since there is no record of a contract. As for the shortening of the duration of tenancy, the implication is that the tenants will not have any incentive to investment on land. In fact, as discussed in section 2.2, Goswami and Bezbaruah (2018) demonstrate that shortening of the duration of tenancy contracts creates a perverse incentive among the fixed-rent tenants to apply inputs like chemical fertilizers to maximize returns within the stipulated short period of contract without caring for the natural fertility of the soil.

Even in states where tenancy reforms were implemented, it appeared that tenancy continued to emerge in one form or the other. Tenancy was completely abolished in Kerala through the Kerala Land Reform Act, 1969 (Herring 1980). However, an evaluation of Kerala's land reform programme suggests that it benefitted mainly large farmers. A substantial portion of land was transferred to relatively big farmers. Besides, the small farmers who leased out land lost the ownership of land (Herring 1983). Further, concealed tenancy emerged as a consequence of the ban on tenancy, and frequent eviction of the tenants became a regular practice (Nair and Menon 2006). On the other hand, 'Operation Barga' in West Bengal that was implemented by the Left Front government in 1977 also failed to emerge as a permanent solution. Theoretically, on the one hand, 'Operation Barga' could improve the bargaining power of the tenants and security of their tenure, and thereby increase productivity (Banerjee et al. 2002). On the other hand, it restricted access to land by the future generations (Ray 1998). Empirically, Banerjee et al. (2002) and Shaban (1987) show that 'Operation Barga' did result in the improvement in agricultural productivity.

The aforementioned discussion suggests that the tenancy reform measures like those undertaken in Kerala and West Bengal cannot provide a long-term or permanent solution to the issues related to the management of tenancy relations. Meanwhile, the context in which these measures were undertaken, and the tenancy laws were passed, has also changed. The grassroot-level agro-economic realities in the countryside, today, are different from what they used to be at the time of passing these laws. The characteristics of the contemporary lessors are different from those of the big landlords of the 1960s and 1970s.

Small and marginal holdings constitute an overwhelming portion of landownership holdings today. In 2012–2013, 85.41 per cent of the ownership holdings belonged to small and marginal holders, and the share of the large holders was only 0.24 per cent (Goswami 2018b). These figures imply that there is little scope of tenancy reform in the conventional sense now. Transferring land from the small and marginal lessors to tillers will create only another class of landless people.

In view of the changing realities and the harmful effects of the existing tenancy laws, a revision of the current tenancy laws is inevitable. Given that the land under lease increased in recent times, and is expected to increase further in the future as discussed in section 2.3, a fresh policy that tackles the triangular challenge of ensuring efficient, egalitarian and sustainable use of these lands is required. This triangular challenge can be overcome, at least to a large extent, by a policy, wherein the focus is on improving access to land rather than transferring ownership of land. In this context, we suggest that restrictive provisions in the tenancy laws are removed, and leasing in and leasing out are made hassle-free by legalizing it.[12] On the one hand, the lessee should be able to use land without the threat of eviction for a reasonably long period of time, and the lessor should be able to lease out without the fear of losing the ownership right, on the other hand. In other words, the use and ownership rights need to be separated. Such a measure will improve the security of tenure and improve the incentives of the tenants to supply adequate efforts. Consequently, efficiency in agricultural operation is expected to improve. As for the

[12] Sharma and Malik (2021) also suggest that legalizing leasing in and leasing out, and making use and cultivation rights on land tradable in the lease market, is a solution to the viability crisis that the Indian agriculture confronts today. They are of the view that legalization of leasing should enable all sections of the rural populace to participate in the lease market. Based on resource endowment, choice and availability of employment opportunities, and ability to take risk, people will decide whether to remain in the farm sector or to shift to the non-farm sector. In other words, legalization of leasing will bring about flexibility in the rural economy. In this context, Reddy and Murty (2021) observe in Andhra Pradesh and Telangana that competitive market forces safeguard the interests of the tenants and lessors, and hence, there is no need to place legislative restrictions on the lease market.

lessors, they may not hesitate to lease out land and also to record the tenancy contracts if there is no fear of losing ownership.[13] Recording of the contracts will safeguard the interests of the tenants.[14] In addition to the above-mentioned discussion, if the lessor does not have the fear of losing the ownership right, he/she may lease out land, especially if agriculture is not viable for him/her, and find an occupation in the non-farm sector. In other words, the proposed measure will improve occupational mobility by releasing land from those who do not want to work on agriculture. Consequently, more land will be available for leasing in, and, thereby, access to land will improve. Furthermore, if the tenants, especially the fixed-rent tenants, can lease in land for a long period, they may not apply inputs indiscriminately that spoil natural fertility of land and may rather adopt a sustainable strategy for cultivation. Such developments, if actually realized, should augur well for overall rural development.

2.6. CONCLUSION

The space for conventional land reforms in India has shrunk due to the ever-increasing fragmentation of landholdings. As a result, the importance of the land rental market to achieve the objective of ensuring efficient, egalitarian and sustainable use of agricultural land has increased than even before. The increase in land under lease as a

---

[13] Assuring the small and marginal lessors that they will not lose the ownership right is a key component of the reform. Efforts to legalize tenancy contracts and thereby to record them can deliver only a limited result as is evident from the experience after the imposition of the Andhra Pradesh (composite) Land Licensed Act, 2011. The objective of this act is to record tenants and give them eligibility cards so that they can access credit, insurance and other transfer payments. However, the coverage of the act has remained very limited (Murty and Reddy 2017) 2011 of the composite state of Andhra Pradesh (AP). The reason for the limited coverage is that the act does not address the fear of losing ownership rights once lands are leased out. Consequently, the lessors do not want the tenants to register the tenancy contracts.

[14] In fact, along with legalization of tenancy, the emphasis of the tenancy reforms should be equally on making tenancy contracts formal through recording so that interests of the tenants are protected.

proportion of operated area in recent times further strengthens this point. Notwithstanding variations, the area under lease has increased in majority of the states.

However, the restrictive provisions in the existing tenancy laws do not help in achieving the objective of utilizing leased-in land efficiently, equitably and sustainably; rather, they create obstacles in this regard. Keeping in mind the changing agro-economic realities in the countryside, the adverse impacts of the existing laws and the current need, we suggest reforms in the current tenancy laws. The reform measure primarily includes separation of the use-right from the ownership rights. It is expected that such a reform will be helpful in bringing about overall rural development.

REFERENCES

Adams, D. W., and N. Rask. 1968. 'Economics of Cost-Share Leases in Less-developed Countries'. *American Journal of Agricultural Economics* 50, no. 4: 935–942.

Banerjee, A. V., P. J. Gertler, and M. Ghatak. 2002. 'Empowerment and efficiency: Tenancy reform in West Bengal'. *Journal of Political Economy* 110, no. 2: 239–280.

Bansal, V., Y. Usami, and V. Rawal. 2018. *Agricultural Tenancy in Contemporary India: A Compendium of Statistical Tables based on NSSO Surveys of Land and Livestock Holdings*. New Delhi: Society for Social and Economic Research.

Bardhan, P. K., and T. N. Srinivasan. 1971. 'Cropsharing Tenancy in Agriculture: A Theoretical and Empirical Analysis'. *American Economic Review* 61, no. 1: 48–64.

Bardhan, P., and A. Rudra. 1980. 'Terms and Conditions of Sharecropping Contracts: An Analysis of Village Survey Data in India'. *The Journal of Development Studies* 16, no. 3: 287–302.

Basu, K. 2005. *Development, Markets, and Institutions*. New Delhi: Oxford University Press.

Bell, C. 1977. 'Alternative Theories of Sharecropping: Some Tests Using Evidence from Northeast India'. *The Journal of Development Studies* 13, no. 4: 317–346.

———. 1990. 'Reforming Property Rights in Land and Tenancy'. *The World Bank Research Observer* 5, no. 2: 143–166.

Bell, C., and P. Zusman. 1976. 'A Bargaining Theoretic Approach to Cropsharing Contracts'. *The American Economic Review* 66, no. 4: 578–588.

Betham-Edwards, M., ed. 1909. *Arthur Young's Travels in France during the Years 1787, 1788, 1789*. London: George Bell and Sons.

Bhaduri, A. 1973. 'A Study in Agricultural Backwardness Under Semi-Feudalism'. *The Economic Journal* 83, no. 329: 120–137.

Bharadwaj, K., and P. K. Das. 1975. 'Tenurial Conditions and Mode of Exploitation: A Study of Some Villages in Orissa'. *Economic & Political Weekly* 10, no, 5/7: 221–223.

Binswanger, H. P., and M. R. Rosenzweig. 1986. 'Behavioural and Material Determinants of Production Relations in Agriculture'. *The Journal of Development Studies* 22, no. 3: 503–539.

Bliss, C., and N. Stern. 1982. *Palanpur: The Economy of an Indian Village*. New Delhi: Oxford University Press.

Byres, T. J. 1972. 'The Dialectic of India's Green Revolution'. *South Asian Review* 5, no. 2: 99–116.

Cheung, S. N. S. 1969. *The Theroy of Share Tenancy*. Chicago, IL/London: The University of Chicago Press.

Cheung, S. N. S. 1989. 'Economic Organization and Transaction Costs'. In *Allocation, Information and Markets*, edited by J. Eatwell, M. Milgate, and P. Newman, 77–82. London: Palgrave Macmillan.

Georgescu-Roegen, N. 1960. 'Economic Theory and Agrarian Economics'. *Oxford Economic Papers* 12, no. 1: 1–40.

Goswami, B. 2012. *Economic Implication of Tenancy: A Study in Assam's Agrarian Set-up*. Unpublished PhD Thesis. Guwahati: Department of Economics, Gauhati University.

———. 2018a. *Economic Analysis of Agrarian Institutions*. Hyderabad: Orient BlackSwan.

———. 2018b. 'Rental Market of Agricultural Land: Changing Context and Need for Tenancy Reform'. In *Indian Agriculture after the Green Revolution: Changes and Challenges*, edited by B. Goswami, M. P. Bezbaruah, and R. Mandal, 29–45. Abingdon: Routledge.

Goswami, B., and M. P. Bezbaruah. 2013. 'Incidence, Forms and Determinants of Tenancy in the Agrarian Set-up of the Assam Plains'. *Economic & Political Weekly* 48, no. 42: 60–68.

———. 2018. 'Revisiting the Tenancy-inefficiency Question with an Inter-temporal Optimisation Framework: Insights from the Agrarian Set-up of Assam Plains in Eastern India'. *Journal of Social and Economic Development* 20, no. 2: 256–273.

Hayami, Y., and K. Otsuka. 1993. *The Economics of Contract Choice: An Agrarian Perspective*. New York, NY: Clarendon Press.

Herring, R. J. 1980. 'Abolition of Landlordism in Kerala: A Redistribution of Privilege'. *Economic & Political Weekly* 15, no. 26: A59–A69.

———. 1983. *Land to the Tiller: The Political Economy of Agrarian Reform in South Asia*. New Haven, CT: Yale University Press.

Himanshu, T. Bharati, and J. Kaur. 2018. 'Tenancy in Palanpur'. In *How Live change: Palanpur, India, and Development Economics*, edited by Himanshu, P. Lanjouw, and N. Stern, 196–237. New York, NY: Oxford University Press.

Johnson, D. G. 1950. 'Resource Allocation under Share Contracts'. *Journal of Political Economy* 58, no. 2: 111–123.

Jones, R. 1831. *An Essay on the Distribution of Wealth and on the Source of Taxation.* London: John Murray.

Kuri, P. K. 2003. 'Factor Market Imperfections and Explanations of Tenancy: Testing of an Econometric Model Using Evidence from Assam of North-East India'. *Indian Journal of Agricultural Economics* 58, no. 2: 234–245.

Laha, A., and P. K. Kuri. 2010. 'Rural Credit Market and the Choice of Tenurial Contracts: A Micro Evidence from Rural West Bengal, India'. *The Bangladesh Development Studies* 33, no. 4: 63–83.

Marshall, A., ed. 1920. *Principles of Economics*. London: Palgrave Macmillan.

Mill, J. S. 1885. *Principles of Political Economy*. New York, NY: Prometheus Books.

Murty, C. S., and M. S. Reddy. 2017. 'AP Land Licensed Cultivators Act in Retrospect and Prospect'. *Journal of Land and Rural Studies* 5, no. 1: 1–11.

Nair, K. N., and V. Menon. 2006. 'Lease Farming in Kerala: Findings from Micro Level Studies'. *Economic & Political Weekly* 41, no. 26: 2732–2738.

Newbery, D. 1975. 'Tenurial Obstacles to Innovation'. *The Journal of Development Studies* 11, no. 4: 263–277.

NITI Aayog. 2016. *Report of the Expert Committee on Land Leasing*. New Delhi: NITI Aayog.

Otsuka, K., and Y. Hayami. 1988. 'Theories of Share Tenancy: A Critical Survey'. *Economic Development and Cultural Change* 37, no. 1: 31–68.

Quibria, M. G., and S. Rashid. 1984. 'The Puzzle of Sharecropping: A Survey of Theories'. *World Development* 12, no. 2: 103–114.

Ramakumar, R. 2000. 'Magnitude and Terms of Agricultural Tenancy in India: A Statewise Analysis of Changes in 1980s'. *Indian Journal of Agricultural Economics* 55, no. 3: 337.

Rawal, V. 2008. 'Ownership Holdings of Land in Rural India: Putting the Record Straight'. *Economic & Political Weekly* 43, no. 10: 43–47.

Ray, D. 1998. *Development Economics*. New Delhi: Oxford University Press.

Reddy, M. S., and C. S. Murty. 2021. 'Land Lease Market under Irrigated and Rainfed Conditions in Andhra Pradesh and Telangana'. *Indian Journal of Agricultural Economics* 76, no. 2: 261–277.

Schickele, R. 1941. 'Effect of Tenure Systems on Agricultural Efficiency'. *Journal of Farm Economics* 23, no. 1: 185–207.

Sen, A. K. 1966. 'Peasants and Dualism with or without Surplus Labor'. *Journal of Political Economy* 74, no. 5: 425–450.

Shaban, R. A. 1987. 'Testing between Competing Models of Sharecropping'. *Journal of Political Economy* 95, no. 5: 893–920.

Sharma, H. R., and S. H. Malik. 2021. 'Land Distribution Structure, Marginalisation of Holdings and Dimensions of Viability Crisis in Indian Agriculture: A State Level Analysis'. *Indian Journal of Agricultural Economics* 76, no. 2: 207–224.

Sharma, N., and J. Dréze. 1996. 'Sharecropping in a North Indian Village'. *The Journal of Development Studies* 33, no. 1: 1–39.

Sharma, N., and J. Dréze. 1998. 'Tenancy'. In *Economic Development in Palanpur over Five Decades*, edited by Peter Lanjouw and Nicholas Stern. New Delhi: Oxford University Press.

Shergill, H. S. 2019. 'Universalisation of Cash Rent Tenancy in Punjab Agriculture: The Causal Factors'. *Indian Journal of Agricultural Economics* 74, no. 4: 552–561.

Smith, A. 1776. *The Wealth of Nations: An Inquiry into the Nature and Causes of the Wealth of Nations*. London: Penguin Classics.

Stiglitz, J. E. 1974. 'Incentives and Risk Sharing in Sharecropping'. *The Review of Economic Studies* 41, no. 2: 219–255.

———. 2004. 'Information and the Change in the Paradigm in Economics'. In *New Frontiers in Economics*, edited by M. Szenberg and L. Ramrattan, 27–67. Cambridge: Cambridge University Press.

Chapter 3

Land Market II

Outright Sale and Issues of Land Acquisition

Madhurjya Prasad Bezbaruah and Faridus Mamun Khan

3.1. INTRODUCTION

Land, along with water, constitutes the most important natural resource required for any agricultural activity to take place. As ownership of land and other factors for agricultural production is rarely endowed in optimal proportions across farm households, markets for land and other factors of production have important roles in altering factor combinations in farming units to more optimal ones. While labour markets enable farm households with labour shortage to acquire additional hands to work in the farms, land markets enable farmers with inadequate or excess availability of land to acquire or shed land for a more effective allocation of land across farms. Transactions between owners and users of agricultural land take place in two types of markets. First, there are the short-term land rental markets where land is acquired on lease for a relatively short period of time, which may range from a crop season to a few years, by those who want to expand their scale of agricultural operation from those who possess land but are unable or unwilling to utilize it fully themselves. In such land rental markets what is transacted is the temporary user right of parcels of land, and the ownership of the land remains with the original holder of it. In the other type of markets, ownership of land is transacted for a longer period either through long-term lease agreements or outright purchase and sale of holding. The land rental markets have been discussed in detail in another chapter of this volume. The focus of this chapter, therefore, is on the land sale market or transactions for outright transfer ownership of landholdings.

Transfer of land through outright change of ownership may take place for agricultural or non-agricultural use of land. With the total geographical area of the country remaining constant over time, the competition among agricultural and non-agricultural sectors for use of the available land resource can be expected to become more intense with the progress of time. Agriculture, traditionally, has been a land-extensive activity. In a developing economy, its primary role has been to produce enough food for ensuring food security of the people in the country. In terms of its share in the gross domestic product (GDP), the importance of agriculture in the Indian economy has been going down steadily over the years.[1] Yet, the significance of agriculture in the economy cannot be claimed to have gone down concomitantly. Despite the momentous shift of the workforce from farm to non-farm sectors since the beginning of the century, agriculture engaged 41 per cent of India's workforce in 2020.[2] As per the 77th round of the National Sample Survey, 54 per cent of the households in rural India were agricultural households in 2018–2019 (National Statistical Office 2021).[3] In recent years, there has been a shift in the preference of Indian consumers away from cereals and other food grains towards

[1] Share of agriculture in gross value added of India has been steadily declining. It stood at 16.1 per cent in 2018–2019 (Economic Survey 2018–2019, Government of India).

[2] Employment in agriculture (percentage of total employment) in India was reported at 41.49 per cent in 2020, according to the World Bank Collection of Development Indicators, compiled from officially recognized sources.

[3] An agricultural household is defined as a household whose production value from all agricultural activities is more than ₹4,000 and having at least one member self-employed in agriculture, either in principal status or in subsidiary status, during the 365 days prior to the survey. Agricultural activities include cultivation of field crops, horticultural crops, fodder crops, plantation, animal husbandry, poultry, fishery, piggery, beekeeping, vermiculture, sericulture, etc. (National Statistical Office, 2021, 4).

vegetables, fruits and livestock products such as meat, milk, fish and eggs (Deshmukh and Vyavahare 2018). In response to this, the composition of agricultural output has also changed in favour of the high-value horticulture and livestock (Paltasingh et al. 2018). Apart from meeting food requirements, agriculture also produces industrial raw materials and exportable items like tea and spices and import substituting commodities like rubber and pulses. Accordingly, the question of reallocating land away from agriculture to non-agricultural uses has to be dealt with carefully.

The demand for land for non-agricultural use has also been increasing rapidly with (a) growing urbanization, (b) the need to improve surface connectivity by expanding road and rail links, (c) the aspiration for India to emerge as a manufacturing hub, and (d) the space required for setting up general infrastructure facilities that go with the development process of an economy. The pertinent question in this context therefore is whether agricultural land can be transferred for non-agricultural use without limiting the role of agriculture in the economy.

Given this backdrop, the remaining parts of the chapter discuss (a) the possibility of agriculture being able to spare land for non-agricultural use, (b) the paradigm of transfer of land among farmers through exchanges in the rural land sale markets and its implication for land acquisition, (c) the complications involved in land transfer and acquisition in India and (d) the attempts towards the formulation of a framework for fairer and speedier acquisition and transfer of land for infrastructure and industrial projects.

3.2. IS THERE ENOUGH LAND TO BE TRANSFERRED AWAY FROM AGRICULTURE?

The possibility of reallocating land from agricultural to non-agricultural use may arise because of the following factors.

Agriculture over the years has been becoming intensive in a number of senses, leading to increasing economization of land. With the expansion of irrigation and development of short-duration photo-intensive varieties, cropping of the same area several times in a year has become

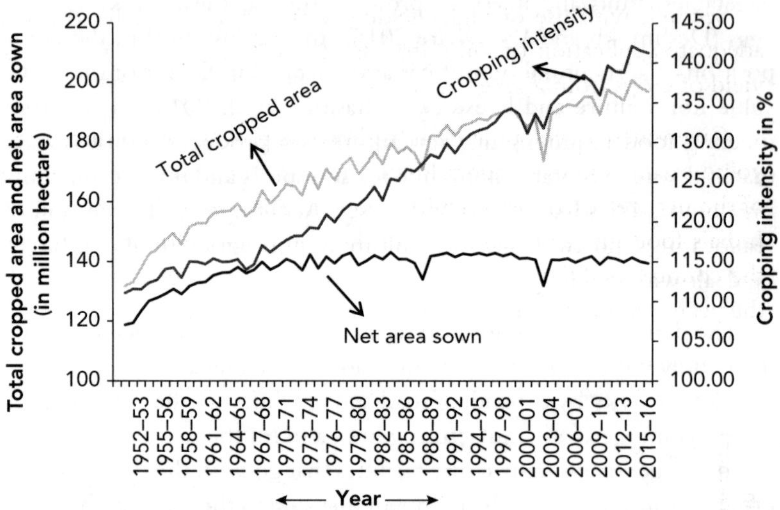

Figure 3.1 *Trends in Net Sown Area, Gross Cropped Area and Cropping Intensity in India*

Source: Authors' construction using data from Government of India (2019).

possible, leading to a growth in cropping intensity. Figure 3.1 presents the upward trend in cropping intensity in India, which started in 1966–1967—the years in which the seeds of the Green Revolution were sown—and the trend continued in the same direction ever since. Figure 3.1 also shows the resulting effective increase in agricultural land (gross cropped area), which went up by 40 per cent in the meantime to reach nearly 200 million hectare mark by 2015–2016, while the physical land surface used in agriculture (technically called the net sown area) remained practically unchanged around 140 million hectares.[4]

---

[4] Gross cropped area (GCA), also known as total cropped area, is the total area sown in a particular year. In calculating GCA, an area is counted as many times as there are sowings in it in the year.

Net area sown represents the total area sown with crops and orchards. Area sowed more than once in the same year is counted only once.

Cropping intensity refers to raising of a number of crops from the same field during one agricultural year.

Cropping Intensity = (Gross Cropped Area/Net Sown Area) × 100.

Second, with use of high-yielding varieties, in combination with adequate application of soil nutrients, it has been possible to increase yield of crops from a given area.

Given these developments, it has become possible to produce larger volumes and values of agricultural output without further expansion of the net area used for agricultural operations. Figure 3.2 shows how India's food grain production and the contribution of agriculture to the country's GDP in absolute real terms have steadily increased over the years despite the net area sown remaining by and large unchanged.

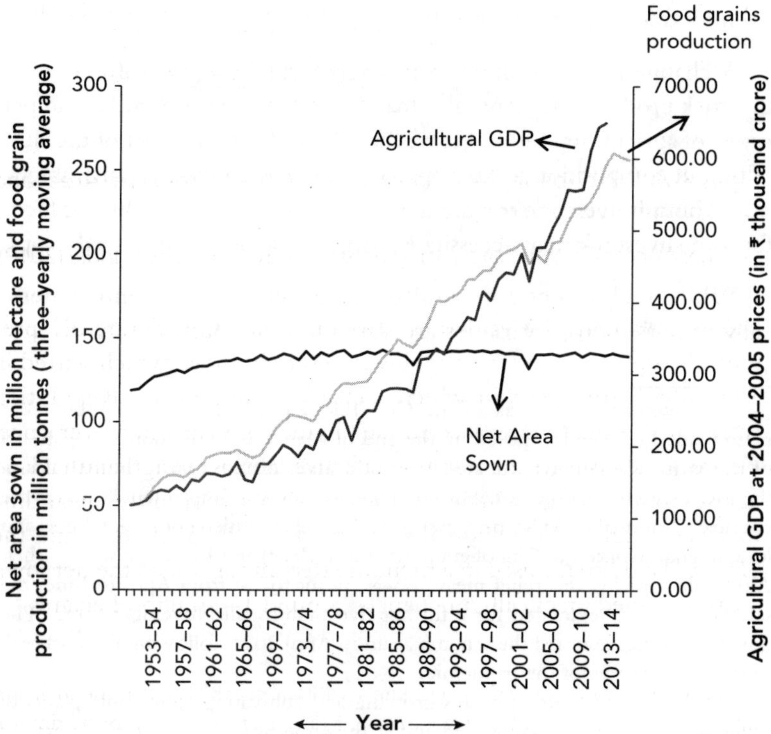

Figure 3.2 *Trends in Food Grain Production, Agricultural GDP at 2004–2005 Prices and Net Sown Area in India*

Source: Author's construction using data from Government of India (2019) and https://niti.gov.in/planningcommission.gov.in/docs/data/datatable/data_2312/DatabookDec2014%202.pdf

Indeed, for the past few decades, India has been carrying such large stocks of food grains, especially wheat and rice, that storage and management of the stocks have been a challenge to the policymakers (Basu 2011; Bhalla 2020; Chand 2009, 2012; Gulati 2013). There has been an attempt to address the issue, along with some other imbalances, that has crept into Indian agriculture, by enacting three farm bills by the Indian parliament (Bezbaruah and Khan 2020). Meanwhile, the excess stock has been of invaluable use in India's strategy of coping with the ongoing COVID-19 pandemic. Since May 2020, governments have been able to distribute free food grains from this stock to the poorer segment of the Indian population, who suffered income deflation and livelihood loss due to the pandemic.[5]

A change in the composition of agricultural output from crops to livestock products may have also made it possible to economize land per rupee of agricultural GDP. However, the land-saving effect of the shift of output composition from crops to livestock is not entirely unambiguous. Though livestock rearing may require less space, producing feeds for some livestock may necessitate a larger area allocation to feed-crops.

While techniques like multi-layered cultivation[6] and genetically modified crop[7] varieties are slated to make further inroads into

---

[5] Following the outbreak of the COVID-19 pandemic and the subsequent nationwide lockdown imposed by the end of March 2020 to contain the spread of the virus, the country initiated free food grain distribution to households at the lower end of income distribution. This measure was implemented under the country's National Food Security Act (NFSA), and it entitled poor households and local migrant workers to 5 kg of grains (rice and wheat) and 1 kg of pulses monthly. Although, initially, this relief measure was meant to last from April to June, the scheme was later extended for a further five months till November 2020. The government has resumed the scheme again in April 2021, following the outbreak of the second wave of the pandemic.

[6] Multi-layered farming means growing and cultivating compatible plants of different heights on the same field and at the same time. It is generally practised in orchards and plantation crops for the utmost use of solar energy even under high planting density.

[7] Genetically modified (GM) crops are plants used in agriculture, the deoxyribonucleic acid (DNA) of which has been modified using genetic engineering methods. The resulting crop can be disease and pest resistant and/or richer in nutritional value. The most commonly genetically modified crops are soy beans, corn, cotton, canola, etc.

agriculture, there are additional reasons to be optimistic about progressive economization of land per unit of agricultural GDP.

Another source for which it may become possible to spare agricultural land for non-agricultural purposes lies in the demographic dynamics of the country. Despite hunger and malnutrition still remaining unacceptably high[8] in India and the world, it is arguable that the 21st century world is no longer a Malthusian one, where population growth outstrips growth in food production, pushing the world towards a catastrophe. With sharply declining fertility rates,[9] population growth rates in India and elsewhere are expected to decline in the coming years so that the world is projected to have less human population by the end of this century than at the present time (Tahvi et al. 2020). India's population is projected to peak by the mid-2040s and steadily decline thereafter. Hence, the requirement to progressively increase food production for meeting the food security needs of a supposedly progressively growing population may not be necessary.

But before we go to the issue of land acquisition and transfer for reallocation of land from agricultural to non-agricultural use, let us take up the nature of transfers of farmland within agriculture through transactions in the rural land sale markets. The patterns of transactions in these markets have implications for formulation of a sound land acquisition policy.

3.3. AGRICULTURAL LAND SALE MARKETS AND THE PATTERN OF LAND TRANSFERS WITHIN AGRICULTURE

One of the much-discussed phenomena in the context of Indian agriculture has been the farm size–productivity inverse relationship. While 'farm size' generally refers to the operational holding of a

[8] As per Global Hunger Index 2020, the percentage of population malnourished in India is 14 per cent. The overall hunger index value (GHI Score), which reflects not only undernourishment but also the extent of malnutrition, is 27.2, which falls in the serious category (Von Grebmer et al. 2020).

[9] As per the National Family Health Survey (NFSH) 5, the total fertility rate (children per woman) declined in India from 2.2 to 2.0 in a matter of just four to five years from 2015–2016 to 2019–2021 (Government of India 2021, 3).

farming unit, 'productivity' in this debate is usually equated to yield of the crop cultivated. Leaving aside the unviable tiny farms and the sharecropping tenant farmers—who generally have other incentive issues—owner-operated and predominantly family labour–run farms, which are typically smaller in size, show higher productivity than the large mechanized farms operating with hired labour. While the more mechanized nature of the latter should have contributed to greater efficiency, substitution of family labour by hired workers often has the opposite effects because of a drop in work intensity and incentives, which outweigh the efficiency gain from greater mechanization. Some other factors have also been suggested for the observed inverse correspondence. According to Ray (1998, 453), it is quite possible that small plots are of higher quality. Good land may be more fragmented in the process of inheritance. Moreover, farmers who sell off land in distress, becoming smallholders in the process, should logically offer to sell off the relatively less fertile parts of the land they own.

Though the empirical evidence on the inverse relation is not unanimous, most studies do confirm a negative correspondence.[10] Given that a trade-off exists between farm size and productivity, the pertinent question in the present context is whether this trade-off influences the pattern of transactions in the land sale market within agriculture. Specifically, whether small landowners are found buying land frequently from rich landowners to exploit productivity gains from the operation of the trade-off. Available empirical evidence suggests that this is not usually the case. While land sale from the relatively rich to the relatively poor is not entirely unheard of, it is typically the other way round in most transactions in the markets for land. This apparent paradox begs an explanation.

---

[10] For instance, Berry and Cline (1979) and Sen (1981) support the inverse farm size–productivity relationship But Walker and Ryan (1990) empirically reject the hypothesis of a negative correspondence between size and productivity. A more recent study, using field data from a nationally representative survey and measuring productivity in terms of yield as well as farm income generated per unit of land, confirms a statistically significant inverse relationship (Gaurav and Mishra 2019).

In a typical Indian rural set-up, the value of land to its holder has at least two components. The first component arises from its usefulness as a factor of production. This component of the value of land amounts to the discounted sum of income streams that will emanate from working the land. The second component arises due to the fact that credit markets in rural India are generally imperfect. In such conditions, it is often necessary to offer land as collateral for securing a loan.[11] The value from this service of the land can be measured by the profitability of the additional loans that can be obtained as a result of mortgaging the land. Under normal conditions, a seller will therefore want to sell the land for a price that is no less than the sum of these two values. If the buyer can buy the land outright from his/her own funds, then he/she reaps both these gains as well and should be willing to pay accordingly for a plot of land. But if the buyer must obtain a loan to buy the land, as most smallholders would, he/she may have to mortgage that very piece of land for the loan. Hence, he/she cannot reap the collateral value of the land until the loan is paid off. Thus, the collateral advantage of a land purchase is pushed back to a distant future when the loan has been repaid. Accordingly, the buyer's present valuation of the land, and hence his/her willingness to pay, is likely to be less than the price the seller is willing to accept. Thus, no transfers generally take place through sale from big landholders to smaller holders (Binswanger et al. 1995; Feder et al. 1988).

Because of the above-discussed reason, the land sale market is rather thin in the sense that land sale transactions are relatively few and infrequent. Most land sales, indeed, appear to be in the form of distress sales that occur from the poor to the rich. By implication, the price at which land is transacted can often be less than its true economic value. A distressed smallholder is unlikely to be able to wait for a better price and will typically be in a weaker bargaining position as compared to the more strongly funded potential buyer.

[11] If credit markets were perfectly competitive, one could obtain all the loans one wanted at some going rate of interest without having to offer land or any other asset as mortgage.

Thinness of the market and the usual distressed condition of the sellers reduce the efficacy of the price of land in the intra-agriculture transfers as a reference point of value of land in designing a compensation package for land acquisition.

3.4. GROWING DEMAND FOR LAND FOR NON-AGRICULTURAL USE AND THE NECESSITY OF LAND ACQUISITION

In July 2021, India completed three decades of launching wide-ranging market-oriented economic reforms. The reform process lifted India to a higher growth trajectory, which was sustained for a long time (25 years) from 1992 to 1993 despite the world economy facing a number of crises in between. The growth process enabled millions of poor Indians to climb up above the poverty line, bringing down the county's poverty headcount ratio to below 20 per cent before the COVID-19 pandemic has queered pitch somewhat. Despite such stellar achievement, the reform process has also had failings. Unlike China, India did not emerge as a major manufacturing nation, limiting the number of job creations for its bulging working-age-group population in the industrial sector. Inequality remained high as the overwhelming majority of the workforce had to remain in the low-paying excessively competitive informal sectors. Critics ascribe such failing of the reform process to the government's inability to push through the necessary reforms in two critical factor markets, namely the labour market and the market for land (Bhagwati and Panagaria 2014). Despite India's otherwise open-arm approach to foreign direct investment (FDI), FDI inflows have been modest as compared to those of China. One of the reasons identified behind relatively smaller FDI inflow and also less-than-expected volume of domestic investments in organized manufacturing has been cited as the difficulty in getting hold of suitable land for setting up production facilities. The National Democratic Alliance (NDA) government led by Prime Minister Narendra Modi has reiterated India's aspiration to become a major industrial power by its call for 'make in India' and *Atmanirbhar Bharat* (self-reliant India). But for this aspiration to be fulfilled, an important necessary condition is to be able to quickly allocate land for setting up of new Industrial units. This leads us to the question of reform of the legal framework for land transfer and acquisition, which has remained largely unchanged for over a century. But to be able to appreciate some finer points in the context, first, a look at the land-use pattern in India can be instructive.

Both Table 3.1 and Figure 3.3 show that over the entire period, the land used for non-agricultural purposes has been increasing steadily without concomitant decrease in the total land available for agriculture. So far, the growing share of land under non-agricultural use, on the aggregate, has expanded at the expense of cultivable wasteland. However, with the structural transformation of the Indian economy gathering momentum since 2000 and with the expected acceleration in the pace of urbanization of the country, the land required for non-agricultural use can be expected to grow at a faster pace in the coming years. Consequently, agriculture, which is currently the largest user of the country's total reporting area, may come under pressure to shed land for non-agricultural uses.

Apart from the expected industrial and urban expansion, the changing composition of agricultural output in favour of horticulture and livestock rearing will also generate greater demand for non-agricultural use of land, as more space will be required for expanding storage and processing facilities for the output of these sub-sectors.

For infrastructure and industrial projects, land is usually required in extensive continuous area. Since no single farmer is likely to possess land in such large quantities, negotiations for land purchase are required to be carried out with a large number of farmers, which, in practice, can be very complicated. A handful of farmers refusing to give up their land at any cost can hold up the land transfer process. Accordingly, government-mediated land acquisition,[12] which implies the acquiring

---

[12] Land acquisition is the act of acquiring of private land by the union or a state government in India for 'public purpose', with specified compensation to the affected landowners. Theoretically, 'public purpose' is supposed to serve the collective interest of the broader community, overriding the private interest of the individual land owners. In practice, 'public purpose' may primarily include industrialization, development of infrastructural facilities and urbanization. Defence projects, infrastructure projects and projects related to housing for the poor, irrespective of whether the project is in public sector, under public–private partnership or private sector, have been specifically mentioned as 'public purpose' projects.

Table 3.1 *Land (in Million Hectares) under Different Land-use Categories in India*

Years Categories	1970–1971	1980–1981	1990–1991	2000–2001	2011–2012	2015–2016
1. Barren and uncultivable land	28.13	19.96	19.39	17.48	17.22	16.94
2. Forest	63.83	67.46	67.81	69.84	71.6	71.87
3. Other uncultivated land (pastures, grazing grounds, orchards, etc.)	17.63	15.57	15.22	14.10	13.47	13.35
4. Net area sown (area under agricultural use)	140.86	140.29	142.87	141.34	140.98	139.51
5. Land usable in agriculture (fallow land)	19.33	24.55	23.37	25.04	25.18	26.72
6. Area under non-agricultural uses	16.48	19.6	21.09	23.75	26.31	27.08
7. Cultivable wasteland	17.50	16.74	15.00	13.63	12.64	12.29
Reporting area (total)	303.76	304.17	304.75	305.18	307.40	307.76

Source: Government of India (2019).

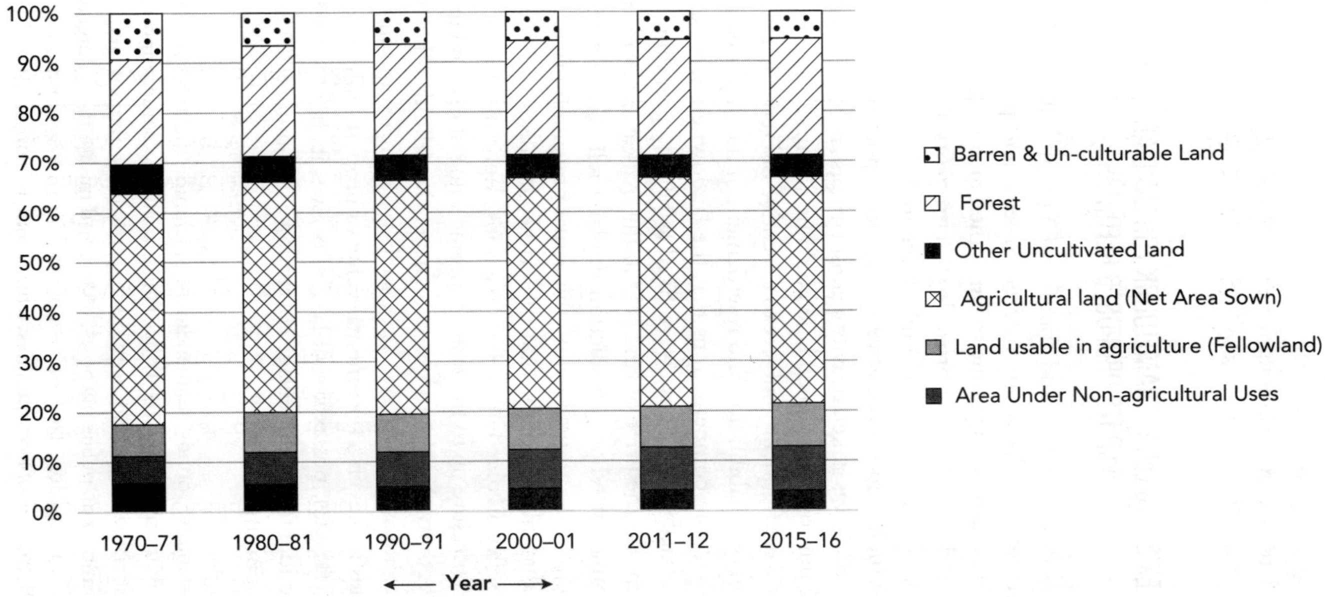

Figure 3.3 *Composition of India's Reporting Area*

Source: Authors' construction using data from Government of India (2019).

of private land by government fiat, albeit with due compensation, becomes necessary.

3.5. EXISTING LEGAL FRAMEWORK FOR LAND ACQUISITION AND ITS PROPOSED REFORMS

The process of acquisition and transfer of agricultural land for non-agricultural use in India is often mired in legal and political tangles. Despite some changes from time to time, the Land Acquisition Act of 1894 (LA) had remained the broad legal framework for land acquisition in India till a new Act came into force in 2013 to replace it. The 1894 Act, which empowered governments to acquire private lands for 'public purpose', was staked heavily against farmers and other landowners. 'Public purposes' for which land could be acquired were not fully defined but were frequently subject to executive discretions. There was no provision of rehabilitation and resettlement of the displaced households. Further, the compensations that the landowners were entitled to were abysmally low. These were fixed as per the prevailing 'circle rates', which was the price of land sold in the market as per records in the circle office in whose jurisdiction the land fell. These rates were generally outdated and well below the actual prevailing price. It may be recalled that thinness of the land sale market and distressed condition of the land seller involved in most transactions imply that the transacted price fails to measure up to the true economic value of the land in terms of its productivity. Furthermore, to a farmer, land holds other values besides its value as a productive asset, such as a security and insurance for bad times and even a sentimental value of property inherited from forefathers. Besides, possession of land also gives its holder a sense of prestige and identity in the village community (Majumder 2019, 5–7). As Bagchi sums up,

> Notwithstanding rounds of amendments, including the 1984 changes, it (Land Acquisition Act 1894) has failed to address some important issues associated with land acquisition particularly forcible acquisitions, definition of 'public purpose', widespread misuse the of 'urgency clause', compensation, lack of transparency in the acquisition process, participation of communities whose land is being acquired and

> virtually no rehabilitation and resettlement package. Further, weak implementation and ineffective administration at the ground level has increased the suffering and anguish of the people. Due to a lack of clear definition of 'public purpose', there has been considerable difference of opinion among various judgments of the Supreme Court, finally resulting into granting very broad discretionary powers to the state in terms of deciding the contours of 'public purpose' under particular circumstances. (Bagchi 2012, 1).

It is no surprise therefore that many land acquisition processes in the past resulted in bitter and long-drawn legal and political contentions. Disputes related to land acquisition and rehabilitation of the Sardar Sarovar Dam,[13] the failed acquisition attempts for Tata Motor's small-car project in Singur,[14] a special economic zone in Nandigram[15] in the state of West Bengal and South Korean company POSCO's[16] steel plant in the state of Odisha are some of the high-profile cases of the recent past.

Given the multitudes of complication in land acquisition process in India, Bhagwati and Panagaria (2014) insist that the crux of the problem

---

[13] The Sardar Sarovar Dam is a concrete gravity dam built on the Narmada River in the state of Gujarat in India. The four Indian states of Gujarat, Madhya Pradesh, Maharashtra and Rajasthan were to receive water and electricity supply from the dam. The construction of the dam began in 1987, but the project was stalled by the Supreme Court of India in 1995 over concerns of displacement of people and ecological damage through the inundation of forests. The dam was later allowed to be completed with lowered height and finally came into operation in 2017.

[14] Land acquisition at Singur, West Bengal, was initiated in 2008 as per the Land Acquisition Act, 1894, for the setting up of an automobile factory by Tata Motors. There was no provision of compensation for he landless agricultural workers, unrecorded sharecroppers and other rural households, who were indirectly dependent for their livelihood on land and agricultural activities. Many landowners had also expressed their unwillingness to give their land. Following a strong opposition to the acquisition process, the project was subsequently moved to Gujarat.

[15] Violence occurred in Nandigram, West Bengal, in 2007, following an attempt to acquire land for a special economic zone (SEZ).

[16] The South Korean conglomerate POSCO signed a memorandum of understanding with the state government of Odisha in June 2005 to construct a steel plant in the state. The project ran into trouble as villagers opposed the acquisition of their land for it.

has been the insufficient compensation fixed as per law. They find that numerous land transfers for projects have been successfully completed in the states of Gujarat, Punjab and Karnataka through direct negotiations between private parties with offers of generous compensations. In these projects, land cost constituted only a tiny proportion of the total project cost. Hence, it was not difficult for the industrialists to offer an attractive price to landowners.

A process of reforming of land acquisition process was finally rolled out in 2007, which resulted in the introduction of a bill to overhaul the prevailing land acquisition laws in the Indian parliament in 2011. After prolonged debates and discussion inside and outside the parliament, a new land acquisition act named as Right to Fair Compensation and Transparency in Land Acquisition, Rehabilitation and Resettlement (LARR) Act came into being. The principal features of the 2013 Act include:

1. an increased compensation to be provided to landowners from 1.3 times the price of land to 2 times the price of land in urban areas, and 2–4 times the price of land in rural areas;
2. compensation to be extended to those families who did not own land, but were dependent on the land for their livelihood;
3. compensation to include measures for rehabilitation of the displaced households;
4. a social impact assessment (SIA) to be conducted for all projects, except those for which land was required urgently. The SIA is to assess such aspects of a proposed acquisition as to whether the project serves public purpose and whether only the minimum area that is required is being acquired besides assessing the social impact of the acquisition; and
5. consent of 80 per cent of landowners for private projects, and 70 per cent of landowners' public–private partnership projects to be first secured for the acquisition process to begin.

The LARR Act was no doubt aimed at ensuring that the land is acquired strictly for public welfare projects, and landowners are adequately compensated and rehabilitated. However, in its concern to be politically correct, the new Act might have over-corrected for the shortcomings of the 1894 Act, as it came to be perceived as making the terms of acquisition too much in favour of the landowners. As a result, land acquisition remained as much in limbo as it used to be before this LARR Act, 2013, came into being. The NDA government that came to power in 2014 aimed to quicken the process of industrialization of the country by bringing in programmes like 'Make in India' and *Atmanirbhar Bharat* to attract domestic and foreign firms to set up their manufacturing units in India. To induce investments by firms in industrial projects, it became an imperative on the part of the government to make the recent legislation more investor friendly. Accordingly, some amendments were proposed to the LARR, and the Right to Fair Compensation and Transparency in Land Acquisition, Rehabilitation and Resettlement (Amendment) Bill, 2015, was introduced in the parliament.

Some of the significant changes proposed in the 2015 Bill are the following:

1. The provision of securing consent of 70–80 per cent of landowners to be exempted for acquiring lands for the five purposes of industrial corridors, public–private partnership projects, rural infrastructure, affordable housing and defence.
2. According to the Act, 2013, if the land remains unutilized for five years, then it needs to be returned to the owner. But according to the proposed amendments, the period after which unutilized land needs to be returned will be five years, or any period specified at the time of setting up the project.
3. According to the 2013 Act, land can be acquired by any private company. But according to the recent ordinance, land can be acquired by any private entity.

Though the bill was easily passed in the lower house of the parliament, it faced bitter political opposition. Apart from opposition parties, some organizations aligned to the BJP, the principal component of the ruling alliance, like Bharatiya Kisan Sangh and Akhil Bharatiya Vanavasi Kalyan Ashram, also expressed their opposition to the amendments in the 2015 bill (Shivananda 2015). As the bill awaits approval in the upper house of the parliament for becoming an Act, some of the state governments, Karnataka and Maharashtra in particular, have gone ahead with their own amendments of the Right to Fair Compensation and Transparency in Land Acquisition, Rehabilitation and Resettlement Act, 2013. But India as a nation is yet to have a settled framework for land acquisition and transfer.

3.6. THE POSSIBLE WAYS FORWARD

The issue of land acquisition cannot be resolved on the basis of compensation linked to a market-determined valuation of the land alone. Besides, the fact remains that the market for land sale is too vitiated by imperfections to reveal a true value of the asset, and land often has many other intrinsic values to its holder, which cannot be captured by market forces. In a country like India where the existing social security for people in the informal sector is so thin that whatever land is held provides a sense of security to the holder for possible bad times. Thus, for farmers, land is not merely an income-generating asset but also an insurance policy. Given that their skills are specific to agriculture, if their land is taken away, most of them may not have any other choice than working as unskilled labourers. Possession of land, by contrast, gives an individual a status and an identity in society. Often, there is emotional attachment to the land as something inherited from forefathers. A sum of money determined with reference to a price recorded in a rather distorted land sale market cannot take into account these different non-marketed values attached to land by farmers. For successful implementation of land acquisition and transfer, it is necessary to devise an acquisition procedure that will take into account all these factors, besides, containing a fair compensation and rehabilitation in lieu of giving up possession of the land. At the same time, the compensations should not be so excessive as to dissuade potential acquirers of the land from going ahead. Finding the right balance is the challenge of the lawmakers.

Some economists have questioned the very basis of the compensation principles underlying the above-described land acquisition laws.

Ghatak and Ghosh (2015) make the point that the compensation rules suggested are arbitrary and not based on sound economic principle or process. Further, neither the LARR Bill, 2013, nor its proposed amendments of 2015 address the issue that once the project will come up the neighbouring farmers whose land will not be acquired are going to reap huge windfalls in terms of an increase in the value of their land—an opportunity that will not be available to farmers whose land will be acquired.

Ghatak (2019) suggests that an auction-based approach can lead to the discovery of a more appropriate price of land to be acquired. Lands owned by different farmers are generally not of uniform quality. Accordingly, there is heterogeneity of land valuations to owners, whereas compensation offers are usually uniform per unit of land. This results in reluctance and even refusal by owners of higher valued land plots to give up their land for acquisition. Ghatak feels that this problem can be avoided in his auction-based approach to land acquisition.

The suggested procedure goes like this: the government will buy some land in and around the project site through an auction. All landowners in the region will be asked to submit asking prices for their plots. Then, the government can start buying land starting from the cheapest offers and then go on to buy the next higher ones. In the process, the government will be buying some of the land in the proposed project site itself and some in the neighbourhood of the site. The remaining project land will then have to be acquired. The price of the last plot purchased can presumably serve as the reference price for the acquisition process. Further, the farmers who will be displaced in the process can be given the option of accepting cash compensation based on the auction revealed price or a plot of land in a nearby location, which the government will have acquired already. Ghatak claims that the process will determine a fair price through a participatory process of competitive bidding, where farmers are free to name their own price. The procedure can thus fill in for missing or imperfect land markets. The suggestion is still in the realm of ideas, and from the way it has been presented, it is not clear how a possible strategic bias arising from landowners' incentive to overstate the price of the land is to be taken care of. Obviously, this and other practical issues may surface in attempting to implement the procedure. Fine-tuning the auction design to take care of these issues will be a challenge. Yet, in the absence of any seemingly superior alternative, Ghatak's suggestion is definitely worth a try. He believes that determining compensation through a land auction and then allowing farmers to choose between land or cash compensation stands a much better chance of satisfying the farmers.

India's recent success in the allocation of coal blocks and telecom spectrum through auctioning inspires some confidence that the auction process may also work more smoothly in the case of land acquisition than the procedures outlined in the Acts (BI India Bureau 2015).

An alternative suggestion for allocating land for large industrial and infrastructure projects is to take the land on a long-term lease rather than outright acquisition of the landholders' ownership over their land. A leasing arrangement not only obviates the need for holders to give up their landownership but also entitles them to a regular stream of rent income, which can be periodically revised with the growing valuation of the land (Aiyar 2012). However, the question of fixing the right amount of rent and getting all farmers in the project site to agree to the lease agreement will remain.

Given the importance and urgency of the issue, it may be worthwhile to try the various alternative ways or some combinations of the different ways to find out context-specific appropriate methods for optimal allocation of land resource among its various alternative uses.

REFERENCES

Aiyar, Swaminathan S. Anklesaria. 2012, 20 June. 'Lease Land, Don't Acquire it'. *Economic Times*. https://economictimes.indiatimes.com/swaminathan-s-a-aiyar/lease-land-dont-acquire-it/articleshow/14284593.cms?from=mdr (accessed on 21 February 2022).

Bagchi, Kanad. 2012, 16 August. 'The Land Acquisition Debate: A Review'. Observer Research Foundation. https://www.orfonline.org/research/the-land-acquisition-debate-a-review/ (accessed on 21 February 2022).

Basu, Kaushik. 2011. 'India's Food Grain Policy: An Economic Theory Perspective'. *Economic & Political Weekly* 46, no. 5. https://www.epw.in/journal/2011/05/

special-articles/indias-foodgrain-policy-economic-theory-perspective.html#:~:text=The%20simultaneous%20occurrence%20of%20high,been%20a%20matter%20of%20concern.&text=While%20we%20no%20doubt%20should,lower%20the%20price%20of%20food (accessed on 21 February 2022).

Berry, R. A., and W. R. Cline 1979. *Agrarian Structure and Productivity in Developing Countries*. Geneva: International Labour Organization.

Bezbaruah, M. P., and Faridus M. Khan 2020. 'MSP, Agricultural Reforms and the Farm Bills'. *Dialogue Quarterly* 22, no. 2. http://www.asthabharati.org/Dia_Oct%20020.pdf (accessed on 21 February 2022).

Bhagwati, J., and A. Panagariya. 2014. *Why Growth Matters: How Economic Growth in India Reduced Poverty and the Lessons for Other Developing Countries*. New York, NY: Public Affairs.

Bhalla, Surjit S. 2020. 'Protesting Farmers Are Arguing for the Perpetuation of Colonial Rule'. *The Indian Express*. https://indianexpress.com/article/opinion/columns/farmers-protest-agri-laws-apmc-mandis-msp-surjit-bhalla-7101406/ (accessed on 21 February 2022).

BI India Bureau. 2015, 10 March. 'Coal and Spectrum Auctions Usher in more "Achhe Din"'. *Business Insider*. https://www.businessinsider.in/coal-and-spectrum-auctions-usher-in-more-achhe-din/articleshow/46517421.cms (accessed on 21 February 2022).

Binswanger, H., K. Deininger, and G. Feder 1995. 'Power, Distortions, Revolt and Reform in Agricultural Land Relations'. In *Handbook of Development Economics*, Vol. 3B, edited by J. Behrman and T. N. Srinivasan. Amsterdam: North Holland.

Chand, Ramesh 2009. 'Wheat Market: The Distortions Caused by Government Intervention'. *Economic & Political Weekly* 44, no. 12: 41–46.

———. 2012. 'Development Policies and Agricultural Markets'. *Economic & Political Weekly*, Review of Rural Affairs 47, no. 52: 53–63.

Deshmukh, M. S., and S. S. Vyavahare. 2018. 'An Analysis of Consumption Expenditure in India'. *European Academic Research* 5, no. 10. https://www.researchgate.net/publication/355188693_An_Analysis_of_Consumption_Expenditure_in_India (accessed on 21 February 2022).

Feder, G., T. Onchan, Y. Chamlamwong, and C. Hongladoran. 1988. *Land Policies and Farm Productivity in Thailand*. Baltimore, MD: Johns Hopkins University Press.

Gaurav, Sarthak, and Srijit Mishra. 2019. 'Is Small Still Beautiful? Revisiting the Farm-size Productivity Debate'. Working Paper No. 74. Bhubaneswar: Nabakrushna Choudhury Centre for Development Studies.

Ghatak, Maitreesh. 2019. Land Market Reforms, In *What the Economy Needs Now*, edited by Abhijit Banerjee, Raghuram Rajan, Gita Gopinath, and Mihir Sharma. New Delhi: Juggernaut Books.

Ghatak, Maitreesh, and Parikshit Ghosh. 2015. 'Land Acquisition Debate: The Price Is Not Right'. https://www.ideasforindia.in/topics/macroeconomics/

land-acquisition-debate-the-price-is-not-right.html (accessed on 21 February 2022).

Government of India. 2019. 'Agricultural Statistics at a Glance 2019'. Ministry of Agriculture and Farmers Welfare, Department of Agriculture, Cooperation and Farmers Welfare, Directorate of Economics and Statistics. https://eands.dacnet.nic.in/PDF/At%20a%20Glance%202019%20Eng.pdf (accessed on 21 February 2022).

Government of India. 2021. *Compendium of Fact Sheets: India and 14 States/Uts Phase-11. National Family Health Survey NFHS-5. 2019–21*. New Delhi: Ministry of Health and Family Welfare, Government of India.

Gulati, Ashok. 2013. 'How to Create Economic Freedom for Agriculture—Can Agriculture Be Unshackled from Government Controls'. In '*State of Economic Freedom in India 2013*', edited by Bibek Debroy and Laveesh Bhandari. https://www.cato.org/sites/cato.org/files/economic-freedom-india-2013/economic-freedom-states-of-india-chapter-1.pdf (accessed on 21 February 2022).

Majumder, Sarasij. 2019. *People's Car: Industrial India and the Riddles of Populism*. Hyderabad: Orient BlackSwan.

National Statistical Office. 2021. 'Situational Assessment of Agricultural Households and Land Holdings of Households in Rural India, 2019'. Ministry of Statistics and Programme Implementation, Government of India.

Paltasingh, Kirtti Ranjan, Phanindra Goyari, and Kiril TochkovIndian. 2018. 'Indian Agriculture after the Green Revolution: An Overview'. In *Indian Agriculture after the Green Revolution: Changes and Challenges*, edited by Binoy Goswami, M. P. Bezbaruah, and Raju Mandal. London/New York, NY: Routledge.

Ray, Debraj. 1998. *Development Economics*. Princeton, NJ: Princeton University Press and Oxford India Paperbacks.

Sen, A. 1981. 'Market Failure and Control of Labour Power: Towards an Explanation of "Structure" and Change in Indian Agriculture: Part 1'. *Cambridge Journal of Economics* 5: 201–228.

Shivananda, Sammith. 2015. 'The Land Acquisition Bill Debate: More Political than Practical'. South Asia@LSE. https://blogs.lse.ac.uk/southasia/2015/03/13/the-land-acquisition-bill-debate-more-political-than-practical/ (accessed on 21 February 2022).

Tahvi, Frank, Kai Fukutaki, Simon I. Hay, Rafael Lozano, Ali H. Mokdad, Vishnu Nandakumar, Maxwell Pierce et al. 2020. 'Fertility, Mortality, Migration, and Population Scenarios for 195 Countries and Territories from 2017 to 2100: A Forecasting Analysis for the Global Burden of Disease Study', 1–22. https://www.thelancet.com (accessed on 21 February 2022).

The New Indian Express. 2021, 27 March. 'Controversy Over Land Acquisition Bill'. https://www.newindianexpress.com/nation/2015/mar/07/Controversy-Over-Land-Acquisition-Bill-All-You-Need-to-Know-725439.html

Von Grebmer, K., J. Bernstein, R. Alders, O. Dar, R. Kock, F. Rampa, M. Wiemers et al. 2020. 'Global Hunger Index: One Decade to Zero Hunger: Linking Health and Sustainable Food Systems'. Bonn: Welthungerhilfe; Dublin: Concern Worldwide.

Walker, T. S., and J. G. Ryan. 1990. *Village and Household Economies in India's Semi-arid Tropics*. Baltimore, MD: Johns Hopkins Press.

Chapter 4

Agricultural Labour Markets

Structure and Functioning

Raju Mandal and Anup Kumar Das

4.1. INTRODUCTION

Unequal endowment of factors of production among the households is a common characteristic of an agrarian economy. More often, it is found that in relation to farmland, labour is abundantly available with smaller farmers, and it is scarce for larger farmers (Ray 2011, 409). As a result, cultivation is carried out with varying land–labour ratios, and usually, a small farm operates with excess labour, whereas labour power is deficient in large farms. Meanwhile, the average size of landholding is getting smaller due to an ever-increasing population pressure and division of land ownership with inheritance, which has resulted in an increase in the number of farmers with surplus labour. Under such circumstances, there is the emergence of the agricultural labour market and land-lease market to correct the unequal distribution of such factors of production. An agricultural labour market facilitates the transfer of the services of manpower from labour-surplus households to labour-deficient households. However, it is a stylized fact that as the economy matures, a segment of agricultural workers moves away to sectors with high productivity and better remuneration. India, an agriculture-dependent economy in terms of workforce participation rate, is not an exception in this regard. For instance, there is a decline of agricultural workforce in India in both absolute and relative terms during the period from 2004–2005 to 2011–2012 (Federation of Indian Chambers of Commerce and Industry 2015). The lower productivity of agriculture, rapid expansion of the non-farm sector, especially the informal sector, farm–non-farm wage gap, preference for regular job and rural–urban migration for better livelihood are some important factors behind the observed decline in labour supply in the farm sector. The Mahatma Gandhi National Rural Employment Guarantee Act (MGNREGA)—a flagship programme of the Government of India that guarantees wage employment of 100 days in a year to unskilled labourers of rural households—has made the problem of labour scarcity in the agricultural sector more acute in recent times (Grover 2014; Gunabhagya et al. 2017). At the same time, the agriculture sector in the country has experienced some changes like increased cropping intensity[1] and spread of farm mechanization,[2] which are likely to affect the demand for farm labour. While intensive cultivation requires the use of farm labour more intensively, farm mechanization reduces the requirement of manpower.

All these dynamics and structural changes in India, in general, and in the agriculture sector, in particular, call for a study of the various emerging aspects of agricultural labour market in the country. Accordingly, the present chapter makes an attempt to discuss the structure and functioning of the agricultural labour market in India in recent times, drawing empirical evidence from both secondary and primary data.

---

[1] As per the data provided by the Agricultural Statistics at a Glance 2020 (Government of India 2021b), cropping intensity in India has increased from 111.07 per cent in 1950–1951 to 143.59 per cent in 2016–2017 (P).

[2] The analysis by Gulati and Juneja (2020) depicts a significant progress of farm mechanization in India, particularly the use of tractors. The availability of farm power in the country increased from 0.25 kilowatt per hectare (kW/ha) to 2.02 kW/ha during1951 and 2017.

The chapter is organized in seven sections. Section 4.2 discusses the functioning of the agricultural labour market with a focus on India. The extent of agricultural labour and its use in India is discussed in section 4.3. Section 4.4 describes the nature and structure of the agricultural labour market in the country. The impact of MGNREGA on the agricultural labour market is explained in section 4.5. This is followed by an analysis of the role of the agricultural labour market on farm production and productivity in section 4.6. Section 4.7 summarizes the important findings of the chapter.

4.2. FUNCTIONING OF AGRICULTURAL LABOUR MARKET

The emergence and functioning of the agricultural labour market in India and other countries are evident from the studies of Som (1961), Vyas and Mathai (1978), Ninan (1984), Banerjee (1989), Unni (1989), Nair (1997), Swamy (1998), Haque (2000), Balasubramanian et al. (2002), Sharma and Kumar (2003), Rajni (2007), Asiwal (2014), Subathra (2015), Salam (1986), Otsuka et al. (1992), Anthony (1993) Lin (1995) Toufique (2005), Hayami and Godo (2014, 329–330), Bedemo et al. (2013), Gupta (2016) and Rahman (2017), among others. Lin (1995) states that a sizable portion of households in rural China participated in the agricultural labour market. Hayami and Godo (2014, 329–330) find the use of hired labour in the farming sector in Philippines, Indonesia and Japan. The increased opportunity for employment in the non-farm sector is the major factor leading to the dependence on hired labour for farming in Japan. The hiring of agricultural labour in Philippines is contract based, and largely for activities requiring more physical labour. The use of hired labour in Pakistan's agriculture is mainly affected by wage, farm size, family labour, fertilizer use, cropping intensity, etc., (Salam 1986). The available literature also shows evidence of the use of hired labour in agricultural operations in other countries like rural Ethiopia (Bedemo et al. 2013), Scotland (Anthony 1993) and Bangladesh (Rahman 2017; Toufique 2005). Thus, the empirical studies from around the world show the functioning of the agricultural labour market in different agrarian economies, and such a market is in fact quite extensive in many of these economies. The variations in the extent of hired agricultural labour use, in turn, depend on a number of factors such as employment opportunity in the non-farm sector (Hayami and Godo 2014, 329–330), existing wage rates (Salam 1986), farm size (Bedemo et al. 2013; Salam 1986), off-farm income (Bedemo et al. 2013), family size (Bedemo et al. 2013), education of the head of the household (Bedemo et al. 2013), family labour (Salam 1986), fertilizer use (Salam 1986) and cropping intensity (Salam 1986).

Agricultural labour market has been functioning in India for a long time. A discussion on factor markets by Swamy (1998) reveals that during the colonial period also, agricultural labour market was functioning in the country. In rural India, agricultural labour has a significant share in the total workers, and it has increased over time (Vyas and Mathai 1978). A study by Som (1961), based on information collected by the first and second Agricultural Labour Enquiry, Ministry of Labour, revealed that during the period from 1950–1951 to 1956–1957, the days of average wage employment in agriculture of both male and female adults increased. However, there was a decrease in the daily wage of casual agricultural labour and an increase in indebtedness of agricultural labour households. The study further depicts the casualization of agricultural labour in India. Moreover, a study by Unni (1989) revealed a rise in the percentage of casual workers in agriculture in the rural parts of the country during the period from 1961 to 1981. It is interesting to note that there has been an increase in the number of agricultural labourers along with a decline in cultivators in the country during the period from 2001 to 2011 (Gupta 2016). This might be because the average monthly income from cultivation is lower as compared to wage income for small and marginal agricultural households. For example, as per the 77th round report of the National Sample Survey (NSS), between July 2018 and June 2019, the average monthly income per agricultural household (for all size classes) from wages was ₹4,063 as compared to ₹3,058 net receipt from crop production (Government of India 2021e).[3]

[3] For the marginal size class of agricultural households, the average monthly net receipts from crop production were around 27.87 per cent of wage income during the period.

The available studies show the existence of agricultural labour markets across the states of India with distinct characteristics in its functioning. For example, the use of hired labour in the agriculture sector of Kerala is found to be quite extensive even among the smallholders (Nair 1997; Ninan 1984). Nair (1997) finds that the actual use of hired farm labour in Kerala is less than the requirements of many farmers, which indicates scarcity of such workers in the state. This kind of labour shortage might be because of the fact that many casual workers from the state have migrated to the Gulf countries. The consequent increase in rural wage rate has attracted many labourers for agricultural operations from other states. This is evident when Dhanya (2016) mentions that, currently, migrant labourers are often hired to meet the demand for casual labourers in the villages of Kerala. Further, the extent of use of agricultural labour across activities was not the same (Ninan 1984). Like Kerala, the agricultural labour market is functioning in Tamil Nadu (Balasubramanian et al. 2002; Prabakar et al. 2011). However, contrary to the usual perceptions, in Tamil Nadu, hiring of female labour for agricultural activities was more than that of male labour, and also the hiring of farm labour was found to be more among farmers with smaller size of landholdings (Balasubramanian et al. 2002). In Himachal Pradesh, the agricultural labour market was functioning primarily under the time rate system without geographical fragmentation and segmentation (Sharma and Kumar 2003). However, there was segmentation in the agricultural labour markets in the state across sex and caste (Sharma and Kumar 2003). The extensive use of agricultural labour by farmer groups of all sizes in eastern and western parts of Uttar Pradesh and the emergence of 'group labour contract' in Meerut were reported by Rajni (2007). The in-migrants constitute such a group to protect their interest and exercise more bargaining power. Thus, Meerut witnessed a change in casual labour contract from individual to group contract. Furthermore, due to non-availability of alternative credit sources, poor farmers become dependent on landowners and thus enter into an interlocked contract. Asiwal (2014) found that agricultural labour market functioning in Jaipur in the state of Rajasthan was localized and non-fragmented in nature, and time rate was the dominant form of such a contract. Furthermore, cash was the prime mode of wage payment but not the only mode.

4.3. THE EXTENT OF AGRICULTURAL LABOUR AND ITS USE IN INDIA

Over the years, the factors like increased population pressure and use of farmland for non-farming activities have reduced the availability of farmland. Consequently, many farmers are becoming landless, and some of them are joining agricultural labour market (Gupta 2016). However, factors like the expansion of non-farm sector, especially informal sector, low agricultural wage and the spread of farm mechanization have caused the shifting of labour from farm to non-farm sector, thereby leading to a scarcity of agricultural labour supply. In recent times, the implementation of MGNREGA is often alleged to have made the labour scarcity for farming activity more severe (Gupta 2016). On the other hand, change in Indian agriculture like increased cropping intensity has improved demand for agricultural labour. All such demand and supply side related changes have affected the size of agricultural labour in the country. In the country, the size of agricultural labour has increased from 27.3 million in 1951 to 144.3 million in 2011 with a compound annual growth rate of 3.2 per cent (Table 4.1). Interestingly, while the percentage share of cultivators in total workers has almost halved from around 50 per cent to 25 per cent during this period, there is an increase in the percentage share of agricultural labour from around 20 per cent to 30 per cent. On the other hand, the size of agricultural labour has grown at a higher rate than those of total workers, agricultural workers and cultivators. The compound annual growth rate of agricultural labour is more than three times that of cultivators, which has grown at the rate of around 1 per cent. This might be due to the gradual decline in the average size of landholdings, more people joining the marginal farm size and landless classes, and cultivation becoming un-remunerative.

There is an increase of both male and female agricultural labourers in India along with a change in their composition. Male agricultural labour (main and marginal) increased from 57.33 million in 2001 to 82.74 million in 2011, and female agricultural labour (main and marginal) increased from 49.45 million to 61.59 million during the same period (Government of India 2017b, 2021a). During 2001–2011, both main and marginal agricultural labourers have increased along with the rise in their shares in the total workers. As per the census data of India,

Table 4.1 *Workers (in Million) in India*

Year	Total Workers	Agricultural Workers	Cultivators	Agricultural Labour
1951	139.5 *(100)*	97.2 (69.68)	69.9 (50.11)	27.3 *(19.57)*
1961	188.7 *(100)*	131.1 (69.48)	99.6 (52.78)	31.5 *(16.69)*
1971	180.4 *(100)*	125.7 (69.68)	78.2 (43.35)	47.5 *(26.33)*
1981	244.6 *(100)*	148 (60.51)	92.5 (37.82)	55.5 *(22.69)*
1991	314.1 *(100)*	185.3 (58.99)	110.7 (35.24)	74.6 *(23.75)*
2001	402.2 *(100)*	234.1 (58.20)	127.3 (31.65)	106.8 *(26.55)*
2011	481.9 *(100)*	263.1 (54.60)	118.8 (24.65)	144.3 *(29.94)*
CAGR	2.3	1.8	0.9	3.2

Source: Adapted from Government of India (2018).
Notes: a) CAGR means compound annual growth rate; b) Figures in the parentheses represent percentage of total workers.

the decadal arithmetic growth rate of main and marginal agricultural labours during 2001–2011 were 35.70 per cent and 34.40 per cent, respectively. As a percentage of the total workers, main agricultural labour increased from 15.79 per cent in 2001 to 17.88 per cent in 2011, and marginal agricultural labour increased from 10.76 per cent to 12.07 per cent during the same period.[4] Thus, in the past decade, there was an additional increase of main agricultural labour than marginal ones in India, depicting a change in the composition of its agricultural

[4] The data on total workers have been taken from Agricultural Statistics at a Glance 2017 (Government of India 2018), and the rest of the information is taken from Office of the Registrar General and Census Commissioner, Government of India (2021d).

workforce. The sex composition of agricultural labour in the country has also changed. The decadal arithmetic growth rates during the period from 2001 to 2011 among the main agricultural labour are 34.38 per cent and 38.14 per cent for male and female, respectively, and among marginal agricultural labour, they are 69.56 per cent and 13.34 per cent, respectively (Government of India 2021d).

The cost of cultivation data for the period 2017–2018 depict a substantial use of agricultural labour in India. The extent of the agricultural labour market can be visualized from the share of hired labour in total manpower used in the cultivation of two major crops of India, namely paddy and wheat as presented in Figures 4.1 and 4.2, respectively. On average, casual labour hour accounts for 52.33 per cent of the total manpower hours used in paddy cultivation in the major paddy producing states of India and attached labour accounts for 0.77 per cent (Figure 4.1). Thus, hired labour—casual and attached labour—accounts for more than half of the manpower hour used for paddy cultivation in the country. The share of hired labour hour in the total manpower hour used per hectare of paddy cultivation ranges from 17.43 per cent (in Himachal Pradesh) to 77.80 per cent (in Kerala) across the major paddy cultivating states of the country, but in most of them it accounts for more than half of the total manpower hours. On the other hand, as observed from Figure 4.2, the share of hired labour (casual and attached) used in major wheat cultivating states was 31 per cent in 2017–2018, and it ranged from 3.61 per cent (in Himachal Pradesh) to 53.94 per cent (in Karnataka) among these states. Thus, from the aforementioned discussion, it is clear that the agricultural labour market is functioning quite extensively in India with wide variations among the states and crops.

A field study of 237 farm households in the Brahmaputra Valley of Assam in the northeast part of India (during November 2017 to February 2018) reveals that 72.57 per cent of the sample farm households participated in the agricultural labour markets. Among the sample participant households, 83.72 per cent are pure demanders, while 4.07 per cent are pure suppliers, and the rest (12.21%) participated as both demander and supplier of agricultural labour. Thus, the participation of farm households in the agricultural labour market is quite extensive—mostly as buyers of agricultural labour for their farm operations.

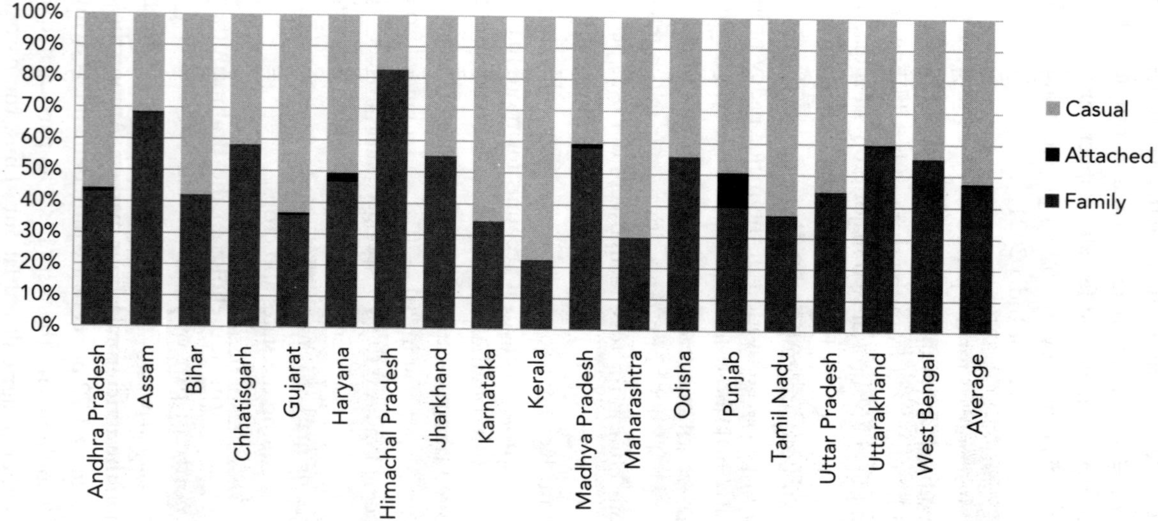

Figure 4.1 *Distribution of Manpower (in hours) Used per Hectare of Paddy Cultivation in India during 2017–2018*

Source: Calculated from Government of India (2021c).

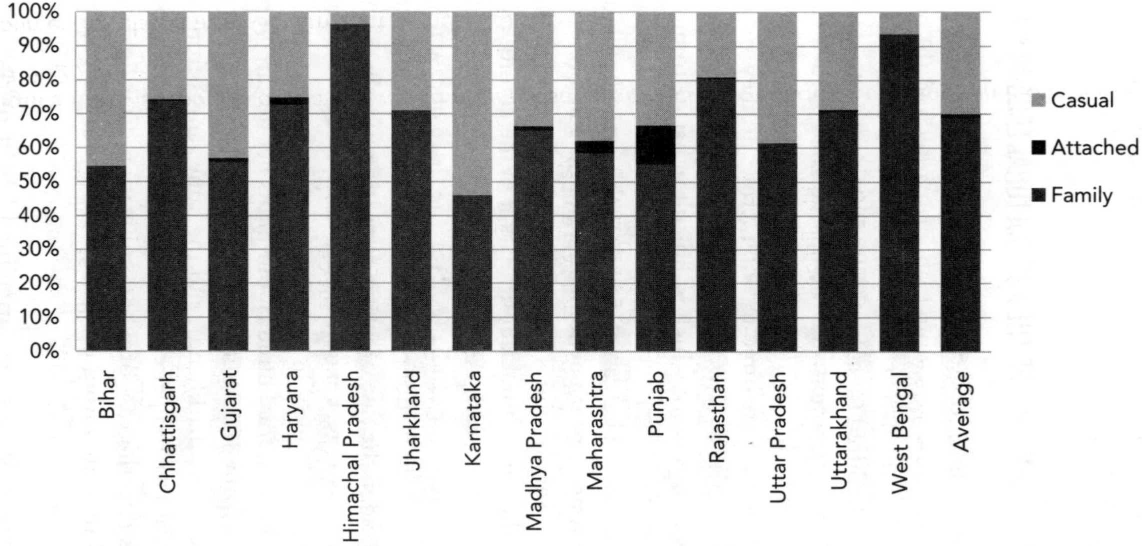

Figure 4.2 *Distribution of Manpower (in hours) Used per Hectare of Wheat Cultivation in India during 2017–2018*

Source: Calculated from Government of India (2021c).

Furthermore, among the sample households, most of the participants in the agricultural labour market belong to small and marginal size groups of operational holdings.

4.4. NATURE AND STRUCTURE OF THE AGRICULTURAL LABOUR MARKET

The functioning of the agricultural labour market is visible broadly in two forms—(a) casual agricultural labour market and (b) permanent agricultural labour market. Under the casual agricultural labour market, labourers are hired for a short period either on a daily basis or for a pre-specified short period, and the task assigned to such labourers is easily observable. In contrast, under the permanent agricultural labour market, labourers are hired for long term, and they are sometimes engaged in supervisory work and also to take the responsibility of risky work as well as work which is difficult in nature to monitor. But the employment of agricultural labour in India mostly takes the form of casual labour. The casualization of the agricultural labour market in India is not a new phenomenon. Studies like Som (1961), Unni (1989), and Sharma and Kumar (2003) already pointed out the casualization of the agricultural labour market in the country, which is even rising over the years. As per the cost of cultivation data for 2017–2018, Government of India (2021c), the share of casual labour hour in total hired labour hours per hectare of paddy cultivation is 98.68 per cent, and in the case of wheat cultivation, this share is 96.69 per cent. This depicts a great extent of casualization of the agricultural labour market in the country in recent times. Across states, the share of casual labour hour in total hired labour hours per hectare of paddy cultivation varies from 81.57 per cent (in Punjab) to 100 per cent (in Himachal Pradesh and Jharkhand), and the same ranges from 74.58 per cent (in Punjab) to 100 per cent (in Himachal Pradesh, Jharkhand and West Bengal) in the case of wheat cultivation. Our field survey data also reveal that the hiring of agricultural labour for cultivation is fully casual in nature in Assam.

Another characteristic of the agricultural labour market in India is its fragmentation. Figure 4.3 presents a gap in the daily average wage of male and female field labour. The daily average agricultural

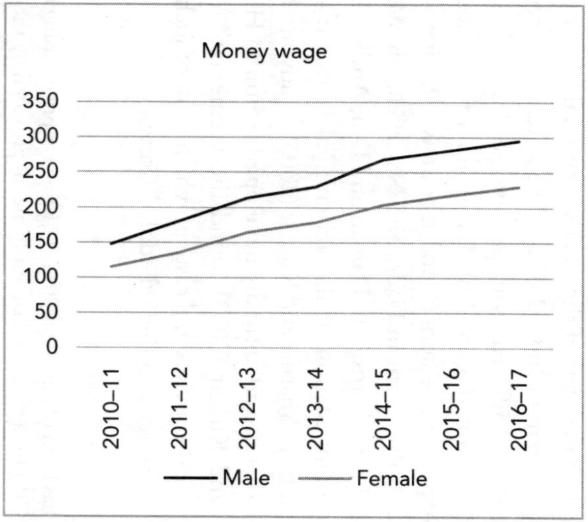

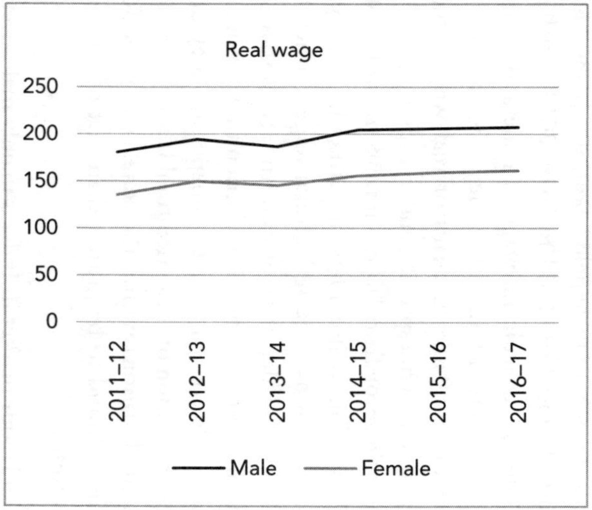

Figure 4.3 *Daily Average Agricultural Wage of Field Labour (in ₹)*

Source: Compiled from Government of India (2015a; 2015b; 2016a; 2016b; 2017a; 2019).

money wage and real wage[5] of male field labour was higher than their female counterparts during 2010–2011 to 2016–2017. Furthermore, the gap in daily average agricultural wage of male and female field labour has been increasing in terms of money wage although it has been found more or less stable in terms of real wage. Figure 4.4 presents the existence of widespread gender gaps in daily average agricultural money wage of field labour among the states of India. Thus, fragmentation of agricultural labour market by sex prevails in India. Moreover, the daily average agricultural wage (money) of field labour, both male and female, was not uniform across states, which reveals geographical fragmentation of the agricultural labour market as well. Our recent field study in the Brahmaputra Valley of Assam also reveals the fragmentation of the agricultural labour market by sex, activities and sample locations within the state. The wage for male farm labour has been found to be greater than that of the female in all the sample locations.

The agricultural labour market in India is mainly male-dominated. As per Census 2011, the male agricultural labour (main and marginal) constituted around 57 per cent of the total agricultural labour force of the country (Government of India 2017b). The state/union territory-wise comparison shows differences in percentage share of male and female agricultural labour (Figure 4.5). Except in a few states/union territories, the share of male agricultural labour was higher. Female agricultural labour is dominant in Dadra and Nagar Haveli, Manipur, Rajasthan, Karnataka, Chhattisgarh, Daman and Diu, Andhra Pradesh and Sikkim. The segmentation of the agricultural labour market in India is also evident from Sharma and Kumar (2003). Studying the agricultural labour market in agriculturally developed region in Himachal Pradesh, Sharma and Kumar (2003) found the segmentation of the agricultural labour market by sex and caste in which most of such labour was male and also belonged to the Scheduled Caste.

[5] The real wage has been obtained (at 2011-12 base year prices) using the consumer price index (CPI) for agricultural labour (general) provided by the Reserve Bank of India (2020).

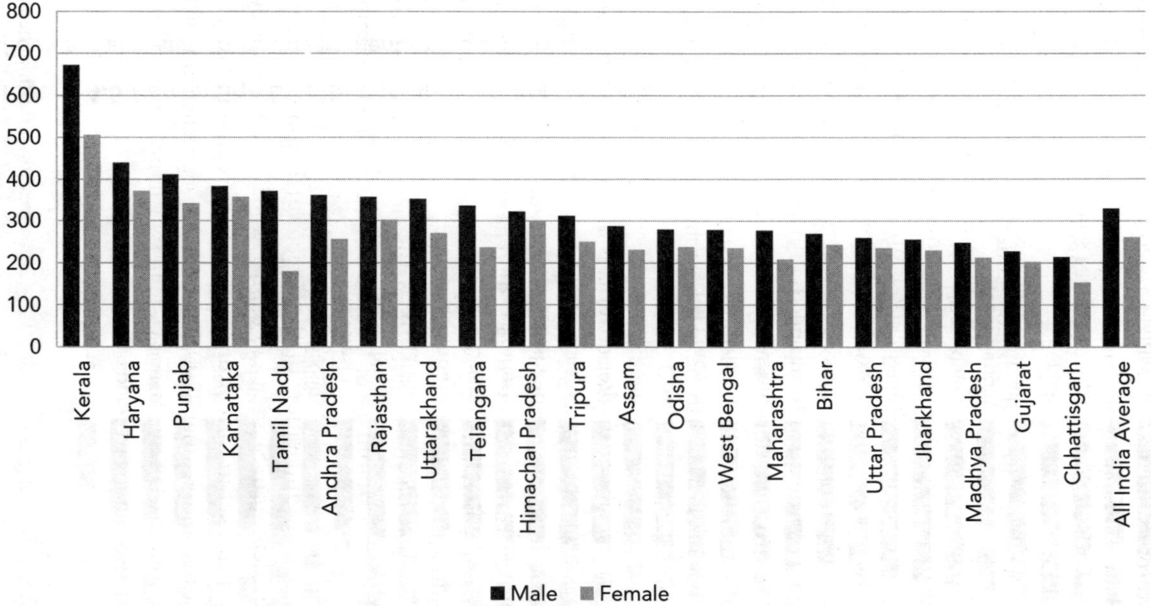

Figure 4.4 *State-wise Daily Average Agricultural Wage (money) of Field Labour in 2018–2019*

Source: Government of India (2020).

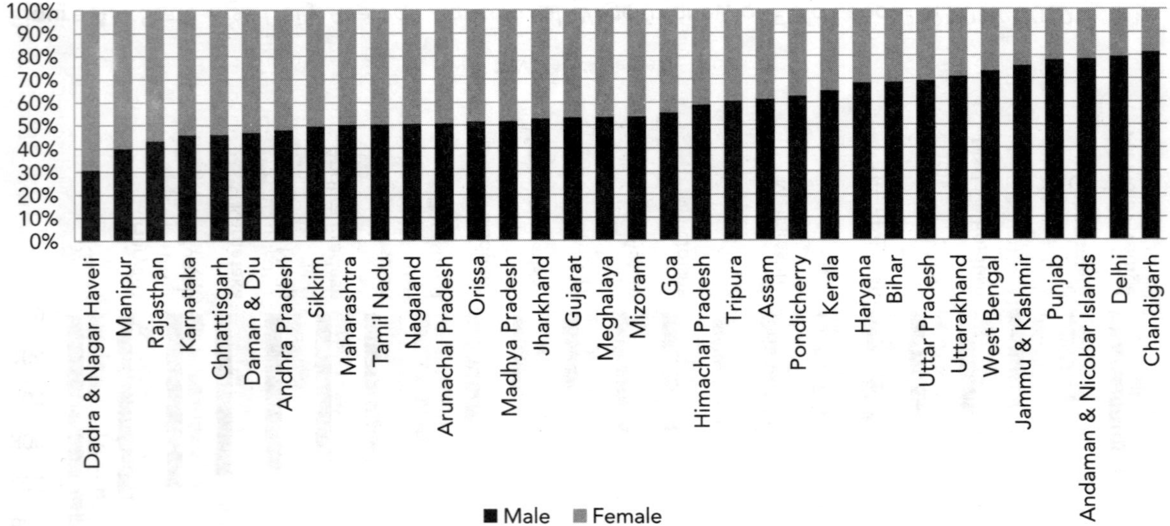

Figure 4.5 *Percentage Distribution of Agricultural Labour (main and marginal) by Sex*

Source: Calculated from Government of India (2017b).

Another feature of the agricultural labour market in India is that it is mostly localized in nature. For instance, Asiwal (2014) found most of the agricultural labourers work within villages in Jaipur (Rajasthan). Likewise, Sharma and Kumar (2003) found that most of the agricultural labourers work within villages in Himachal Pradesh. Our field data also reveal such a type of localized functioning of the agricultural labour market in the Brahmaputra Valley of Assam. However, hiring of labour for farm operation even from other states is also taking place in some parts of the country, which are deficit in agricultural labour like Punjab and Kerala. In this regard, the emergence of 'group labour contract' in Meerut (Uttar Pradesh) constituted by in-migrants from other states may be noted (Rajni 2007).

Another important feature of the agricultural labour market in India is that it is interlocked with other factor markets. Interlocking of the agricultural labour market with other factor markets is evident in states such as Himachal Pradesh (Sharma and Kumar 2003), Rajasthan (Asiwal 2014), Uttar Pradesh (Bardhan and Rudra 1978; Rajni 2007), West Bengal (Bardhan and Rudra 1978; Haque 2000) and Bihar (Bardhan and Rudra 1978). A study in Himachal Pradesh by Sharma and Kumar (2003) found a great extent of interlocking of factor markets between labour and credit, and labour and land. Around 65 per cent of the casual agricultural labour households were found to be involved in interlocking of labour–land and labour–credit markets. However, the interlocking of labour and credit markets is more prevalent than that of labour and land markets. In the case of labour–credit interlocking, although there was zero explicit rate of interest on borrowed money, the employers appropriated a higher implicit interest rate in the form of many small unpaid jobs. It was found that the probability of involvement in such interlocked transactions increases with family size and decreases with age of the labourer. Interlocking of land–labour and labour–credit markets in Bihar, Uttar Pradesh and West Bengal was also reported by Bardhan and Rudra (1978) when they depicted the incidence of 'bonded labour' as an outcome of labour–credit interlocking. A system, known as 'Dadan', was found by Bardhan and Rudra (1980) in West Bengal under which loan (cash or grains) was taken in the lean season by the labourer from a potential employer on the basis of commitment for labour at a required time in the future, and this is a typical form of labour–credit interlocking. The incidence of labour–credit and labour–land interlocking is also present in Rajasthan, and the former is quite extensive in the state (Asiwal 2014). Due to the non-availability of alternative credit sources, poor farmers in Uttar Pradesh become dependent on landowners and thus enter into an interlinked contract (Rajni 2007). Rajni (2007) found two types of interlinked transactions in Uttar Pradesh, namely (a) land, labour and credit contracts of landless–lessees and (b) credit–labour linkages of casual labour households. The interlocking of labour, land and credit markets in West Bengal is also evident from Haque (2000). But as observed by him, the interlocked transactions are not always unproductive and exploitative in nature. Haque (2000) found that the interlocked arrangement of labour–land and credit in West Bengal is working well, whereas the same arrangements in tribal and other backward villages of Bihar are very much exploitative. Haque (2000), in this context, stated that whether the interlocking transactions in factor markets would be exploitative hinges upon the nature of rural power structure.

The transaction of agricultural labour in India is found basically in two forms: (a) time-rate form and (b) area-based form. While wage rate is fixed based on the duration of working hours under the time-rate form, the same is fixed in the case of the latter on the basis of area of farmland in which a labourer is to carry out an assigned activity like tilling and harvesting. Among the two forms of agricultural labour hiring prevalent in the country, time-rate form was found to be dominant in Himachal Pradesh (Sharma and Kumar 2003) and in Jaipur (Asiwal 2014). Our primary data from the Brahmaputra Valley of Assam also reveals the dominance of hiring of agricultural labour under the time-rate system.

4.5. THE MAHATMA GANDHI NATIONAL RURAL EMPLOYMENT GUARANTEE ACT AND AGRICULTURAL LABOUR MARKET

The MGNREGA, 2005—the flagship programme of the Government of India—since its implementation in February 2006 aims at providing livelihood security by promising at least 100 days of wage employment for unskilled labourers to every rural household in a year. This employment guarantee by the government has quite expectedly impacted the labour market in India, especially in the rural areas in different ways. Since most of the landless people and even the marginal farmers in the rural areas are engaged as agricultural workers, they are likely to be affected the most by the programme. There are a number of empirical studies available by now in different parts of the country with evidence of mixed impact of the programme in the rural areas, particularly in the agricultural labour market. The most obvious effects of it are found in the form of participation of rural folk (especially the women), supply of agricultural labourers and the agricultural wage rate.

One notable impact of MGNREGA in the rural areas is that it has increased the rural labour participation rate, particularly for women, by making attractive and convenient work opportunities easily accessible (MoRD 2012). The programme with its inherent characteristics of being local and promising employment guarantee at the same wage rate between genders has facilitated participation of more women in the rural labour market. Moreover, while other types of available works are biased against the women in terms of wage rate, the programme by providing wage parity has resulted in the reduction of wage disparities between men and women agricultural workers. Azam (2012), and Chakraborty and Singh (2018), using nationally representative data from NSS find that MGNREGA has a positive impact on the labour force participation rate, which is found to be more pronounced for females.

With a continuous increase in the rural population, there has been an increase in the number of rural landless and marginal farmers, majority of whom had no option but to get themselves engaged in low-skilled wage employment in the farm and non-farm activities. The hypothesis about MGNREGA creating scarcity of agricultural labourers and boosting their wages stems from the fact that the programme promises unskilled wage employment to every rural household and thus has the possibility of creating competition with the farm sector for low-skilled casual workers. This might be accentuated by the positive wage differentials of MGNREGA and agricultural labourers in some parts of the country as reported by some studies. That is why notwithstanding the positive impact of MGNREGA on agriculture and livelihoods of the vulnerable segments like small, marginal and landless households in rural areas (Nagaraj et al. 2016), the programme is often alleged to have created scarcity of labour in the farm and non-farm sectors, thereby pushing the rural wage rate and reducing the profitability and income of the farmers. The evidence of this, however, is inconclusive. Some argue that this labour scarcity is partly because of a relatively higher wage rate of MGNREGA and partly because of a preference for MGNREGA works over others due to its less toil, less supervision and provision of other facilities (Thadathil and Mohandas 2012). Ravi and Engler (2013), analysing household data in Andhra Pradesh, find that in the initial years of the programme, it predominantly attracted non-agricultural labour (78%) because works under the programme were concentrated in the dry summer months when demand for agricultural labour was low. But over time, more households have started participating as labourers in the programme who would have participated as agricultural labourers (55.3%) if the MGNREGA did not exist. This suggests broader labour market distortions in rural areas where the Act is not just viewed as an employment guarantor for people during slack agriculture season but as an alternative to agricultural labour work (Ravi and Engler 2013).

The introduction of MGNREGA, with the provisions of minimum and equal wages for male and female workers, brought about not only an increase in the overall agricultural wages but also reduction in the male–female wage differentials (Reddy et al. 2014). Moreover, it has also offered a better bargaining power to agricultural labourers. Berg et al. (2018) while studying the impact of MGNREGA on agricultural wages—using district-level monthly data from 18 states of India over the period from May 2000 to June 2011—find that the programme, on average, increased real daily agricultural wages by 4.3 per cent per year. However, the effect cannot be generalized as it was concentrated in some states, and in the agricultural peak season when the demand for agricultural labour is high. Likewise, Nagaraj et al. (2016), in their study on Telangana and Maharashtra, find that there has been a gradual increase in the real wages of both farm and non-farm workers, especially after the implementation of

MGNREGA. But the growth in average daily wage rates of male farm workers has been quite fast after MGNREGA in both the states as compared to almost negative growth rate before its implementation. However, they observe that the programme cannot be held solely responsible for the scarcity of male labour for farm work. This is because while both the farm and non-farm wages have increased by almost three times during the MGNREGA implementation in some areas, MGNREGA wage has increased only by half of it. They further add that the shortage of male labour for farm work became more prominent, which seems to be compensated by a higher female labour participation in some major crops, thus confirming the feminization of labour. Furthermore, the proportion of hired labour has reduced at a much faster rate than the family labour with the adoption of farm mechanization (Nagaraj et al. 2016).

However, it is difficult to argue conclusively that the shortage in agricultural labour is due to MGNREGA. The shortage of agricultural labourers and their diversion from farms may be due to factors other than MGNREGA (MoRD 2012). Alha (2017), on the basis of a field-level evidence from two villages of Rajasthan, finds that the role of MGNREGA in creating the shortage of labour for agricultural operations seems minimal because work availability under the programme does not clash with the agricultural season in the villages. He further notes that the shortage in agricultural labour (if there is any at all) and their diversion from farms is because of factors outside MGNREGA like migration and emerging better non-farm opportunities either with higher wages or with a steady income flow in nearby villages and towns. Similarly, Murthy and Indumati (2011) note that the macro-level data on season-wise employment under MGNREGA do not support the hypothesis that the programme weans away labour force from agricultural activities and creates labour shortage. According to them, it is the relative increase in non-farm wages rather than MGNREGA wages that is contributing to the higher scarcity of agricultural labour. In a similar line, Kajale and Shroff (2011) in their study on Maharashtra opine that it is difficult to segregate the effect of MGNREGA on labour shortage in agriculture from that of non-farm activities, spread of education, etc. Varshney et al. (2018) find no systematic evidence of any impact of public works employment in MGNREGA on wages and crowding out of casual labour in agriculture. Similarly, according to Reddy et al. (2014), the level of agricultural wages was higher even before the launching of the scheme under MGNREGA in the agriculturally well-endowed regions, and their labour demand in the peak season was met by seasonal migration of labour from labour-surplus regions. This suggests that the impact of the scheme under MGNREGA on agricultural wages in such areas was not much, except in pockets where the migrant labour flow declined. Similarly, Dhanya (2016), using primary data, find that the programme has had a limited effect on the labour market in Kerala in terms of the substitution between works as well as adding to the labour force in general. However, the programme offered a fall-back option to the workers by shifting to it in the event of non-availability of work in their regular occupations (Dhanya 2016). The high wages in alternative works act as a disincentive for substituting with MGNREGA works. He further adds that MGNREGA has resulted in the shortage of women labour force engaged in pre- and post-harvesting operations in agrarian districts of Wayanad and Idukki. As a result, wages for women labour force involved in this work have increased, which were earlier only marginally higher than the MGNREGA wages (Dhanya 2016). Moreover, there may be a decline in the supply of agricultural labourers due to the following: first, the provision of welfare schemes like food subsidies seem to make people complacent and undersupply their labour on many occasions (Murthy and Indumati 2012). Second, the chances of getting employed in agricultural wage labour decrease as one rises in the consumption distribution (Kijima and Lanjouw 2005).

Thus, the MGNREGA definitely has had some impact on the agricultural labour market in terms of labour force participation, scarcity of labour and wages. However, there are wide variations and heterogeneity across the country as far the nature and magnitude of such impacts are concerned. While some studies try to hold the programme responsible for scarcity of agricultural labour and increased farm wage, others claim that the increase in the agricultural wage is due to factors other than MGNREGA. Thus, the impact of MGNREGA on the agricultural labour market is still debatable and inclusive.

4.6. AGRICULTURAL LABOUR MARKET AND FARM PRODUCTION AND PRODUCTIVITY: A CASE STUDY

The role of the agricultural labour market is evident from different studies, which reveal a large-scale dependency on hired labour for agricultural operations. The large extent of use of hired agricultural labour in India in recent times could be seen from Figures 4.1 and 4.2. More importantly, even small and marginal farmers are dependent on hired agricultural labour. As per the field investigation in the Brahmaputra Valley of Assam, around 70 per cent of sample farmers of all size groups have hired labour for farm operation, and the man-days of hired agricultural labour used per sample household is around 58 days in the reference year. Per hectare of gross crop area, hired agricultural labour used by sample farmers is around 45 man-days. The small and marginal farmer accounts for around 89 per cent of sample agricultural labour hiring-in farmers. Similarly, around 59 per cent of the man-days of hired farm labour is used by such farmers. However, a higher percentage of large farmers are dependent on hired agricultural labour as compared to the small and marginal farmers.

The agricultural labour market plays a significant role in raising production and productivity of the agricultural sector. The negative impact of the declining share of agricultural workers in total workers on yield and cropping intensity is reported by Prabakar et al. (2011). Availability of agricultural labour for hiring-in can augment the farm production and productivity-enhancing practices. The regression analysis,[6] based on field survey data, depicts that the wage of agricultural labour has a significant negative impact on cropping intensity and crop diversification (Table 4.2). As low wage indicates availability of relatively more farm labour for hiring in, the negative impact of wage implies significant positive impact on cropping intensity and crop diversification of farm labour availability facilitated by the agricultural labour market.

[6] The cropping intensity has a lower limit, and crop diversification has both lower and upper limits. In the data set, in the case of both cropping intensity and crop diversification, there are clusters of observations as lower end, and hence, left-censored Tobit regression model has been used for both the indicators of better farm practices.

Table 4.2 *Impact of Availability of Hired Farm Labour on Cropping Intensity and Crop Diversification*

Variables	Cropping Intensity		Crop Diversification	
	Coefficients	RSE	Coefficients	SE
Wage	−0.33[b]	0.16	−0.001[b]	0.00
Cropping intensity	—	—	0.003[c]	0.00
Availability of family labour	1.41	2.20	0.022[a]	0.01
Extent of ploughing mechanization	0.13	0.14	0.00	0.00
Farm size	−4.22	3.31	0.045[c]	0.01
Extent of tenancy	−3.44	12.53	0.04	0.04
Education of head of household	−0.49	1.13	0.00	0.00
Age of head of household	0.46	0.29	0.00	0.00
Principal source of income	28.87[c]	9.10	0.108[c]	0.03
Extent of irrigation	0.07	0.14	0.00	0.00
Access to finance	3.82	10.04	−0.02	0.03
Access to extension	28.07[b]	12.88	0.06	0.04
Extent of HYV seeds	−0.15	0.13	—	—

Type of cultivator	1.24	7.70	0.03	0.03
Morigaon	−33.67[c]	12.50	0.104[b]	0.05
Darrang	−112.54[c]	17.43	0.04	0.04
Lakhimpur	33.18[a]	18.19	0.204[c]	0.06
Constant	172.14[c]	45.44	0.04	0.14
F	7.06[c] (16,212)		—	
LR chi^2	—		184.91[c] (16)	
No. of observations	228		236	

Source: Field study.
Note: RSE: Robust standard error, SE: standard error; [c], [b] and [a] Represent significance at the 1 per cent, 5 per cent and 10 per cent levels, respectively; and figures in parenthesis presents degrees of freedom.

4.7. CONCLUSION

Along with the different agrarian economies of the world, in the small and marginal landholding preponderant agriculture in India, the agricultural labour market is functioning for a long time. Agricultural labour comprises a significant proportion of the manpower used for farming even by farmers belonging to the smaller size group. However, the extent of the agricultural labour market is varied across states and crops. The use of agricultural labour is expanding over the years in the country, and presently, the share of agricultural labour in total workers is more than that of cultivators. Moreover, the growth rate of agricultural labour is higher than those of total workers, agricultural workers and cultivators. There has been also a change in the composition of agricultural labour in the country. The agricultural labour market in India is largely casual and fragmented in nature. Agricultural wage of male field labourers is higher than their female counterparts throughout the country. Agricultural wage is also not uniform across states. Apart from fragmentation, the agricultural labour market is segmented by gender, caste and geographical locations. In most of the states and union territories, the agricultural labour market is male dominated. Further, the agricultural labour market is localized in nature, and it is confined mostly within villages. There is also interlocking of the agricultural labour market with other factor markets such as the land-lease market and credit market. However, it has been observed that interlocking arrangements of labour–land and labour–credit are not so much exploitative everywhere.

The MGNREGA has had some impact on the agricultural labour market in terms of labour force participation, scarcity of labour and wages. However, there are wide variations and heterogeneity across the country as far as the nature and magnitude of such impacts are concerned. While some studies try to hold the programme responsible for the scarcity of agricultural labour and increased farm wage, others claim that the increase in the agricultural wage is due to factors other than MGNREGA. Thus, the impact of MGNREGA on the agricultural labour market is still debatable and inclusive.

The agricultural labour market facilitates correction of mismatch in the factor endowments by transferring labour from labour-surplus households to farm households with relatively more land. Moreover, the said market also plays an important role in the development of agricultural sector by facilitating farm production and productivity enhancing practices. For example, regression analysis of farm-level primary data from the Brahmaputra Valley of Assam reveals that the agricultural labour market plays an important role in raising cropping intensity and crop diversification by provisioning the farm labour for hiring. While the agricultural labour market contributes to agricultural development significantly, there are some imperfections in functioning of such a market. Interlocked transaction in agricultural labour market with other factor markets, especially with credit markets, is a serious case of market imperfection in India. In this regard, more government initiatives for greater penetration of institutional credit to the farm sector can be a policy option.

REFERENCES

Alha, A. 2017. 'Impact of MGNREGA on a Tightened Labour Market'. *Social Change* 47, no. 4: 552–564.

Anthony, Richard. 1993. 'The Scottish Agricultural Labour Market, 1900–1939: A Case of Institutional Intervention'. *The Economic History Review* 46, no. 3: 558–574.

Asiwal, Ramesh Chand. 2014. 'A Socio-economic Study of Agricultural Labour Markets in the First Dusky-Decade of the New Millennium—An Exploratory Analysis of Jaipur (Rajasthan)'. Unpublished Thesis, Swami Keshwanand Rajasthan Agricultural University, Bikaner.

Azam, M. 2012. 'The Impact of Indian Job Guarantee Scheme on Labor Market Outcomes: Evidence from a Natural Experiment'. IZA Discussion Paper No. 6548, World Bank.

Balasubramanian, K., P. Tamizoli, and S. Murugakani. 2002. 'Labour, Market Linkages and Gender: Case Study of a Village in Tamil Nadu'. *Economic & Political Weekly* 37, no. 43: 4390–4396.

Banerjee, Nirmala. 1989. 'Trends in Women's Employment, 1971–1981: Some Macro-Level Observations'. *Economic & Political Weekly* 24, no. 17: WS10–WS22.

Bardhan, P., and A. Rudra. 1978. 'Interlinkage of Land, Labour and Credit Relations: An Analysis of Village Survey Data in East India'. *Economic & Political Weekly* 13, no. 6&7: 367–384.

Bardhan, P., and A. Rudra. 1980. 'Types of Labour Attachment in Agriculture: Results of a Survey in West Bengal, 1979'. *Economic & Political Weekly* 15, no. 35: 1477–1484.

Bedemo, Amsalu, K. Getnet, and B. Kassa. 2013. 'Determinants of Household Demand for and Supply of Farm Labour in Rural Ethiopia'. *Australian Journal of Labour Economics* 16, no. 3: 351–367.

Berg, E., S. Bhattacharyya, D. Rajasekhar, and Manjula, R. 2018. 'Can Public Works Increase Equilibrium Wages? Evidence from India's National Rural Employment Guarantee'. *World Development* 103: 239–254.

Chakraborty, L., and Y. Singh. 2018. 'Fiscal Policy, as the "Employer of Last Resort": Impact of MGNREGS on Labour Force Participation Rates in India'. NIPFP Working paper series No. 210. New Delhi: National Institute of Public Finance and Policy.

Dhanya, V. 2016. 'Implications of MGNREGS on Labour Market, Wages and Consumption Expenditure in Kerala'. RBI Working Paper Series. Mumbai: Department of Economics and Policy Research, Reserve Bank of India.

Federation of Indian Chambers of Commerce and Industry. 2015. 'Labour in Indian Agriculture: A Growing Challenge'. https://ficci.in/spdocument/20550/FICCI-agri-Report%2009-03-2015.pdf (accessed on 26 June 2021).

Government of India. 2014. 'Agricultural Wages in India 2010–2011'. https://eands.dacnet.nic.in/PDF/AgriculturalWagesinIndia2010-11.pdf (accessed on 26 June 2021).

Government of India. 2015a. 'Agricultural Wages in India 2011–2012'. https://eands.dacnet.nic.in/AgriWages2011-12.pdf (accessed on 26 June 2021).

Government of India. 2015b. 'Agricultural Wages in India 2012–2013'. https://eands.dacnet.nic.in/AgriWages2012-13.pdf (accessed on 26 June 2021).

Government of India. 2016a. 'Agricultural Wages in India 2013–2014'. https://eands.dacnet.nic.in/AgriWages2013-14.pdf (accessed on 26 June 2021).

Government of India. 2016b. 'Agricultural Wages in India 2014–2015'. https://eands.dacnet.nic.in/AgriWages2014-15.pdf (accessed on 26 June 2021).

Government of India. 2017a. 'Agricultural Wages in India 2015–2016'. https://eands.dacnet.nic.in/AgriWages2015-16.pdf (accessed on 26 June 2021).

Government of India. 2017b. 'Agricultural Statistics at a Glance 2016'. https://eands.dacnet.nic.in/PDF/Glance-2016.pdf (accessed on 26 June 2021).

Government of India. 2018. 'Agricultural Statistics at a Glance 2017'. https://eands.dacnet.nic.in/PDF/Agricultural%20Statistics%20at%20a%20Glance%202017.pdf (accessed on 19 August 2021).

Government of India. 2019. 'Agricultural Wages in India 2016–2017'. https://eands.dacnet.nic.in/AgriWages2016-17.pdf (accessed on 26 June 2021).

Government of India. 2020. 'Agricultural Wages in India 2018–2019'. https://eands.dacnet.nic.in/PDF/AWI%20Final%202018%2019.pdf (accessed on 26 June 2021).

Government of India. 2021a. 'Agricultural Statistics at a Glance 2011'. Directorate of Economics and Statistics. https://eands.dacnet.nic.in/latest_20011.htm (accessed on 22 August 2021).

Government of India. 2021b. 'Agricultural Statistics at a Glance 2020'. Directorate of Economics and Statistics. https://eands.dacnet.nic.in/PDF/Agricultural%20Statistics%20at%20a%20Glance%20-%202020%20(English%20version).pdf (accessed on 28 August 2021).

Government of India. 2021c. *Directorate of Economics and Statistics*. https://eands.dacnet.nic.in/Cost_of_Cultivation.htm (accessed on 23 June 2021)

Government of India. 2021d. 'Office of the Registrar General and Census Commissioner, India'. https://censusindia.gov.in/2011census/B-series/B_7.html (accessed on 26 June 2021).

Government of India. 2021e. 'Situation Assessment of Agricultural Households and Land and Livestock Holdings of Households in Rural India, 2019'. Ministry of Statistics and Programme Implementation, National Statistical Office. http://mospi.nic.in/sites/default/files/publication_reports/Report_587m.pdf (accessed on 10 December 2021).

Gulati, A., and R. Juneja. 2020. 'Farm Mechanization in Indian Agriculture with Focus on Tractors'. ZEF Discussion Papers on Development Policy No. 297, Germany. https://www.econstor.eu/bitstream/10419/229975/1/zef-dp-297.pdf (accessed on 28 August 2021).

Gunabhagya, A. T. Joshi, S. S. Patil, and G. N. Maraddi. 2017. 'Agricultural Labour Shortage: An Abysmal to Agriculture in North Eastern Karnataka'. *Economic Affairs* 62(4): 589–594.

Gupta, N. 2016. 'Decline of Cultivators and Growth of Agricultural Labourers in India from 2001 to 2011'. *International Journal of Rural Management* 12, no. 2: 179–198.

Grover, D. K. 2014. 'Rapporteur's Report on Labour Scarcity in Agriculture and Farm Mechanisation'. *Indian Journal of Agricultural Economics* 69, no. 3: 438–449.

Haque, T. 2000. 'Contractual Arrangements in Land and Labour Markets in Rural India'. *Indian Journal of Agricultural Economics* 55, no. 3: 233–252.

Hayami, Y., and Y. Godo. 2014. *Development Economics from the Poverty to the Wealth of Nations*. New Delhi: Oxford University Press.

Kajale, J., and S. S. Shroff. 2011. *Impact of NREGA on Wage Rates, Food Security and Rural Urban Migration in Maharashtra*. Report submitted to the Ministry of Agriculture. Pune: Gokhale Institute of Politics and Economics, Agro-Economic Research Centre.

Kijima, Y., and P. Lanjouw. 2005. 'Economic Diversification and Poverty in Rural India'. *Indian Journal of Labour Economics* 48, no. 2: 349–374.

Lin, Justin Yifu. 1995. 'Endowments, Technology, and Factor Markets: A Natural Experiment of Induced Institutional Innovation from China's Rural Reform'. *American Journal of Agricultural Economics* 77, no. 2: 231–242.

Ministry of Rural Development (MoRD). 2012. 'Report of the Committee on Revision of MGNREGA Operational Guidelines'. Report submitted to the MoRD. New Delhi: Government of India.

Murthy, P. S. S., and S. Indumati. 2011. 'Economic Analysis of MGNREGA in the Drought–prone States of Karnataka, Rajasthan and Irrigation–dominated State of Andhra Pradesh'. *Agricultural Economics Research Review* 24: 531–536.

Nagaraj, N., C. Bantilan, L. Pandey, and N.S. Roy. 2016. 'Impact of MGNREGA on Rural Agricultural Wages, Farm Productivity and Net Returns: An Economic Analysis Across SAT Villages'. *Indian Journal of Agricultural Economics* 71, no. 2: 176–190.

Nair, M. K. Sukumaran. 1997. 'Rural Labour Market in Kerala: Small Holder Agriculture and Labour Market Dynamics'. *Economic & Political Weekly* 32, no. 35: L45–L52.

Ninan, K. N. 1984. 'Labour Use in Agriculture: Case Studies of Tapioca and Paddy'. *Economic & Political Weekly* 19, no. 51/52: A199–A204.

Otsuka, Keijiro, H. Chuma, and Y. Hayami. 1992. 'Land and Labor Contracts in Agrarian Economics: Theories and Facts'. *Journal of Economic Literature* 30, no. 4: 1965–2018.

Prabakar, C., K. S. Devi, and S. Selvam. 2011. 'Labour Scarcity—Its Immensity and Impact on Agriculture'. *Agricultural Economics Research Review* 24: 373–380.

Rahman, Rushidan Islam. 2017. 'Changes in the Situation of Agricultural Labourers in Bangladesh'. *The Bangladesh Development Studies* 40B, no. 3&4: 137–157.

Rajni, Vijaya. 2007. 'Casual Labour Contracts of Agricultural Labourers in East and West Uttar Pradesh'. *Economic & Political Weekly* 42, no. 2: 154–160.

Ravi, S., and M. Engler. 2013. 'Workfare as an Effective Way to Fight Poverty: The Case of India's NREGS'. https://ssrn.com/abstract=1336837 or http://dx.doi.org/10.2139/ssrn.1336837 (accessed on 27 August 2021).

Ray, Debraj. 2011. *Development Economics*. New Delhi: Oxford University Press.

Reddy, D. N., A. A. Reddy, and M. C. S. Bantilan. 2014. 'The Impact of Mahatma Gandhi National Rural Employment Guarantee Act (MGNREGA) on Rural Labor Markets and Agriculture'. *India Review* 13, no. 3: 251–273.

Reserve Bank of India. 2020. 'Handbook of Statistics on the Indian Economy 2019–2020'. https://rbidocs.rbi.org.in/rdocs/Publications/PDFs/0HBS202024D4CA0CC03F4674B040F7DEDE7E5360.PDF (accessed on 26 June 2021).

Salam, Abdul. 1986. 'Farm Labour Use and Its Determinants Results from a Farm Survey in Pakistan'. *Pakistan Economic and Social Review* 24, no. 1: 1–21.

Sharma, H. R., and V. Kumar. 2003. 'Functioning of Agricultural Labour Market: Micro Evidence from an Agriculturally Developed Region of Himachal Pradesh'. *Indian Journal of Agricultural Economics* 58, no. 4: 695–714.

Som, Ranjan Kumar. 1961. 'Agricultural Labour in India'. *The Economic Weekly* 13, no. 8: 263–270.

Subathra, C. 2015. 'Scenario of Cultivators and Agricultural Laborers—A Study'. *International Journal of Research* 2, no. 10: 1133–1139.

Swamy, Anand V. 1998. 'Factor Markets and Resource Allocation in Colonial Punjab'. *The Journal of Development Studies* 34, no. 3: 97–115.

Thadathil, M. S., and V. Mohandas. 2012. 'Impact of MGNREGS on Labour Supply to Agricultural Sector of Wayanad District in Kerala'. *Agricultural Economics Research Review* 25, no. 1: 151–155.

Toufique, Kazi Ali. 2005. 'Farm Size and Productivity in Bangladesh Agriculture: Role of Transaction Costs in Rural Labour Markets'. *Economic & Political Weekly* 40, no. 10: 988–992.

Unni, Jeemol. 1989. 'Changes in Women's Employment in Rural Areas, 1961–83'. *Economic & Political Weekly* 24, no. 17: WS23–WS31.

Varshney, D., D. Goyel, and J. V. Meenakshi. 2018. 'The Impact of MGNREGA on Agricultural Outcomes and the Rural Labour Market: A Matched DID Approach'. *The Indian Journal of Labour Economics* 61, no. 35: 589–621.

Vyas, V. S., and G. Mathai. 1978. 'Farm and Non-Farm Employment in Rural Areas: A Perspective for Planning'. *Economic & Political Weekly* 13, no. 6/7: 333–347.

Chapter 5

Groundwater Markets

Functioning and Issues

Mrinal Kanti Dutta and Jitu Tamuli

5.1. INTRODUCTION

Increased use of groundwater in India's agricultural sector since the beginning of the Green Revolution is a direct outcome of efforts to achieve food security and increased crop output. While higher use of groundwater for irrigation is considered to have a direct bearing on the depleted groundwater reserve, there are instances of emergence of certain institutions, which can help in better utilization of the scarce resource of groundwater. One such institution is the groundwater markets or water markets. In view of the overwhelmingly large number of resource-poor farmers in the small and marginal category (Government of India 2015)[1] and land fragmentation in the country (Government of India 2006; NSSO 2014), benefits of the investment in groundwater extraction are said to be better realized, and optimal utilization of water resources can be ensured in cases where water is

[1] As per the National Sample Survey (NSS) 77th Round (2019), around 86.80 per cent of the total operational holdings in India fall under the 'small and marginal' categories of size classes, which measure less than 2 hectares in size (Government of India 2021). Further, these holdings are not just uneconomically sized but are, often, fragmented (Government of India 2006, 2021; NSO 2021; NSSO 2014).

shared or sold to willing buyers than owning water-extracting devices (WEDs) individually.

The water market evolves when water is treated as an economic good. In the literature, there are two lines of definition of water markets. The first one refers to water markets that involve annual or permanent transfer of the water use rights between a willing buyer and a willing seller in exchange for compensation determined by supply and demand, the cost of mobility, the reliability of the supply and the cost of mitigating any environmental and third-party effects (Simpson 1994). This is generally known as the formal water market in which the concept of water right is defined in a stricter sense. Such water markets require some institutional arrangements like a well-equipped physical delivery system for water, information and transparency regarding price and availability of water and administrative framework and user-based management system (Asad et al. 1999).

The second variant of water market refers to a localized village-level informal arrangements for water transactions, whereby owners of WEDs (e.g., pump sets or tube wells) sell water or irrigation services[2] to neighbouring farmers at prices mostly determined by the incremental cost of pumping (Shah 1991, 1993). It is usually believed that the owners of the WEDs have some excess water extraction capacity, which is normally sold to willing buyers in the neighbourhood. Some

---

[2] There was a long debate on the terms 'water markets' or 'market for irrigation services'. Since, in the water market, water is not sold *per se*, farmers sell water from their own water extraction mechanism (WEM), it is often argued that it is a market for irrigation service (Palmer-Jones, 2002). However, as Shah and Ballabh (1997) note,

> Many researchers have contested the use of the term 'water market' for such transaction because, in principle, the water they pump is not their private property and what well owner sell is merely the services of their pump sets. It is argued therefore, that these are best referred to as pump rental markets. Technically this seems rights. However, the term water market persists in scholarly literature as also in farmers' usage. One reason is the simplicity of the phrase 'water market'; but probably a more correct reason is that the water they pump is theirs, and others in the village including buyers do not have any serious objection as long as their right to extract water in future is not encouraged. (Shah and Ballabh 1997; A-189)

informal norms and customs dominate water transactions, which also result in diverse arrangement in the payment system of such markets. Social relationship between the seller and the buyers also has an influence on the nature of transaction in such water markets. Thus, informal water markets based on informal contract enforcement have none of the institutional characteristics that formal water markets have.

Although different authors have tried to define informal water markets based on specific characteristics, it was Pant (1992) who had brought out the definition of informal water markets and underlying conditions for the existence of the market in a very precise manner. He defines water market as 'a market that refers to sale of water versus hire of private pump sets or boring'.[3] According to him, water markets are likely to exist in a situation where the following four conditions are satisfied:

1. The buyers perceive irrigation through purchase of groundwater as the most agreeable alternative in comparison to other sources of irrigation.
2. The water supplier has pumping capacity in excess of his/her own requirements and perceives water sales a profitable proposition
3. Willing buyers are available within the command area of the suppliers' irrigation equipment in case the pump set is fixed (in the case of mobile pump sets, there is no fixed command, and their managerial control is more important).
4. Buyers are able physically to gain access to the water.

Going by the above-mentioned definition, water markets can be considered as 'residual markets' as the owners of WEDs should have some excess pumping capacity.

The prevalence of formal water markets is mostly observed in countries such as the United States, Australia, Spain, Peru, Chile, Mexico, South Africa, North Africa, Brazil and Georgia (Bate 2002; Bjornlund

[3] Adapted from Ballabh and Shah (1989), *Groundwater Markets: A Review of Issues Evidence and Politics,* paper presented in the workshop on Efficiency and Equity in Ground Water Use and Management, Institute of Rural Management, Anand, 30 January—1 February 1989.

and McKay 1998, 2002; Isley and Middleton 2003), while informal water markets are pervasive in the irrigated areas of Asian countries, namely Pakistan, India, Bangladesh, (Meinzen-Dick 1998; Rinaudo and Stosser 1997; Saleth 1996, 1998; Shah 1991, 1993), Indonesia, Jordan (Meinzen-Dick and Mendoza 1996) and China (Zhang et al. 2006). Thobani (1997), however, has pointed out the widespread existence of informal water markets in Mexico before the introduction of formal tradable water rights. The World Bank (1999) also has pointed to the existence of informal water markets in Mexico, alongside the more recent formal water markets.

In India, initial efforts to create irrigation infrastructure were taken up as a government initiative. The medium and large-scale irrigation projects in the traditional sites of the Green Revolution came up with investment in the public sector. However, with relatively easier funding from banks and other financial institutions later on, there were initiatives for private investment in groundwater irrigation in the country. In certain cases, private investment in groundwater irrigation was encouraged through public policies as well (e.g., shallow tube wells (STWs) in Assam in the late 1990s were installed under different schemes of National Bank for Agriculture and Rural Development—NABARD and World Bank). However, with the spread of the Green Revolution to different regions, and land being fragmented and agricultural plots being scattered, the resource-poor farmers found it relatively difficult and uneconomic to carry out relatively lumpy investment in such irrigation technology. With the emergence of water markets later on, however, these farmers found it relatively easy to purchase water from WED owners and irrigate their agricultural fields rather than investing in such technology. As mentioned already, water markets are considered to be widespread in India. However, the spread of the market seems to be varying considerably based on the agro-climatic condition and many other socio-economic parameters. Availability of water resources is one such important factor in determining the pace of growth of the water market. Normally, in regions where supply of water is high, the pace of development of the water market is considered to be rapid. However, contrary to this assertion, in the eastern Indian states of Odisha, Bihar and West Bengal, groundwater markets are stated to be highly underdeveloped, in spite of abundance of easily accessible groundwater reserve (Shah 1993). Assam is another state in eastern India, where the spread of groundwater market is found to be relatively slow.

The present chapter is an attempt to examine the nature and functioning of water markets in India, taking the case of Assam. It also tries to highlight the issues associated with the growth of such markets. The chapter makes use of available literature and secondary data for analysing groundwater markets for the country. While, for the study on water market in Assam, the authors make use of some primary data, which were collected by the second author from selected farm households in Nagaon and Morigaon districts of Central Brahmaputra Valley Zone (CBVZ) a few years back.

The chapter comprises five sections, including the introduction. Section 5.2 discusses the status and dimension of groundwater markets in India based on available secondary data and literature. Section 5.3 is devoted to examining the issues of groundwater markets in India, focusing mostly on the issues of efficiency, reliability, energy use and interlocking of factor markets. Section 5.4 examines the issues of water markets in a water-abundant region taking the case of Assam and attempts to examine how the issues are different from those in water-scarce regions. Finally, section 5.5 concludes the chapter by summarizing the discussion.

5.2. GROUNDWATER MARKETS IN INDIA

Agricultural development in India is largely dependent on development of irrigation. The country has witnessed a more than threefold increase in the net irrigated area from 21 million hectares in 1950–1951 to 68 million hectares in 2013–2014; the share of groundwater irrigation through wells has been rising substantially from 28 per cent to 62 per cent. The main contribution in this came from a rapid growth in tube well irrigation, the share of which rose from 18.55 per cent in 1966–1967 to 73.91 in 2012–2013 in well irrigation (Gandhi 2011; MOSPI 2017). This indicates the overwhelming significance of groundwater irrigation in India's irrigation scenario, and within that the contribution of tube well irrigation technology. Groundwater accounts for more than 60 per cent of the irrigated area in the country at present. However, the availability of the resource is not uniform across the country; rather, it is highly concentrated in specific locations. Out of the total replenishable groundwater reserve of 431.42 bcm in the country, the Ganga basin alone accounts for nearly 40 per cent and none of the other basins even crosses 10 per cent of the total reserve (Gandhi and Bhamoriya 2011).

The spread of groundwater irrigation in the country, triggered by the Green Revolution, is accompanied by notable growth of an institution known as groundwater markets. Although water trading can be traced back to the 1920s, a systematic documentation of the practice began only in the late 1960s (Saleth 1998). Spread of groundwater irrigation and resultant emergence of water markets are closely linked with the property rights issue of groundwater. As rights over groundwater in India are automatically bestowed on those having rights over land, groundwater irrigation is normally within the reach of those possessing land. A landowner can legally draw any amount of water as he/she wants unless the geo-hydrological condition or technology limits it (Gandhi 2011). The consequence of such a legal framework is that only the landowners can own groundwater in India. The landless households or tribes that may have community rights over land, as such, will not have access to groundwater irrigation. Under the present circumstances of property rights, ensuring access to groundwater irrigation for all the needy farmers is a huge challenge. The emergence and development of groundwater market is expected to overcome this problem substantially (Dutta 2011; Jeet 2005). As water markets in India are localized village-level institutions, they are greatly influenced by the prevailing customs and socio-economic conditions.

Saleth (1998) notes that 'Although water markets in India are localized, fragmented and vary in terms of maturity, they are an evolving institution with substantial efficiency and welfare effects'. Narain (1997) in this regard notes, 'The emergence of groundwater markets could perhaps best be viewed as a response to the pattern of development of ground water in the country, which has largely left behind a vast chunk of farmers who are unable to afford water extraction mechanisms'.

Regarding the participants in water markets, studies are not unanimous. Past studies show that the well owners with less holdings have a higher extent of participation than those who own larger holdings (Shah and Raju 1988). In addition, many studies maintained that small and marginal farmers tend to be water buyers, while the large and medium farmers tend to be water sellers (Singh and Singh 2003). However, recent studies have pointed out that this need not necessarily be true. There are instances when a large chunk of water sellers are found belonging to small and marginal farmers category under the prevailing condition of land fragmentation and operational holding not being contiguous (Dutta 2007; Tamuli 2014).

The spread and existence of groundwater markets is not uniform across the country. In some states such as Gujarat, Maharashtra, Haryana, Andhra Pradesh, Tamil Nadu, Uttar Pradesh (UP), Punjab and West Bengal, the presence of such markets is reported to be more widespread (Saleth 1996). Many studies have pointed out that although the occurrence of groundwater markets is more widespread in these states, development of the market is more pervasive in Gujarat (Dubash 2000, Gandhi and Bhamoriya 2011; Mohanty and Gupta 2002, Narain 1997). Water markets in Gujarat are stated to have existed for as long 70–80 years (Narain 1997; Shah 1991). However, compared to these agriculturally developed states, in water abundant regions in Eastern India, namely eastern UP, Bihar, Odisha, Assam, etc., the presence of such markets is very thin (Dutta 2011, 2012; Shah 1991). The differences in the occurrence of groundwater markets are the result of a number of factors such as rainfall, groundwater supply, cropping pattern, cost and availability of electricity and development of tube wells under private ownership to name some of them (Saleth 1994; Shah 1993).

There is no macro-level estimate on the size of groundwater markets in India. Several micro studies, however, illustrate the degree of variation in the use of water trading in the country. In terms of the area irrigated through groundwater markets, estimates vary from 30 to 80 per cent depending on the location. Based on a number of micro studies on water markets, Shah (1993) has estimated that more than 50 per cent of the gross area irrigated by private modern WEDs is served by groundwater markets. Saleth (1998) using a methodology based on pump sets rental data, put the figure at 6 million hectares or 15 per cent of the total area irrigated by groundwater. Mohanty and Gupta (2002), assuming a contribution of irrigated cultivation to total output at US$230 per hectare/per year, have estimated the total value of output due to water sales to be US$1.38 billion/per year. Further, there is a great degree of variation in the size of groundwater markets among different states. In northern Gujarat, nearly 80 per cent of the total irrigated acreage is served by water markets (Shah 1993), while in eastern and western parts of UP, it is 73 and 79 per cent, respectively (Pant 2004). On a similar note, around 40–60 per cent of irrigated land in Allahabad district of UP is reported to be irrigated through water markets (Shankar 1992a). However, this figure is much lower at about 30 per cent in Vaigai Basin of Tamil Nadu (Janakarajan 1993, 1994).

Although the water markets in the country are informal in nature, and local customs and practices prevail, there is variation in its operation from region to region. For example, in case of the basis of water charge realized, there are differences in the approach. Overall, literature has pointed out the prevalence of three different bases on which water charge is realized in India, namely hourly rate, volume-based rate and area-based rate. Overwhelming majority of the empirical studies in India, however, have pointed out the dominance of hourly rate in water transaction where water charge is decided based on the number of hours the pump is used for irrigating the field (e.g., Hussain et al. 2005; Jha and Sinha 2008; Janakarajan 1993; Khair et al. 2012; Pant 1992; Palmer-Jones 1993; Satyasai et al. 1997; Shah and Ballabh 1997 etc.). Instances of volume-based and area-based approaches for deciding the water charge are also found in different parts of the country.

The property rights issue of groundwater has resulted in an increasing concern relating to the growth of water market in India. Many studies have concurred that the penetration of informal water markets lead to over exploitation of the groundwater resources with serious inter-temporal externalities in the form of declining water tables, higher pumping costs, lower well yield or even abandonment of wells, especially in the water-scarce regions (Janakarajan 1993; Meinzen Dick 1998; Moench 1992; Mondal and Majumdar 2008; Narain 1997; Saleth

1994, 1996; Shah 1993; Singh 2002). Since individual farmers are more concerned with their private gains and costs and may completely ignore social cost (negative externality) of over-exploitation of groundwater resources, growth of groundwater markets may aggravate aquifer depletion (Saleth 1998). As the landowners have the right to extract groundwater beyond any limit until it is available, pricing of water fails to reflect true scarcity value of groundwater resulting in over-exploitation of the resource. This ultimately may result in allocative inefficiency, inequity in resource use and ecological unsustainability (Narain 1997; Saleth 1996). This negative externality associated with the growth of water market is already very intensive in water-scarce or dry regions in India (Chandrakanth et al. 2004; Moench 1992, 2000; Scott and Shah 2004). Reports of conflicts arising over the use of groundwater among the farmers in many parts of India are widespread in literature (Cullet 2012; Foster and Gardunu 2004; Janakarajan and Moench 2006).

5.3. ISSUES OF GROUNDWATER MARKETS IN INDIA

The major issues that have dominated the studies on informal groundwater markets in South Asia and for that matter in India include equity, reliability of the water markets, efficiency in groundwater use along with the other inputs, impact of the market in the enhancement of income and sustainability of the groundwater resource. As these are interconnected with the use of groundwater irrigation in agriculture, some of these issues are discussed along with the issues of use of groundwater irrigation.

5.3.1. Equity

One of the prominent issues dominating the discussion of groundwater markets in India is the equity issue, whereby the growth of water markets is expected to increase access to water for the participants in the market. Owning a WED and extracting groundwater require relatively lumpy initial investment and it is normally beyond the capacity of the resource-poor small and marginal farmers. The emergence of water markets may overcome this problem by supplying irrigation water to those neighbouring willing farmers who consider water buying to be the best available option under such a scenario. With these markets remaining informal and traditional principles deciding water transaction and transaction taking place both in terms of cash and kind, the buyers (farmers) find this option more feasible.

Studies on water markets are unanimous in acknowledging the favourable impact of water markets in terms of extension of opportunity to equitable access to groundwater irrigation to the small and marginal farmers. Water markets are also found to ensure generation of gains for the buyers across different agro-climatic conditions. These gains include higher and risk-free income realization and employment through increase in crop yield, cropping intensity, changing cropping pattern in favour of high-value crops and use of modern agricultural technologies, which are considered scale neutral (Dutta 2011; Joshi 2005; Khanna 2006; Khair et al. 2012; Gandhi 2011; Meinzen-Dick and Mendoza 1996, 1998; Palmer-Jones 2001; Pant 1991, 1992, 2005; Shah 1988, 1991, 1993, Singh 2002; Zhang et al. 2006). Water markets by way of ensuring access to groundwater can help in the reduction of poverty and ensure economic development. Evidence indicates that improved water supply can generate many positive externalities in the overall household micro-economy. In areas dependent on irrigated agriculture, the reliability of groundwater and the resulting higher crop yield generally achieved, often enables farmers with smallholdings to considerably increase their incomes (Moench 1993). In this regard, Singh and Singh (2003) in a study in western UP have observed water distribution to be relatively equitable for small and marginal farmers engaged in water trading in the cultivation of sugarcane. The positive impact of well irrigation goes beyond those who own them as it also increases and stabilizes the demand for associated inputs, including labour. As asserted by Gandhi (2011), the expansion of well irrigation can have a ripple effect in the rural areas, including creating more employment.

5.3.2. Reliability

One of the serious issues in irrigated agriculture is reliability of water supplied to the field, which basically indicates supply and availability of irrigation water for the targeted users at the time of requirement.

While publicly owned canal irrigation systems are found to be unreliable insofar as irrigation supply is concerned due to a host of issues, groundwater seems to be relatively free from these issues (Dutta 2011). However, privately owned and supplied groundwater irrigation can be unreliable at times due to the nature of the resource and the issues of property rights.

Water markets are normally considered to be residual in nature, indicating the fact that water is sold by the owners of WEDs after meeting their own requirements. Obviously, buyers are subject to inadequate water supply when needed under these circumstances, indicating non-reliability of provision of water to the buyers (Meinzen-Dick 1998).

Findings of different studies in India and other parts of South Asia on the issue are not similar. Meinzen-Dick (1998) is one researcher who examined the issue of reliability of water market systematically in Pakistan. The researcher found that the private groundwater market was a less reliable source of water when the farmers needed it the most. Meinzen-Dick identified a host of factors such as capacity of the tube wells, social status of the buyers and age of the buyers as significant factors affecting reliability of groundwater markets in the country.

Hussain et al. (2005) in their study on water market in Pakistan found the market unreliable for the buyers. According to them, buyers found the market unreliable when they purchased water from small-capacity, electric-powered tube wells. In order to improve reliability of the water market, they emphasized on increasing tube well density by assisting small and marginal farmers to purchase tube wells. They were also of the opinion that regular supply of electricity could help in getting an access to reliable supply of water.

Singh and Singh (2003) reporting from a study in UP, however, found that almost all the respondents under self-users and self-users + sellers forms of water market had realized adequate availability of water and control on water supply throughout the year in the case of diesel-operated water extraction mechanisms (WEMs). A good number of buyer farmers were also found to be experiencing the same, indicating that water was largely reliable under market arrangement for all categories of market participants. The study had also found diesel-operated WEMs to be relatively more reliable as compared to electric-operated WEMs, but the water buying cost was much higher for diesel-operated WEMs than electric-operated WEMs (₹7 per hour) due to high cost of water extraction.

In our survey in Nagaon and Morigaon districts in CBVZ of Assam, around 62 per cent of water buyers found the water supply non-reliable due to a host of reasons. One of the prominent reasons for this is the high concurrent demand for irrigation water at the time of sowing of the crop. As the installed capacity of the irrigation system is fixed, supplying water to all the neighbouring farmers at the same time becomes extremely difficult.

5.3.3. Efficiency

Another important issue in groundwater irrigation is the issue of efficiency in water use. Efficiency can be defined as achieving maximum output from a given level of input mix. From the point of view of available literature, efficiency in water use under the water market can be looked into in terms of utilization efficiency[4] as well as technical efficiency (TE).[5]

---

[4] Utilization efficiency can be defined as optimizing utilization of installed irrigation potential of water-extracting devices. Groundwater extraction water pumps are normally associated with a fixed irrigation potential. For example, a five HP capacity machine engaged for extraction of groundwater has a capacity of irrigating up to 2 hectares of land. Utilization efficiency in that sense can be measured in terms of maximizing utilization of installed irrigation potential of these machines. In other words, utilization efficiency for these machines can be measured in terms of utilization rate, which is nothing but the ratio of net area irrigated to net irrigable area expressed in percentage for the particular scheme or machine.

[5] Technical efficiency refers to a situation where with a given technology and a set of inputs, a producer (a farmer in our case) is able to produce the maximum possible output. Technical efficiency is divided into two types: output-oriented technical efficiency and input-oriented or input-conserving technical efficiency (Kalirajan and Shand 1994, 1999). Output-oriented technical efficiency is defined as the maximum output that can be produced for a given set of inputs. Alternatively, input-oriented technical efficiency measures the amount of minimum inputs required to produce a given level of output. That is, producers are regarded

In one of the earlier studies in Nagaon district of Assam, Dutta (2012) reported relatively better utilization efficiency of STW-based irrigation schemes primarily because of the emergence of groundwater market in the district.

The emergence and growth of the water market are expected to contribute positively towards attaining higher TE by making water available at the time of requirement for those farmers participating in such a market. Some of the categories of participants in these water markets may be in the form of 'only buyers', 'only self-users + sellers' and 'self-user + sellers + buyers'. However, in most of the cases, the water market is found to be residual in nature, which results in inadequate provision of water in buyers' plots. Hence, there may obviously be differences in the attainment of TE between buyers' and sellers' plots or between buyers' plots and owner's plots.

Examining the impact of groundwater markets on attainment of TE in the eastern dry zone of Karnataka, Manjunatha et al. (2011a, 2011b) have reported that the farmers who had participated in the market have achieved higher TE scores on their plots than those who have remained outside the market. However, they have noted the differences in the attainment of TE score among owners of tube wells, water buyers and water sellers. Srivastava et al. (2009) in their study on the impact of groundwater market on water–use efficiency for 100 sample farm households in the Central Plain Zones of UP have found that both buyers and owners of WEMs are technically inefficient in water–use, as the actual use of irrigation water is found to be much higher than the optimum level. Khanna (2006) has noted the difference in TE scores between owner and buyers, where buyers' plots are the least efficient than the plots owned and operated by the owner of tube wells.

In our study on water markets in Nagaon and Morigaon districts of Assam, the minimum and maximum estimated output-oriented TE score for all farmers' plots were found to be 0.514 and 0.983, respectively. The average TE score was 0.941.

---

technically inefficient if they use more inputs than required to produce a given level of output.

The study did not find any remarkable difference in the average TE scores achieved on the plots of 'only buyers' and 'only self-users + sellers'. The average TE score on plots of these two categories of groundwater users was found to be 0.94. This finding is a little deviation from results of other studies on water market where the researchers have found buyers' plots to be technically less efficient than that of 'self-user + sellers' (Khanna 2006; Manjunatha 2011a, 2011b). However, a notable difference is found in the minimum TE scores. While the minimum TE scores on buyers' plots were found to be 0.547, the same was 0.805 on self-user-cum-sellers' plots. That the buyers' plots are equally technically efficient cannot be accepted at least in the case of a few buyers who had recorded a very minimum TE scores as compared to the 'self-user + sellers'.

Besides, plots owned and operated by the 'self-user + sellers + buyers' had recorded the highest TE scores (0.982) among all groundwater users. The fact that plots operated by the 'self-user + sellers + buyers' are technically more efficient than those plots of 'self-users' implies that farmers participating in the groundwater market are more efficient in input use than the non-participants.

The average TE scores on both marginal and small plots were found higher than the average TE scores of semi-medium and medium plots. It indicates that input use is relatively more effective on small and marginal plots than the medium plots. This is probably due to the fact that on relatively smaller plots, the farmers can have better control on the input combination; hence, the farming is more effective.

5.3.4. Market Imperfection and Monopoly Power

Some Indian studies have pointed out the presence of market imperfections in the water market in the form of monopoly power enjoyed by the water sellers-cum-big landlords (Janakarajan 1993; Satyasai et al. 1997; Shah 1993). In the case of water markets, the very nature of the market can give rise to some kind of imperfection/monopoly power. First, a seller in the market has to have ownership over a WED, which requires some initial capital investment. Obviously, relatively richer and wealthier farmers will have an advantage over here. Resource-poor farmers, with no access to formal credit from financial institutions, will naturally be deprived from participating in such markets. Second, with fragmented holdings and agricultural plots being scattered, the water-buying farmers will not have many options of purchasing water from other sellers. This might give some kind of local monopoly power to the water sellers. Acharyya et al. (2018), however, have observed that in the case of groundwater irrigation, monopoly markets may promote some kind of efficiency as well. First, with lesser number of water sellers in the market, less amount of groundwater extraction will take place, minimizing the common property resource problem. Second, since there is a long-term specific relation between a water seller and a buyer, from the perspective of incomplete contract theory, it is more efficient that the irrigation and cultivation are carried out by the same individual.

With the monopoly power, the sellers are found to charge water rates higher than the incremental cost of pumping (e.g., 2.5–3 times the marginal cost and 1.25–1.8 times of average total cost) and thereby appropriate sizeable amount of profits (Shah 1999). Acharyya et al. (2018) have also observed some degree of market imperfections in the water market in the three districts of West Bengal. According to them, water sellers in the state resort to collusive oligopoly where the owners of WEDs, based on their catchment area, divide the market among themselves, with the condition that no water seller will try to sell water in another seller's demarcated area.

There is also non-price discrimination, whereby sellers refuse to supply water to the buyers during crucial periods, based on various socio-economic factors, which are mostly non-market in nature, which, in turn, makes the market unreliable for the buyers (Meinzen-Dick 1998).

5.3.5. Energy Use and Groundwater Markets

Groundwater use for irrigation is also subject to availability of energy source. With the Green Revolution, the country has seen changes in the policy for energy use. With an objective of increasing the use of irrigation in agriculture, many states had enacted policies subsidizing (or waiving) electricity charge for irrigation. Many of the traditional sites of the Green Revolution such as Punjab, Haryana, UP had either waived electricity charge for irrigation or subsidized it. While such a move had a positive influence on the use of electricity for irrigation, at the same time, it had encouraged over-exploitation of the precious resource groundwater because of artificially lowering down of cost of extraction. The policy on energy use, however, is not uniform across states in the country.

According to some studies, out of a total of 20 million operational groundwater wells in India, more than 70 per cent rely on electricity, 26 per cent are diesel-powered and the remaining ones depend on wind, solar, animal power and other energy sources. However, since pumps on the deepest tube wells (which require higher energy per unit water) are predominantly electric, 85 per cent of the groundwater pumping energy is provided by electricity (Gandhi and Bhamoriya 2011). Hence, electricity pricing policies can have serious consequences for India's agriculture sector. (Sidhu et al. 2020)

5.3.6. Interlocking of Factor Markets

Water markets are closely linked with other rural markets like credit markets and land tenancy markets (Acharyya 2020; Acharyya et al. 2018; Fujita and Hossain 1995; Jacoby et al. 2004; Kajisa and Sakurai 2005; Palmer-Jones 1994; Saleth 1998). Due to the prevailing socio-economic conditions in rural areas, the same group of people has to perform different roles in different rural markets. For example, the landlord may have to function not only as a provider of land in land rental market, he/she may also have to function as the loan provider for the farmer. The same landlord may act as water seller in the water market. The overwhelming presence of the same person in different rural markets gives him some kind of local monopoly power, which is found to be exercised by him in different forms. Prospective water buyers may have to carry out additional work at no cost to get access to water from such a monopolist water seller.

Looking at the presence of tenancy among farmers under different structures of water markets is important as access to water by the small and marginal farmers critically depends on whether the farmers lease in land or not from the water sellers (Meinzen-Dick 1994, 1998). Empirical studies have pointed out that some of the buyers had to render some additional services for getting access to irrigation water like operating the pump or irrigating the well owner's field to water sellers in addition to payment of water charge (Janakarajan 1993, 1994).

5.3.7. The Issue of Property Rights and Water Markets

Besides these aspects, the unresolved question overlying the recent debate on groundwater markets is the apprehension that informal water markets may lead to over-exploitation of the groundwater resources with serious ramifications on inter-temporal externalities in the form of declining water tables, higher pumping costs, lower well yield or even abandonment of wells, especially in the water-scare regions (Janakarajan 1993; Meinzen Dick 1998; Moench 1992; Narain 1997; Saleth 1994, 1996; Shah 1993; Singh 2002). Since individual farmers are more concerned with their private gains and costs and may completely ignore social cost of over-exploitation of groundwater resources, growth of groundwater markets may aggravate aquifer depletion (Saleth 1998). However, one implication of such deliberation is the property rights issue of groundwater in India.

As per the law, the ownership of groundwater in India is attached to land, and the landowners have the right to extract groundwater beyond any limit until it is available. The immediate consequence of such a legal framework is that only the landowners can own groundwater in India. The landless households or tribes that may have community rights over land will have no private control over groundwater (Gandhi 2011). Under such a situation, pricing of water fails to reflect true scarcity value of water, resulting in over-exploitation of the resource. This ultimately may result in allocative inefficiency, inequity in resource use and ecological unsustainability (Narain 1997; Saleth 1996). The rich landlords can be water lords and indulge openly in extraction and selling of as much water as they wish (Singh 2002). Although the problems may not seem to be so intense in the water-abundant regions, the possibility that unregulated groundwater abstraction can eventually lead to local problems of groundwater over-exploitation cannot be ruled out. The lack of well-defined property rights, the invisibility and the complex flow characteristics of groundwater make it very difficult to monitor its use (Singh 2002).

5.4. GROUNDWATER MARKETS IN ASSAM

As is already discussed, the growth of groundwater market in India is not uniform across regions, and, as such, issues of such markets in different regions may vary considerably. To see the nature and working of water markets across locations, a case study of water markets in Assam is presented in this section. Assam in the north-eastern part of India is considered to possess relatively large groundwater reserves with heavy monsoon precipitation facilitating easy replenishment. The Central Groundwater Board (CGWB) of India has estimated the net availability of annual replenishable groundwater in the state at 21.43 bcm, out of which 11.25 per cent is extracted for all purposes (industrial, domestic and agriculture; Government of India 2020). With a view to tap the availability of groundwater for agricultural use in the state, there were initiatives through government agencies for the rapid growth of groundwater-based minor irrigation schemes in the late 1990s of the previous century. (For instance, the compound annual growth rates (CAGRs) of total minor irrigation structures in the state was 11.40 per cent during 1986–1987 to 1993–1994, which increased to 16.08 per cent during 1993–1994 to 2000–2001, while the same for India was 6.99 per cent during 1993–1994 to 2000–2001 [MoWR 2001, 2005]). Among all the groundwater structures in the state, the growth of STWs under private ownership was found to be the highest. As per the Minor Irrigation Census 2000–2001 of the Government of India, about 98 per cent of total STWs installed in Assam was under individual ownership. With expansion of groundwater irrigation, the practice of water transactions between owners of WED with excess capacity with neighbouring farmers began paving the way for the emergence of groundwater market in the state (Dutta 2012). While the groundwater market in the state has grown in significance, literature on groundwater irrigation and groundwater market is found to be relatively scarce.

The case study is based on a survey of 198 farm households from the CBVZ of the state, comprising the districts of Nagaon and Morigaon. The survey reveals that the water market is functioning quite extensively in rural Assam. About 90.91 per cent of the sample farmers are engaged in water transaction. The nature of water market in the state is found to be largely seasonal with farmers engaged in the transaction of water for cultivation of summer rice, which is grown primarily using groundwater in the winter season when there is hardly any rainfall.

Various issues relating to the nature and functioning of the water market in the state is presented in the following subsections with a comparison of results of studies from other parts of India.

5.4.1. Market Arrangement

The field survey found six alternative market arrangements for water trade in the study area, namely 'self-users + sellers', 'buyers', 'self-users + sellers + buyers', 'self-users + buyers', 'pure sellers' and 'self-users'.[6] The distribution of different categories of farmers in the market shows that majority of the buyers (98.36%) belong to small (41.54%) and marginal (56.82%) category of farmers. Buyers in the semi-medium

---

[6] **Self-users + sellers**: Farmers with independent or joint ownership (or both) of tube wells use water for cultivating their own plots as well as selling water to needy farmers in the vicinity of the tube well after meeting their own requirements.

Buyers: The farmers who buy water from the nearest tube wells usually adjacent to their agricultural plots. However, there is the possibility of water purchase from any distant source when there is facility for water conveyance.

Self-users + sellers + buyers: The owners of tube wells, who cultivate their agricultural plots with water from own tube wells, sell water to willing buyers after meeting their own requirement and buy water from other tube wells in another location when their cultivable land is fragmented.

Self-users + buyers: The farmers with independent ownership or joint ownership of tube wells use water from their own tube wells for their own use in one plot and buy water from other tube wells in other plots.

Pure sellers: This refers to a situation in which some farmers have invested on tube wells, not to meet their own irrigation requirement, but for using it primarily for selling water to other farmers.

Self-users: Farmers with individual or joint ownership of tube wells and use it for cultivation on own plots are referred to as self-users.

category are only 5.13 per cent. The fact that pure buyers in the water market are generally the small and marginal farmers is reported by almost all studies on the water market. Viewed from this point, it can be inferred that the market has been quite successful in ensuring equity in access to groundwater for the small and marginal farmers in the state.

However, in the case of sellers, out of the total sample of 'self-users + sellers', about 65.78 per cent belong to small and marginal category, whereas 28.86 and 5.15 per cent, respectively, are in semi-medium and medium categories. It implies that the majority of the water sellers are concentrated in the category of small and marginal farmers. This is in contrast with the findings of majority of the existing literature on water markets, which have reported that the water sellers are usually the large farmers, whereas buyers are small farmers. Though the number of sellers in large or medium farm category is low, the size of their holdings is greater than the buyers. The average size of operational holdings of the buyers is 0.9 hectares, while the minimum and maximum sizes of operational holdings are 0.20 and 3.08 hectares, respectively. But the average size of operational holdings of the sellers in all categories (except the 'pure sellers') remains higher than the average size of operational holdings (1.35 hectare) for all the market participants.

Further, a few members of the group 'pure sellers', though, do not hold any cultivable land, are in the possession of STWs and are engaged in water selling. This category of water sellers owns the tube well primarily for selling water to other farmers for earning additional income. This seems to be a new dimension of the market and has not been mentioned by Pant (1992) while elaborating the conditions for existence of groundwater market. Thus, on the seller's side, it shows that the market has helped some of the tube well owners to sell water by taking groundwater pumping as an additional source of income. Thus, it suggests that the market is 'not residual' to buyers in all cases against the popular belief that the water market is residual in nature.

5.4.2. Mode of Payment

Three different rates of water transactions dominate the literature in water markets, namely hourly rate, volume-based rate and area-based rate. Overwhelming majority of the empirical studies in India have pointed out prevalence/dominance of hourly rate in water transaction, where water charge is decided based on the number of hours the pump is used for irrigating the field (e.g., Hussain et al. 2005; Janakarajan 1993; Jha and Sinha 2008; Khair et al. 2012; Palmer-Jones 1993; Pant 1992; Satyasai et al. 1997; Shah and Ballabh 1997). However, in the case of our case study, water charge is found to be realized based on the area approach. Here, water charge is based on the total amount of area irrigated. This deviation in the approach may be due to the fact that the water market in the state is seasonal in nature, catering to the requirements of the farmers in cultivation of summer rice during rain-free months. Since there is not much variation in hydrological conditions, geological conditions, the soil, crop cultivated and the method of cultivation, this approach may be the best under the prevailing condition.

The water charge realized is found to be in combination of both cash and kind with a dominance of non-cash transaction. Under non-cash transactions, majority (about 66.49%) of the total sample farmers are found to have paid a fixed charge. This phenomenon has an important implication for the development of groundwater markets in the study area. Shah (1991) in his seminal work on water market opined that the prevalence of non-cash transaction is 'an artifact of early stage of water market development', and drive towards maturity will '....give way to one or two standard and widely used contract; and outright cash payment gains precedence over crop sharing contracts'. Viewed from this angle, the water market observed in the study area may be considered to be in its early stage of development. However, not all available literature supports Shah's assertion. Although Choudhury (1990) had similar observations on water charge, Dubash (2000) has found no empirical evidence in support of Shah's proposition. In fact, he concluded, referring to Aggarwal (1999), that non-cash transactions in the water market are widely dominant and stubbornly persistent over time.

5.4.3. Water Charge Realized and Energy Use

Depending upon the type of fuel/power used for the operation of the pumps, water charge realized may vary. The price of both the forms of fuel, namely diesel and electricity, is subject to government policy and price movement in the market, and as such, price of the fuel varies from time to time. For example, based on findings of a number of studies from Punjab, UP and Gujarat, Saleth (1998) has concluded that the hourly rates vary from about US$0.10–US$1.30 for electric pumps and US$0.20–0.60 for diesel pumps. Like other studies on water markets in the country, our study has also noted the difference in water charges depending on the type of fuel/power used. In our study area, the average water charge, under the fixed charge in-kind payment system is 7.47 quintals per hectare, the minimum and maximum being 5.97quintals/hectare and 11.95 quintal/hectare, respectively, when water is bought from the diesel-operated tube well. The water charge is almost double, that is, 13.65 quintal per hectare, when the water is bought from the electric-operated tube wells. The prevalent rates for output sharing among a few sample buyers are found to vary from one-third to two-thirds of the total produce. This rate is almost the same as reported in other studies on water markets. For example, Kajisa and Sakurai (2005) in a study in Madhya Pradesh found it to be ranging from 30 to 40 per cent. Similarly, Fujita and Hossain (1995) in their study of water markets in northwest Bangladesh have found it to be either 33 or 40 per cent. The relatively higher range of water charge under the output sharing mode of transaction may point to the possibility of Marshallian inefficiency in water contract as pointed out by Kajisa and Sakurai (2005).

Variation in prices in both cash and kind forms of water contract among a few sample buyers is observed at the village level in our survey. While this variation is found to be 33 per cent of the average water charge, the variation is found to be less as compared to findings of Janakarajan (1994), who found a large variation in pricing both within and between villages in a study covering 27 villages in southern Tamil Nadu. Prasad (1991) in his study on water market in Bihar also has noted the presence of a large variation in water charges practised by the water sellers who belong to large landholding class. A large variation in prices has also been reported by Kajisa and Sakurai (2005) in their study on water markets with inputs from six villages in Madhya Pradesh. Since there are a few cases of price variation among buyers belonging to same villages, the market may be considered to be relatively competitive at the village level. This finding of the study is more akin to findings of some other studies, which find the market competitive in states such as Andhra Pradesh, Punjab, West Bengal, UP and Odisha (Saleth 1998).

5.4.4. Interlinkage of Water Markets with Other Markets

As mentioned already, water markets are closely linked with other rural markets like financial markets and land markets. In our survey, it is found that about 31.95 per cent of the total sample water buyers have leased in land from the water sellers, and about 42.27 per cent of the total sellers have leased out land to the water buyers. This shows that the water market is intertwined with the land-lease market. However, no landlord has been found to be apparently varying water charges between his tenants and other buyers. This finding is not in line with the findings of Jacoby et al. (2004) and Dubash (2002), who observed a differential treatment meted out by water sellers to the tenants and other buyers. Both these studies reported about water sellers favouring tenant buyers in transaction.

5.4.5. Reliability of Water Market

Groundwater market being largely a residual market is often found to be failing to meet the water demand of the buyers during the period of high demand (Bhandari and Pandey 2006). Thus, non-availability of groundwater in sufficient quantities to the self-users + sellers for their own use as well as for sale and inadequate supply faced by the water buyers, when needed, indicate non-reliability of groundwater markets in fulfilling farmers' needs for irrigation. In our survey, on the supply side, the availability of water to the self-users + sellers is conditioned by a limited number of factors such as condition of the pump sets, relative scarcity of groundwater due to simultaneous drafting by all the farmers and irregular supply of electricity. However, from the buyers' point of view, as high as 62 per cent of the total sample buyers found the market unreliable in meeting their own needs. This number is found to be high when compared to the findings of Meinzen-Dick (1998). The buyers found it unreliable as their respective sellers could not supply water due to the presence of multiple buyers at the same time. As against this, the tenants of the water sellers have reported the market to be reliable, indicating that reliability of the water market is conditioned by the existing land tenure system. Moreover, personal relationship between the buyers and the sellers is also found to be playing a role in the reliability of the market. Most of the buyers finding the market reliable in the survey are found to be having a personal relationship with their existing sellers.

5.4.6. Flexibility in the Water Contract

Palmer-Jones (1993), Meinzen-Dick (2000) and Dubash (2002) have outlined the complexity in the nature of water contracts, which is mostly governed by the social processes. This lends the water sellers some market power to charge different prices from different buyers (Jacoby et al. 2004; Pant 2004; Shah 1993; Shah and Ballabh 1997; Wood 1995). Although sample sellers are not found to have charged different water charges from different buyers, some of them have been found to have given concession on water charges to some of their buyers who are either their siblings or relatives. This finding resembles the results of Shah (1993).

5.4.7. Overdues in the Payment of Water Charge

The studies on water market report that there always remains an overdue in the payment of water charge by the water buyers (Khanna 2006). In this field study in Assam, a few buyers have been found to be defaulters in making payment of water in time. Out of a total of 97 water sellers, about 55.67 per cent have reported that there remains an overdue in the payment of water charge. The sample buyers, who are the relatives of the sample water sellers, are the highest defaulters, which is about 44.45 per cent of the total defaulters. This is followed by buyers, who are neither the relatives nor the tenants of the water sellers. This is found to be about 37.04 per cent of the defaulters. Compared to these two groups, the number of tenants who failed to make payment on time is less, which is 9.26 per cent of the total defaulters. A few buyers, who are tenants and relatives of the water sellers, have also been found to be defaulting on payment of water charge. Though a majority of buyers have remained defaulters for a year, out of the total defaulters, about 38.88 per cent are permanent defaulters. Among the permanent defaulters, about 57.14 per cent are relatives of the sample water sellers.

5.4.8. Water Charges and Other Services Rendered by the Buyers

The nature and mode of operation of the village-level groundwater market also state that the payment of water charge does not always guarantee access to water (Wood 1995). In addition to water charge, some of the buyers are required to render some additional services to the water sellers like operating the pump and irrigating the well owner's field (Janakarajan 1993, 1994). In the present study, about 35.05 per cent of the buyers are found to provide some sort of free services to their respective water sellers in addition to the water charge paid. The buyers are required to provide these services in order to maintain a cordial relationship with the sellers, so that they are provided with timely supply of water at the time of requirement. The presence of this type of preferential treatment has also been reported by Narayanamoorthy (1991) in water markets in Pudukkottai district of Tamil Nadu. From this analysis, it may be concluded that market practices are not purely based on conventional economic model, which is endogenous to the water market. Instead, the water sellers exercise some monopoly power,[7] though not reflected in the water charges, through some other means, which are exogenous to the market system. Here, some comparison can be drawn—: First, the market in the study area is like the market in Gujarat (Shah 1993) and Tamil Nadu (Janakarajan 1994), where the market is found to be more oligopolistic and monopolistic in nature; Second, it resembles the observation made by Saleth (1998) that '....in a market where the buyers and sellers have about the same sized farms and share a common socio-economic background is likely to be

[7] Monopoly power is related to price. But in the literature of water market this is explained based on the degree of exploitation exercised by the water sellers on the buyers.

more equitable and less exploitative'. Third, the market in the study area is less exploitative like the same in the case of Madhya Pradesh where Kajisa and Sakurai (2005) have found in a study that the sellers' behaviour is not exploitative.

5.4.9. Common Pool Nature of Groundwater and Its Depletion

Groundwater being a common pool resource, its extraction is associated with negative externality in the form of reduction in the amount available for other users. The market-induced groundwater depletion is extensively reported from the water-scarce regions of India such as Tamil Nadu, Andhra Pradesh and Gujarat. (Chandrakanth et al. 2004; Moench 1992, 2000; Scott and Shah 2004). Many studies have reported a dispute over the use of groundwater in such regions, owing mainly to the scarcity of the resource (Janakarajan and Moench 2006; Shah 1993). In areas with abundant groundwater reserves and heavy monsoon precipitation ensuring easy replenishment like Assam in eastern India, this problem may not appear to be so serious. However, the possibility that unregulated groundwater withdrawal can eventually lead to local problems of groundwater over-exploitation cannot be ruled out. In the context of the state of Assam, no such dispute over the use of groundwater has been observed. Yet most of the market participants (about 43.75% of the sample water sellers who have faced non-availability of water) reported a failure of the pump sets in delivering sufficient water when all the pump sets in the field are operated concurrently, indicating that there is relative scarcity of groundwater in some locations. Owing to this, a few farmers have expressed their apprehension that unfettered penetration of pump sets may cause conflict over the use of groundwater. Such a situation calls for proper regulation of operation of water markets even in areas richly endowed with groundwater.

5.5. CONCLUSION

This chapter has made an attempt to examine the functioning of groundwater market in India along with its related issues with the help of available data and literature and a case study in Assam. The discussion in the chapter indicates that water markets are quite active and extensive in agriculture in India. Although the nature and functioning of the water market are found to be similar across different regions in the country, there are some variations in its mode of operation in different locations. A few emerging issues of the market are also reported by recent studies. As the water sellers normally have to have excess capacity to be able to sell water, the water market is usually considered to be residual in nature. However, our case study from Assam has shown that in certain locations in the state, people have owned and installed tube wells with the sole aim of selling water to needy farmers in the neighbourhood for earning additional income. This phenomenon refutes the very notion of 'residuality' of water market, which is widely reported in literature. In addition, contrary to the usual notion that sellers in the water market belong to large and medium farmer category, the case study for Assam has shown that an overwhelming majority of the sellers belong to small and marginal farmer category, indicating that owning large farm holding is not the necessary condition for selling water in the groundwater market. As these are village-level localized markets, local socio-economic conditions and social processes determine the pattern of water transactions. Again, although overdrafting of groundwater is not an issue in water-abundant regions, unlike in water-scarce regions, there is apprehension that an unregulated spread of the water market may lead to overdrafting of groundwater and associated negative externalities even in richly endowed regions. Under these circumstances, there is a need to have some kind of regulation in the extraction and use of groundwater for irrigation and on operation of water markets in these regions. Of course, these regulations can be location-specific taking into account the specific characteristics of the local environment and requirements of the people.

REFERENCES

Acharyya, A. 2020. 'Groundwater Market and Agricultural Tenancy: A New Form of Collective Inter-Linkage in West Bengal'. *Indian Journal of Agricultural Economics* 75, no. 4: 375–384.

Acharyya, A., M. Ghosh, and R. N. Bhattacharya. 2018. 'Groundwater Market in West Bengal, India: Does It Display Monopoly Power'? *Studies in Microeconomics* 6, no. 1–2: 1–25.

Aggarwal, R. M. 1999. 'Risk Sharing and Transactions Costs in Groundwater Markets: Evidence from Rural India'. Mimeo. College Park, MD: Department of Agriculture and Resource Economics, University of Maryland.

Asad, Musa, Luiz Gabriel Azevedo, Karin E. Kemper, and Larry D. Simpson. 1999. *Management of Water Resources Bulk Water Pricing in Brazil*. Washington, DC: The World Bank.

Bate, R. 2002. 'Water—Can Property Rights and Markets Replace Conflict'? In *Sustainable Development: Promoting Progress or Perpetuating Poverty?* edited by J. Morris. London: Profile Books.

Bhandari, H., and S. Pandey. 2006. 'Economics of Groundwater Irrigation in Nepal: Some Farm-level Evidences'. *Journal of Agricultural and Applied Economics* 38, no. 1: 185–199.

Bjornlund, H., and J. McKay. 1998. 'Factors Affecting Water Prices in a Rural Water Market: A South Australian Experience'. *Water Resources Research* 34, no. 6: 1563–1570.

———. 2002. 'Aspects of Water Markets for Developing Countries: Experiences from Australia, Chile and the US'. *Environmental and Development Economics* 7, no. 4: 769–795.

Chandrakanth, M. G., B. Alemu, and M. G. Bhat. 2004. 'Combating Negative Externalities of Drought: A Study of Groundwater Recharge through Watershed'. *Economic & Political Weekly* 39, no. 11: 1164–1170.

Choudhury, M. J. 1990. 'The Adoption of Tubewell Technology in Pakistan'. *Pakistan Development Review* 29, no. 3–4: 291–303.

Cullet, P. 2012. 'Groundwater: Towards a New Legal and Institutional Framework'. In *Water Conflicts in India: Towards a New Legal and Institutional Framework,* edited by Philippe Cullet, Suhas Paranjape, Himanshu Thakkar, M. S. Vani, K. J. Joy, and M. K. Ramesh. Pune: Forum for Policy Dialogue on Water Conflicts in India; Geneva: International Environmental Law Research Centre.

Dubash, N. K. 2000. 'Ecologically and Socially Embedded Exchange: "Gujarat Model" of Water Markets'. *Economic & Political Weekly* 35, no. 16: 1376–1385.

Dutta, M. K. 2007. 'Management of Groundwater Irrigation through Water Markets'. *ICFAI Journal of Environmental Economics* 5, no. 4: 28–43.

———. 2011. *Irrigation Potential in Agriculture of Assam*. New Delhi: Concept Publishing Company.

———. 2012. 'Institution of Ground Water Market for Management of Groundwater Resource: A Study from Assam in Northeast India'. Paper presented at the 56th Australian Agricultural and Resource Economics Society (AARES) Annual Conference, Fremantle, Western Australia, 7–10 February.

Foster, S., and H. Gardunu. 2004. 'Tamil Nadu: Resolving the Conflict over Rural Groundwater Use Between Drinking Water and Irrigation Supply'. In *GW MATE: Case Profile on Sustainable Groundwater Management Lessons from Practice*. Washington, DC: World Bank. http://www.worldbank.org.gmate (accessed on 10 March 2012).

Fujita, K., and F. Hossain 1995. 'Role of the Groundwater Market in Agricultural Development and Income Distribution: A Case Study in a North West Bangladesh Village'. *The Developing Economics* 33, no. 4: 442–463.

Gandhi, Vasant P., and Vaibhav Bhamoriya. 2011. 'Groundwater Irrigation in India: Growth, Challenges, and Risks'. In *India Infrastructure Report 2011—Water: Policy and Performance for Sustainable Development,* edited by IDFC, 90–117. New Delhi: Oxford University Press.

Government of India. 2006. *Serving Farmers and Saving Farming: Revised Draft National Policy for Farmers.* New Delhi: National Commission on Farmers, Ministry of Agriculture, Government of India.

Government of India. 2020. *Ground Water Year Book—India 2019–2020.* Report of the Central Ground Water Board, Government of India. http://cgwb.gov.in/Ground-Water/GW%20YEAR%20BOOK%202019-20%20ALL%20INDIA%20FINAL%20752021%20(1).pdf (accessed on 21 February 2022).

Government of India. 2021. *Situational Assessment of Agricultural Households and Land and Holdings of Households in Rural India, 2019.* Report of the Ministry of Statistics and Programme Implementation, National Statistical Office, New Delhi.

Hussain, Z., H. Badar, and M. F. Hussain. 2005. 'Rural Water Markets in Pakistan: Prevalence, Problems and Prospects'. *European Journal of Scientific Research* 9, no. 2. https://www.academia.edu/Rural_Water_Markets_in_Pakistan_Prevalance_Problems_and_Prospects (accessed on 11 February 2013).

Isley, P., and R. J. Middleton, Jr. 2003. 'Water Markets in Georgia: An Overview of Ongoing Sales of Water'. Water Policy Working Paper No. 2003-006. https://www.issuelab.org/resources/4724/4724.pdf (accessed on 21 February 2022).

Jacoby, H. G., R. Murgai, and S. Ur Rehman. 2004. 'Monopoly Power and Distribution in Fragmented Markets: The Case of Groundwater'. *The Review of Economic Studies* 71, no. 7: 783–808.

Janakarajan, S. 1993. 'Trading in Groundwater: A Source of Power and Accumulation'. In *Costs and Productivity of Irrigation in Tamil Nadu,* edited by Planning Commission of India, Government of India.

———. 1994. 'Trading in Groundwater: A Source of Power and Accumulation'. In *Selling Water: Conceptual and Policy Debate over Groundwater in India,* edited by M. Moench. Ahmedabad: VIKSAT.

Janakarajan, S., and M. Moench. 2006. '"Are Wells a Potential Threat to Farmers" Well-being? Case of Deteriorating Groundwater Irrigation in Tamil Nadu'. *Economic & Political Weekly* 41, no. 37: 3977–3978.

Jeet, Inder. 2005. *Groundwater Resources of India: Occurrence, Utilization and Management.* New Delhi: Mittal Publications.

Jha, U. M., and R. K. Sinha. 2008. 'Role of Water Markets in Groundwater Management in Bihar and Jharkhand'. In *Glimpses of Indian Agriculture: Macro and Micro Aspects,* Vol. 2, edited by S. M. Jharwal. New Delhi: Academic Foundation.

Joshi, P. K. 2005. 'Ground Water Management: Problems and Opportunities'. In *Institutionalising Common Pool Resources,* edited by D. K. Marothia. New Delhi: Concept Publishing Company.

Kajisa, K., and T. Sakurai. 2005. 'Efficiency and Equity in Groundwater Markets: The Case of Madhya Pradesh, India'. *Environmental and Development Economics* 10, no. 6: 801–819.

Kalirajan, K. P., and R. T. Shand. 1994. *Economics in Disequilibrium: An Approach from the Frontier.* New Delhi: Macmillan India Limited.

———. 'Frontier Production Functions and Technical Efficiency Measures'. *Journal of Economic Surveys* 13, no. 2: 149–172.

Khair, S. M., S. Mushtaq, R. J. Culas, and M. Hafeez. 2012, March. 'Groundwater Markets under the Water Scarcity Conditions: The Upland Balochistan Region of Pakistan'. *Agricultural Systems* 107: 21–32.

Khanna, G. 2006. 'Technical Efficiency in Production and Resource Use in Sugar Cane: A Stochastic Production Function Analysis'. HEI Working Paper No 15/2006. Geneva: Graduate Institute of International Studies.

Manjunatha A.V., S. Speelman, M. G. Chandrakanth, and V. G. Huylenbroeck. 2011a. 'Can Groundwater Markets Promote Efficiency in Agricultural Production'? Paper presented in the 13th Biennial Conference of the International Association for the Study of the Commons (IASC), Hyderabad, 10–14 January.

———. 2011b. 'Impact of Groundwater Markets in India on Water Use Efficiency: A Data Envelopment Analysis Approach'. *Journal of Environmental Management* 92, no. 1: 2924–2929.

Meinzen-Dick, R. 1994. "Groundwater Markets in Pakistan: Participation and Productivity", Research Report No. 105, International Food Policy Research Institute, Washington D. C., USA.

Meinzen-Dick, R. 1995. 'Timeliness of Irrigation: Performance Indicators and Impact on Agricultural Production in the Some Irrigation System, Bihar', *Irrigation and Drainage Systems,*.9, 4: 371-387.

Meinzen-Dick, R. and M. Mendoza. 1996. 'Alternative to Water Allocation Mechanisms: Indian and International Experiences', *Economic and Political Weekly,*. 31, 13: 25-30.

Meinzen-Dick, R. S. 1998. 'Groundwater Markets in Pakistan: Institutional Development and Productivity Impacts'. In *Markets for Water: Potential and Performance,* edited by K. W. Easter, M. W. Rosegrant, and A. Dinar. Boston, MA: Kluwer Academic Publishers.

Meinzen-Dick, R., and M. Mendoza 1996. 'Alternative to Water Allocation Mechanisms: Indian and International Experiences'. *Economic & Political Weekly* 31, no. 13: A25–A30.

Meinzen-Dick, R. S. 2000. 'Public, Private and Shared Water: Groundwater Markets and Access in Pakistan', in B. Randolph et al. (Eds.), *Negotiating Water Rights,* Intermediate Technology Publications, UK.

Moench, M. 1992. 'Chasing the Water Table: Equity and Sustainability in Groundwater Management'. *Economic & Political Weekly* 27, no. 51–52: A171–A177.

———. 2002. 'When Management Fails: Evolutionary Perspectives and Adaptive Frameworks for Responding to Water Problems'. Working Paper. Boulder, CO: Institute for Social and Environmental Transitions.

Moench, M. (1993), 'Chasing the Water Table: Equity and Sustainability in Groundwater Management, Gujarat India', Paper Presented at the Workshop on Political Theory and Policy Analysis, 513, North Park, Indian University, Bloomington, Indiana.

Mohanty, N., and S. Gupta. 2002, August. 'Breaking the Gridlock in Water Reforms through Water Markets: International Experience and Implementation Issues for India'. Working Paper Series. New Delhi: Julian L. Simon Centre for Policy Research.

Mondal, R. C., and D. Majumdar. 2008. 'Role of Water Markets in Groundwater Management in West Bengal'. In *Glimpses of Indian Agriculture: Macro and Micro Aspects*, Vol. 2, edited by S. M. Jharwal. New Delhi: Academic Foundation.

Narain, V. 1997. 'India's Water Crisis: Avenues for Policy and Institutional Reform'. *TERI Information Monitor on Environmental Science* 2, no. 1: 1–6.

Narayanamoorthy, A. 1991. "Deep Borewell Water Business in Pudukkottai District, Tamil Nadu: some Empirical Evidence:, *Indian Journal of Agricultural Economics,* 46, no. 3: 380-81.

National Sample Survey Organisation (NSSO). 2014. *Key Indicators of Situation Assessment of Agricultural Households*. New Delhi: Ministry of Statistics and Programme Implementation.

National Statistical Office (NSO). 2021. *Situational Assessment of Agricultural Households and Land and Holdings of Households in Rural India, 2019*. New Delhi: Ministry of Statistics and Programme Implementation.

Palmer-Jones, R. 1993. 'Groundwater Market in South Asia: A Discussion of Theory and Evidence', Paper Presented at the Workshop on "Water Management: India's Groundwater Challenge" at VIKSAT, Ahmadabad, December 1993.

Palmer-Jones, R. 1993, December. 'Groundwater Market in South Asia: A Discussion of Theory and Evidence'. Paper Presented at the Workshop on 'Water Management: India's Groundwater Challenge' at VIKSAT, Ahmadabad.

Palmer-Jones, R. 2001. 'Irrigation Services Markets in Bangladesh: Private Provision of Local Public Goods and Community Regulation', Paper Presented at Symposium on Managing Common Resources: What is the Solution?, Lund, Sweden, 10-11, September 2001.

Pant, N. 1991. 'Groundwater Resources Issues in Eastern India', in Meinzen-Dick, R. and M. Svendsen (Eds.) *Future Directions for Indian Agriculture – Research and Policy Issues,* International Food Policy Research Institute, Washington D.C., USA.

Pant, N. 1992. *New Trend in Indian Irrigation*. New Delhi: Ashish Publishing House.

Pant, N. 2004. "Trends in Groundwater Irrigation in Eastern and Western UP", *Economic and Political Weekly,* 39, 31: 3463-3468.

Pant, N. 2005, "Control and Access to Groundwater in UP", *Economic and Political Weekly,* June 25, 40, no.26: 2672-2680.

Prasad, J. 1991. 'Development and Performance of Groundwater Markets: A Study in a Village of North Bihar'. *Indian Journal of Agricultural Economics* 46, no. 3: 377–392.

Rinaudo, J. D., and P. R. T. Strosser. 1997. 'Linking Water Market Functioning, Access to Water Resources and Farm Production Strategies: Example from Pakistan'. *Irrigation Drainage System* 11, no. 3: 261–280.

Saleth, M. 1994. "Towards a New Water Institutions: Economics, Law and Policy', *Economic and Political Weekly,* 29, 39: 147-155.

Saleth, M. 1996. *Water Institutions in India: Economics, Law and Policy*. New Delhi: Institute of Economic Growth, Common Wealth Publishers.

———. 1998. 'Water Markets in India: Economic and Institutional Aspects'. In *Markets for Water: Potential and Performance,* Vol. 15, edited by K. W. Easter, M. W. Rosegrant, and A. Dinar, 187–205. Springer US Series: Natural Resource Management and Policy. http://link.springer.com/chapter/10.1007%2F978-0-585-32088-5_12 (accessed on 29 November 2013).

Satyasai, K. J. S., P. Kumar, and Mruthyunjay. 1997. 'Terms of Transactions in Groundwater Markets: A Study in Anantapur Districts of Andhra Pradesh'. *Indian Journal of Agricultural Economics* 52, no. 4: 751–759.

Scott, C. E., and T. Shah. 2004. 'Groundwater Overdraft Reduction through Agricultural Energy Policy: Insights from India and Mexico'. *Water Resource Development* 20, no. 2: 149–164.

Shah, T. 1988. "Externality and Equity Implications of Private Exploitation of Groundwater Resources", *Agricultural Systems*, 28, no. 2:119-139.

Shah, T. 1991. 'Water Markets and Irrigation Development in India'. *Indian Journal of Agriculture* 46, no. 3: 335–348.

———. 1993. *Groundwater Markets and Irrigation Development: Political Economy and Practical Policy*. Mumbai: Oxford University Press.

Shah, T. and V. Ballabh. 1997. 'Water Markets in North Bihar: Six Village Studies in Muzaffarpur District', *Economic and Political Weekly,* 32, no. 52: 183-190.

Shah, T., and V. Ballabh. 1997. 'Water Markets in North Bihar: Six Village Studies in Muzaffarpur District'. *Economic & Political Weekly* 32, no. 52: A183–A190.

Shah, Tushaar, and K. Vengama Raju. 1988. 'Groundwater Markets and Small Farmer Development'. *Economic & Political Weekly* 23, no. 13: A23–A28.

Shankar, K. 1992a. 'Water Markets in Eastern UP'. *Economic & Political Weekly* 27, no. 18: 931–933.

———. 1992b. *Dynamics of Groundwater Irrigation*. New Delhi: Segment Books.

Sidhu, Balsher Singh, Milind Kandlikar, and Navin Ramankutty. 2020. 'Power Tariffs for Groundwater Irrigation in India: A Comparative Analysis of the Environmental, Equity, and Economic Tradeoffs'. *World*

Development 128: 104836. https://www.sciencedirect.com/science/article/pii/S0305750X19304851 (accessed on 12 June 2021).

Simpson, L. D. 1994. 'Are "Water Markets" a Viable Option'? *Finance and Development* 31, no. 2: 30–32.

Singh, D. 2002. 'Water Markets in Fragile Environments: Key Issues in Sustainability'. *Indian Journal of Agricultural Economics* 57, no. 2: 180–196.

Singh, D. R., and R. P. Singh. 2003. 'Groundwater Markets and the Issues of Equity and Reliability to Water Access: A Case of Western Uttar Pradesh'. *Indian Journal of Agricultural Economics* 58, no. 1: 115–127.

Srivastava, S. K., R. Kumar, and R. P. Singh. 2009. 'Extent of Groundwater Extraction and Irrigation Efficiency of Farms under Different Water-Market Regime in Central Uttar Pradesh'. *Agricultural Economics Research Review* 22, no. 1: 87–98.

Tamuli, J. 2014. 'Institution for the Use of Groundwater in Assam: A Study of Groundwater Markets with Special Emphasis on Structure, Determinants, Reliability and Efficiency'. Unpublished PhD Thesis. Guwahati: Department of Humanities and Social Sciences, Indian Institute of Technology Guwahati.

Thobani, M. 1997. 'Formal Water Markets: Why, When and How to Introduce Tradable Water Rights'. *The World Bank Research Observer* 12, no. 2: 164–179.

Wood, G. D. 1995. *Private Provision after Public Neglect: Opting Out with Pumpsets in North Bihar*. Bath: Centre for Development Studies, University of Bath.

World Bank. 1999. *Mexico Policy Options for Aquifer Stabilisations*. Washington, DC: The World Bank.

Zhang, L., J. Wang, and J. Huang. 2006. 'Groundwater Entrepreneurs in China: Selling Water to Meet the Demand for Water'. Paper presented at the International Association of Agricultural Economists Conference, Gold Coast, Australia, 12–18 August.

Chapter 6

Rental Market of Farm Machineries and Equipment

Anup Kumar Das

6.1. INTRODUCTION

The scope of increasing agricultural production through the expansion of cultivable area is getting reduced due to increased population pressure on land, the supply of which is inelastic in nature. Consequently, intensive utilization of farmland becomes important to raise agricultural production. Farm mechanization that facilitates enhancement of agricultural production through intensive and productive utilization of farmland has therefore gained importance. The use of farm machineries such as tractors, power tillers and pump sets enhances cropping intensity (Agarwal 1984; Rao 1972; J. Singh 2006; Verma 2006) and productivity in agriculture significantly (Rao 1972; Roy and Blase 1978; Verma 2006). Farm mechanization helps in timely cultivation, maintaining the quality of operation, increasing the productivity of factors like land and labour, reducing the cost of cultivation and risks of weather and non-availability of labour, all of which raise agricultural output (G. Singh 2006, J. Singh 2006). However, farm mechanization is constrained by factors like small and fragmented landholdings and poor economic conditions of the farmers. For instance, the use of ploughing machinery in a farm requires the farmland to be of a viable minimum size.

Likewise, the heavy farm machineries, which are expensive in nature, are not accessible to the poor farmers. In such situations, the emergence of well-functioning rental markets of such farm capital goods can facilitate mechanized farming even by small and marginal farmers. The poor farmers, for whom procurement of such machinery is not possible, can still mechanize their farm operations by hiring in these machines. Rental markets of farm machineries can also promote the owner-users of these machineries. For instance, in a country like India, the farm size of many farmers, who are capable of procuring heavy farm machineries like tractors and power tillers, is not large enough for optimum utilization of the capacity of these machineries. Therefore, it is conceivable that such a mismatch between the farm size and capacity of the farm machineries discourages the purchase of machineries only for own farm operation. However, the possibility of hiring out the excess capacity of farm machineries encourages the ownership of such capital goods by farmers for whom farm machineries are affordable but landholdings are insufficient to fully utilize their capacity, thereby making farm mechanization more extensive. Furthermore, the difficulty in rearing of draft animals due to factors such as declining grazing land, shortage of manpower and recurrent occurrence of floods makes rental markets of ploughing machinery more significant. Rath (2015) in this regard states that the difficulties to maintain bullocks result in increasing use of either hired tractors for ploughing or hiring of bullocks and plough by small farmers.

While these markets have emerged and started playing an important role in mechanization of farming operations, especially of small farms, understanding of their functioning is not widespread. This chapter presents a discussion on the extent and nature of functioning of rental markets of farm machinery, and their contribution to farm production, along with limitations of these markets.

In this context, it is worth noting that another form of rural factor market started emerging in some parts of the country in the 1990s, which has also been contributing to machination of operations in smaller farms. Notable among these is the markets for second-hand tractors in Punjab (Singh and Rangi 2008). As working efficiency of tractors gets reduced after using them for some time, many large farmers with relatively better access to resources tend to replace the old tractors with new ones. The used tractors are disposed of in the market for second-hand tractors where the buyers are typically the smaller farmers who cannot afford to own a new one and for whom the used tractors are still good enough for relatively smaller-scale operations. Important as these markets are, their existence requires the presence of a class of large farmers who periodically replace their used tractors even before the lives of the machines are over. Accordingly, such markets are thriving only in states like Punjab, where large farmers still constitute a substantial part of the farming community. The second-hand markets for tractors in those parts of the country where small farmers predominate are understandably too thin to be of major impact. The focus of this book being small farm agriculture, the second-hand markets in tractors are not pursued any further here.

The remaining part of the chapter has been organized into five sections. Section 6.2 discusses the functioning of the rental markets of farm machineries and equipment and their extent in India. The forms and determinants of participation in such markets are presented in section 6.3. A discussion on rental market of farm machineries and equipment and consolidation of landholdings in India is incorporated in section 6.4. Section 6.5 examines the imperfections in the rental market of farm machineries and equipment and the role of custom hiring centres. Section 6.6 summarizes the overall findings of the chapter along with policy implications.

6.2. THE FUNCTIONING OF FARM MACHINERIES AND EQUIPMENT RENTAL MARKETS IN INDIA

The disproportionate possession of factors of production by households induces the emergence and functioning of various factor markets in agriculture such as land market, labour market, water market and credit market. In this context, Ray (2011) states that agricultural input markets are likely to emerge as a consequence of the unequal distribution of the factors of production. Apart from correcting the imbalances in factor endowments (Birthal and Singh 1991; Lin 1995; Singh et al. 1991), such markets reduce income inequality as well (Benjamin and Brandt 1997).

The inequality in factor endowments is a common feature of most of the rural households in India, and hence, different factor markets are functioning in the agriculture sector in the country. In India, small and fragmented landholdings have been one of the major challenges confronting the agriculture sector. Small and fragmented landholdings make it inconvenient to use the heavy machinery in farm operations (J. Singh 2006) and also reduce the incentives to invest in farm machineries like tube wells for groundwater irrigation (Dobbs and Foster 1972). Dutta (2007) finds small and fragmented landholdings as a factor limiting the fuller utilization of potential created under the shallow tube wells (STWs) in Assam. Vaidyanathan (1986), in this context, states that the profitability of innovation and their adoption is affected by both size and pattern of landholdings. Taking the groundwater as the best example, Vaidyanathan (1986) states that the cost of constructing wells and installing pump sets tends to be higher relative to returns in small and highly fragmented landholdings as compared to the large and consolidated landholdings. The development of the groundwater market in Haryana–Punjab–western Uttar Pradesh through tube wells took place after land consolidation where the average size of holdings being relatively large. On the other hand, in the eastern part of the Gangetic plain, the private rate of returns to well irrigation is less, where the average size of landholdings is of smaller size, and they are highly fragmented. To do away with the consequences of small and fragmented landholdings, in the post-independence period, certain measures were taken by the Government of India to consolidate landholdings as an important part of land reforms. However, consolidation of landholdings remained largely unimplemented (Kapila 2011; Misra and Puri 2004). Despite the fact that the success of consolidation of landholdings in India is quite limited and the average size of individual landholding is increasingly becoming smaller (*Indian Journal of Agricultural Economics* 2014), the functioning of factor markets has facilitated the adoption of better farm practices, including the spread of mechanization. As in countries like China (Lin 1995) and Nepal (Sharma and Goswami 2020), the hiring-in use of farm capital goods is going on in different parts of India. Agarwal (1984) and Roy and Blase (1978) report the use of hired tractors in Punjab in India. In the Nagpur district of western Rajasthan, owners of tractors were found to practise hiring out as an instrument of minimization/elimination of underutilized tractor services (Jodha 1974). Recent studies by Das and Bezbaruah (2017), and Das (2019) and Goswami (2016) depict the functioning of rental markets of farm machinery in Assam.

The use of different farm machineries and equipment by a good number of farmers of all size groups in India is visible from the data provided by the All India Report on Input Survey 2016–2017 of the Government of India. For instance, as per data provided by the *All India Report on Input Survey 2016–2017* (Government of India 2021a), the number of operational holdings using tractors, power tillers, pump sets (diesel/electric), combine harvester (tractor operated) and combine harvester (self-propelled) are 72.293 million, 18.878 million, 45.962 million, 7.001 million and 4.502 million, respectively, and they account for 49.45 per cent, 12.91 per cent, 31.44 per cent, 4.79 per cent and 3.08 per cent, respectively, of the total operational holdings.[1] The percentage of operational holdings using wooden plough, mould board plough, cane crusher (animal/power) and sprinklers are 30.26 per cent, 12.95 per cent, 2.01 per cent and 3 per cent, respectively (Government of India 2021a). Across the size classes, the use of such capital goods is highest in marginal holdings, followed by the small holdings. There is an increase in the number of operational holdings, using some of the farm machineries and equipment. As per the All India Report on Input Survey 2011–2012 (Government of India 2016), the number of operational holdings using tractors and power tillers are, respectively, 61.133 million and 7.954 million and the corresponding figures are reported to be 72.293 million and 18.878 million, respectively, in the *All India Report on Input Survey 2016–2017* (Government of India 2021a). However, the number of operational holdings using wooden plough and mould broad plough has reduced during 2011–2012 to 2016–2017. As observed, during the period, the number of small and marginal operational holdings using heavy farm machinery like tractors and power tillers has also increased. Given the size of landholdings and financial condition of most of the farmers in the country, it is understandable that the own use of farm machineries and equipment,

[1] Percentages are calculated considering the figures rounded in thousands.

especially the heavy machineries like tractors and power tillers, would be quite limited and use of such farm machinery to a great extent is through hiring, which is evident from Table 6.1. The percentages of operational holdings using farm capital goods by hiring to the total operational holdings using such capital goods range from 92.56 per cent to 11.64 per cent across all the capital goods presented in Table 6.1. In terms of the percentages of operational holdings using farm capital goods by hiring to the total operational holdings using such capital goods, the most extensively hired farm capital good is tractor-powered combine harvester (92.56%), followed by self-propelled combine harvester (90.47%), tractor (83%) and power tiller (78.44%), respectively. Across size groups, the percentages of operational holdings using tractors by hiring to the total operational holdings using such capital goods are highest for the marginal farmers (88.62%) and lowest for the large farmers (45.14%). Likewise, the hiring use of power tillers is most extensive among the marginal farmers (83.54%) and least extensive among the large farmers (44.33%). In the case of other capital goods, except wooden plough, the marginal farmers are hiring the most, followed by the small farmers, and it is least in the case of the large farmers. Except in case of wooden plough, the percentage of operational holdings using capital goods by hiring to the total operational holdings using such capital goods bears an inverse relation with the size of operational holdings with respect to all the farm capital goods under consideration. Thus, it appears that in India, the rental markets of different farm machineries and equipment are functioning, and they are more extensive in the case of heavy farm machinery such as combine harvesters, tractors and power tillers. Further, participation in such markets is most widespread among marginal farmers, followed by small farmers, and there is an inverse relation between the size of operational holdings and the extent of hiring use of most of the farm machineries and equipment.

As per the cost of cultivation data provided by the Government of India, in 2017–2018, the share of average cost on hired machinery per hectare of paddy acreage was 88.95 per cent of the operational cost on machinery (Figure 6.1). Across the major paddy cultivating states of India, the percentage of average cost on hired machinery per hectare of paddy acreage ranges from 52.44 per cent to 99.72 per cent of the

Table 6.1 *Estimated Number (in Thousands) of Operational Holdings in India Using Some Agricultural Machineries and Equipment by Hiring*

Size Groups	Wooden Plough	Mould Board Plough	Pump Sets (Diesel/ Electric)	Power Tiller	Tractor	Cane Crusher (Animal/ Power)	Sprinklers	Combine Harvester (Tractor Powered)	Combine Harvester (Self-propelled)
Marginal (below 1 ha)	3,470 (11.74)	2,939 (26.90)	11,016 (40.35)	1,0418 (83.54)	41,633 (88.62)	1,074 (68.80)	328 (20.65)	3,767 (94.67)	2,153 (93.24)
Small (1–2 ha)	1,035 (12.48)	1,178 (26.44)	2,034 (20.63)	2,784 (75.53)	11,085 (80.89)	416 (65.10)	112 (8.64)	1447 (93.29)	905 (91.23)
Semi-medium (2–4 ha)	484 (10.60)	596 (23.46)	840 (14.35)	1,152 (62.20)	5,215 (68.81)	236 (54.63)	66 (7.49)	857 (90.21)	618 (88.16)
Medium (4–10 ha)	147 (8.89)	212 (23.14)	231 (8.92)	410 (53.04)	1807 (52.45)	112 (41.48)	28 (5.53)	356 (80.00)	338 (81.84)
Large (10 ha and above)	15 (8.29)	21 (21.21)	20 (5.57)	43 (44.33)	265 (45.14)	15 (34.88)	4 (3.77)	53 (69.74)	58 (68.24)
All size groups	5,151 (11.64)	4,946 (26.12)	14,141 (30.77)	14,807 (78.44)	60,005 (83.00)	1,853 (62.92)	538 (12.29)	6,480 (92.56)	4,073 (90.47)

Source: Computed from Government of India (2021a).
Note: Figure in ( ) presents percentage of operational holdings using farm capital goods by hiring to the total operational holdings using such capital goods.

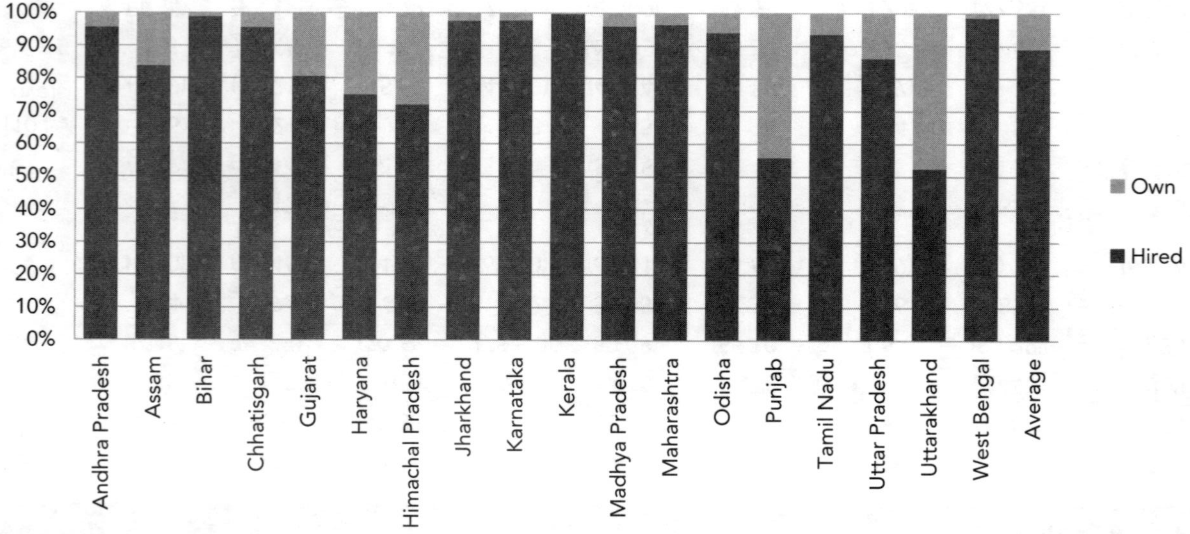

Figure 6.1 *Composition of Operational Cost on Machinery for Paddy Cultivation in India during 2017–2018*

Source: Government of India (2021b).

operational cost on machinery. In fact, in each major paddy cultivating state of the country, farmers incur more cost on hired machinery than the operational cost on own machinery. Furthermore, the share of cost on hired machinery in the total cost of cultivation has shown a positive trend in most of the major paddy cultivating states of the country (Figure 6.2). Therefore, it is evident that the rental markets of farm machineries and equipment are not only functioning in the country but also their extent is becoming widespread over the years.

Two independent case studies in the Brahmaputra Valley of Assam by Das and Bezbaruah (2017) and Das (2019) also confirm the functioning of rental markets of the farm machineries. However, the extent of participation in such markets is different across the types of machinery. For instance, the percentage of farm households that participated in the rental market of ploughing machinery was around 78 per cent against about 35 per cent in that of irrigating machinery (Das and Bezbaruah 2017). The observed lower participation in irrigating machinery rental than that in ploughing machinery is perhaps due to the factors like the less expensive nature and the lesser requirement and mobility of the former than the latter type of farm machinery as pointed out in the study. Das and Bezbaruah (2017) and Das (2019) further show that the participation rates in the rental market of ploughing machinery in the Brahmaputra Valley have been rising sharply.[2] As per the latter study, all the surveyed households participated in the rental market of ploughing machinery, whereas the corresponding figure was around 78 per cent as per the former study. The participation in rental markets of farm machinery by farm households is mostly in the form of pure buyer. However, a few participants in ploughing machinery rental are both buyers and sellers, while there is hardly any pure seller. Only a very small portion of participants is found to be pure sellers in the rental market of irrigation machinery. The fact that there is the absence of pure sellers in the case of ploughing machinery and an insignificant percentage in the case of irrigating machinery depicts that cultivators procure such machinery mainly for own use and hire out the excess capacity.

[2] Sample districts of the studies are not the same.

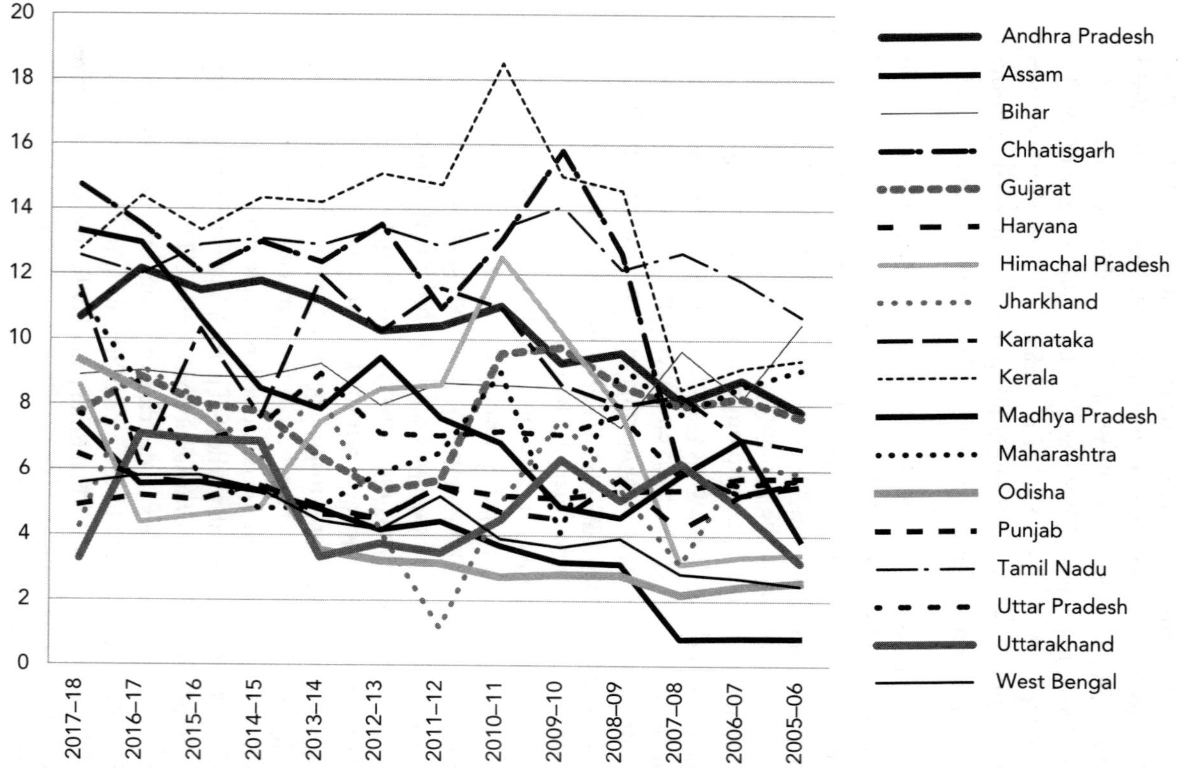

Figure 6.2 *Share of Hired Machinery Cost in Total Cost of Paddy Cultivation per hectare*

Source: Government of India (2021b).

6.3. FORMS AND DETERMINANTS OF HIRING

The functioning of rental markets of farm machineries and equipment in India is found in different forms across different locations. Das (2019), utilizing the information gathered through a primary survey of 121 farm households in the Brahmaputra Valley of Assam during January–February 2016, finds three different forms of functioning of the rental markets of ploughing machinery. The forms of rental markets of ploughing machinery found to be operative in the study area are—(a) area based (b) daily based and (c) hourly based. However, the rental market of ploughing machinery is found to be functioning in all the sample districts only in area-based form, and other two forms were present only in one sample district. Thus, it appears that the area-based form of the rental market of ploughing machinery is the common form in the study area. Furthermore, looking into the hiring in of ploughing machinery across the forms, the area-based form was found to be dominant in terms of both households hiring in such machinery and rounds of hiring per plot of cultivated land. In terms of the area (considering the round of ploughing) in which hired ploughing machinery is used, daily-based hiring is preferred by a rental user over the other two forms of hiring. Das and Bezbaruah (2017) find that the rental markets of farm machinery—ploughing and irrigation—are informal in nature. A subsequent study of the rental market of ploughing machinery by Das (2019) also reveals the informal nature of such markets. Moreover, cash is the only mode of payment of rent for ploughing machinery (Das 2019; Das and Bezbaruah 2017), and in the case of irrigation machinery, payment of rent is made in both cash and kind (Das and Bezbaruah 2017).

In functioning and spreading of rental markets of farm machineries and equipment, access to credit plays a vital role. The role of access to credit is varied across the forms of credit. Credit can be classified based on the sources as institutional and non-institutional. The latter form of credit is found to encourage both own use and hiring use of farm machineries and equipment. Das (2016) finds that a good portion of farm machineries and equipment was purchased with the help of borrowed money from both institutional and non-institutional sources.

Many of the farm machineries and equipment, especially the heavy farm machinery, which are more expensive in nature, are purchased with the help of non-institutional credit and hired out by their owner. Thus, non-institutional credit encourages the participation of farm households in the rental markets of such farm machinery and equipment as suppliers. Apart from this, it is evident from the study by Das (2016) that non-institutional credit has a significant positive impact on hiring use of ploughing machinery. Institutional credit, on the other hand, encourages the own use of farm machinery and has no significant role in their hiring use. The point to be noted here is that institutional credit promotes ownership of farm machineries and equipment more for which rental markets are more extensive. As ownership facilitates participation as the suppliers in rental markets, institutional credit plays the role of raising the number of participants in such markets as the suppliers. Apart from credit, farm size encourages the own use of ploughing machinery but discourages hiring use (Das 2016). As owners of ploughing machinery hire out the excess capacity of such machinery, participation in rental markets as the suppliers is more for the large-sized group of farmers. The ownership of draft animal discourages the owner-user of machinery but encourages their hiring use (Das 2016). However, the intensity of hiring use of ploughing machinery is reduced by the ownership of both draft animal and ploughing machinery (Das 2019). A study on factors determining the purchase decision of pump set service in Nepal by Sharma and Goswami (2020) depicts access to extension service, share of area under high-yielding varieties (HYVs) in total cropped area, availability of pump sets, caste of farmers and locational characteristics as the determinants. The chances of purchase of services of pump set increase for farmers with larger share of area under HYVs; it is obvious as those crops are more water dependent. The probability of purchase of services of pump set is more among the farmers having access to extension services than the farmers without such services. Another factor which affects the hiring in of pump set is its availability. Higher availability of pump sets in a locality raises the purchase of services of such farm machinery. The caste of the farmers also determines the hiring use of pump set machinery services. It is found that the farmers belonging to the caste category of relatively more backward classes in terms of financial condition purchase less services of pump sets. Furthermore, locational characteristics like the presence of canal irrigation and wetland reduce the requirements to purchase the pump set services in such areas.

6.4. RENTAL MARKETS AND CONSOLIDATION OF LANDHOLDINGS

As stated earlier, in order to do away with the problems associated with small and fragmented landholdings such as low farm mechanization, inefficient farm operation, low production and productivity of agriculture, consolidation of landholding measures were initiated as a part of land reforms in India. However, constrained by many factors, the implementation of consolidation of landholdings was observable only in few states, and thus, it remained largely unimplemented in the country as a whole. Even though consolidation of landholdings remains pending, farm mechanization is taking place and spreading over time, and the emergence and functioning of rental markets of farm machinery have a great role in it. The field study by Das and Bezbaruah (2017) in the Brahmaputra Valley in the northeastern part of India revealed that 82.42 per cent of users of ploughing machinery among the sample farm households were hiring users, and this percentage was 61.90 per cent in the case of sample irrigating machinery users (Table 6.2). Area-wise, hired ploughing and irrigating machineries were used in 56.76 per cent of gross ploughed area and 49.80 per cent of gross irrigated area, respectively (Figure 6.3). This shows that the use of both ploughing and irrigating machineries is substantially through hiring in, and it has been made possible by the functioning of rental markets for such machineries. In the absence of such markets, the rental users could not have mechanized their farm operation and even, the extent of owner-users of farm machinery would have been less than observed. Given the farm size, it is understandable that the capacity of farm machinery, specifically the ploughing machinery, is more than the farmland of the owner of such machinery. In the absence of opportunities to hire out the excess capacity of farm machinery, many of the farmers may not have gone for investment on such farm capital goods. The hiring-in use of ploughing machinery was found in the case of farmers belonging to any size group. However, irrigating machinery was found to be used through hiring in by farmers of all size groups other than the size

Table 6.2 *Users of Farm Machinery across Size Classes of Operational Holdings (in Hectare)*

	Ploughing			Irrigating		
Size Class	Total Users	Owner Users	Pure Hiring Users	Total Users	Owner-Users	Pure Hiring Users
<1	81 (100.00)	3 (03.70)	78 (96.30)	49 (100.00)	15 (30.61)	34 (69.39)
1 to 2	67 (100.00)	16 (23.88)	51 (76.12)	39 (100.00)	16 (41.03)	23 (58.97)
2 to 3	19 (100.00)	5 (26.32)	14 (73.68)	11 (100.00)	05 (45.45)	06 (54.55)
3 to 4	6 (100.00)	5 (83.33)	1 (16.67)	02 (100.00)	01 (50.00)	01 (50.00)
4 to 5	6 (100.00)	1 (16.67)	5 (83.33)	02 (100.00)	02 (100.00)	00 (00.00)
5 ≥	3 (100.00)	2 (66.67)	1 (33.33)	02 (100.00)	01 (50.00)	01 (50.00)
All	182 (100.00)	32 (17.58)	150 (82.42)	105 (100.00)	40 (38.10)	65 (61.90)

Source: Compiled from Das and Bezbaruah (2017).
Figure in ( ) presents percentage to the total uses of respective machinery.

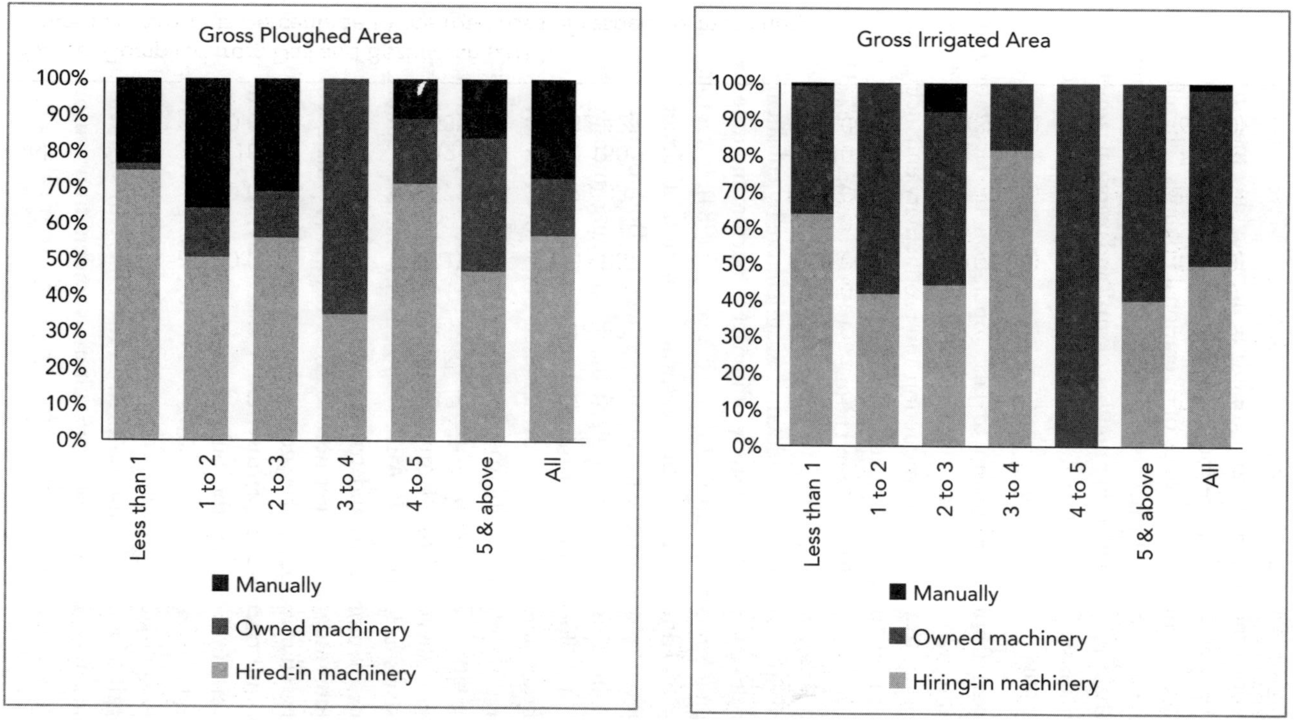

Figure 6.3 *Distribution of Gross Ploughed and Irrigated Areas by Type*

Source: Compiled from Das and Bezbaruah (2017).

group of 4–5 hectares of operational holdings. More importantly, 86 per cent of the farmers who were hiring in ploughing machinery and 87.69 per cent who were hiring in irrigating machinery belonged to small and marginal size groups of operational holdings. Therefore, the functioning of rental markets of farm machinery has been facilitating farm mechanization by larger number of small and marginal farmers—the dominant size group of farmers—as compared to farmers of the larger size groups.

Apart from contribution to farm operation by facilitating and spreading farm mechanization, the rental markets of farm machinery contribute towards farm production and productivity enhancing practices. In this context, Roy and Blase (1978) found that tractor farms, including both owner-users and hiring-in users of tractors, realized higher cropping intensity and yield than the non-tractor farms. Tractorization contributes in raising the production of agriculture by enhancing intensive cultivation. From the study of impact of tractors and tube wells on cropping intensity in Punjab, India, by Agarwal (1984), it was found that as compared to the use of bullocks, the realization of higher cropping intensity was associated with the use of tractors. Both owner-users and hiring-in users of tractors realized higher cropping intensity than the users of bullocks, although this advantage was found to be statistically significant only in the case of owner-users of tractors. A study by ITES, Madras, shows that an increase in productivity on tractor owning and hiring farms varied from 4.1 per cent to 54.8 per cent (Verma 2006). As per a survey of 815 farming households belonging to 85 villages of 7 states in India by NCAER (1980), as compared to bullock farms, tractor-owning farms and tractor-using farms realized higher yields, cropping intensity and per hectare gross income (Verma 2006). It was reported that the per hectare gross income derived by the tractor-owning farms and tractor-using farms were, respectively, 63 per cent and 31 per cent higher than the bullock-owing farms. Likewise, cropping intensity of tractor-owning farms and tractor-using farms exceeded by 12 per cent and 8 per cent, respectively, than bullock-operated farms. Thus, the role of the use of hired-in machinery in augmenting production and productivity of agriculture is evident from various studies on farm mechanization. Apart from these, there are also a few studies that specifically dealt with the rental markets of farm machinery and its impact on production and productivity of agriculture. Based on primary data collected from 232 farm households in the Brahmaputra Valley in Assam of Northeast India, Das and Bezbaruah (2017) found that apart from owner-users of tilling and irrigating machineries, pure hiring-in users realized higher cropping intensity, crop diversification and yield as compared to the non-users of such machinery.[3] As per the regression analysis, such advantages of hiring-in users over non-users of irrigating machinery were found to be statistically significant although not so in the case of tilling machinery.[4] Given that hiring-in users were participants in the rental markets of tilling and irrigating machineries, the role of such markets in enhancing agricultural production and productivity is visible quite clearly. A recent study of rental markets of pump sets in the central and western parts of Nepal plains by Sharma and Goswami (2020) also depicted a similar role of such markets in facilitating intensive and diversified cultivation. Based on the survey of 291 farm households, Sharma and Goswami (2020) found that the hiring-in users of pump sets realized higher cropping intensity and more crop diversification than non-users and even owner-users, and the differences were found to be statistically significant. Thus, the positive impact of rental markets of farm machineries and equipment in raising production and productivity of agriculture is also evident from both the studies by Das and Bezbaruah (2017) and Sharma and Goswami (2020).

From the discussion in this section, it is found that rental markets of farm machineries and equipment have facilitated farm mechanization even by small and marginal farmers, and, directly or indirectly, such markets contribute to the adoption of production and productivity-augmenting practices. In India, rental markets of farm machineries and equipment are functioning and contributing to farm mechanization along with production and productivity of agriculture, and, hence, it appeared that such markets have substituted, at least to some extent, the long-pending consolidation of landholdings measure of land reform in the country.

[3] Refer to Figure 4 of Das and Bezbaruah (2017).

[4] Refer to Tables 8–10 of Das and Bezbaruah (2017).

Besides contributing to farm mechanization and production and productivity-improving practices, the functioning of the rental markets of tilling machinery enable farming in areas where rearing of draft animal is difficult. As per the field study, during November 2013 to January 2014, in the Brahmaputra Valley, it was found that in a sample village, frequent occurrence of floods had made rearing of bullocks difficult, and hence, farmers carried out their cultivation using hired tilling machinery (Das 2015). As own uses of tilling machinery are not affordable for all farmers and rearing of bullocks was difficult because of frequent incidences of floods in the area, farming would not have been possible for them had the rental markets of such machinery not functioning.

Since rental markets of farm machinery help in mechanized cultivation, employment may be impacted by the functioning of such markets. There may be displacement of human labour from the sector, on the one hand, while with an increase in cropping intensity and crop diversification, on the other hand, one may expect the generation of additional employment opportunities. The impact of rental markets of farm machinery on employment is yet to be examined. However, we can have an idea about the impact of the rental market of such machinery on employment to some extent by looking into the impact of farm mechanization on it. Although there is a debate on the effect of tractorization of agriculture on employment, it is evident from studies that the reduction of labour employment caused by it is quite nominal. In a review-based study, Verma (2006) stated that the net human labour displacement in agricultural operations resulting from farm mechanization was not significant, and even the displacement of human labour was more than compensated by the enhanced demand for such labour brings by multiple cropping, intensive cultivation and higher yields. Furthermore, demand for labour for manufacturing, servicing, distribution, repair and maintenance as well as other complementary jobs substantially increased due to mechanization, and thus, there was also the generation of non-farm employment (Verma 2006). Rise in employment due to the use of tractors in farm operation was also stated by Roy and Blase (1978). More importantly, while the new generation of farm households is becoming less willing to take up the laborious work of manual agriculture owing to the spread of education (Kuri 2003), tractorization encourages the educated persons to join cultivation. There are instances of educated persons working elsewhere earlier, joining cultivation due to tractorization (Chopra 1974).

6.5. IMPERFECTIONS IN THE RENTAL MARKET OF FARM MACHINERIES AND EQUIPMENT AND CUSTOM HIRING CENTRE

It is evident that the rental markets of farm machinery have a great role in diffusing of farm mechanization and production and productivity improving practices. However, the efficiency and equity implication of these emerging factor markets in agriculture is dependent on the absence of any major imperfection in their functioning. There are two readily conceivable sources of imperfections of these markets. The first is the possible presence of market power or monopoly elements. The suppliers in such factor markets are usually the bigger landholders having a greater impact in their locality and, hence, by exercising their influence, such suppliers of farm machineries and equipment may realize higher rental rates. Second, as most of the suppliers of the capital goods are users, it is explicable that those suppliers will rent out machinery only after finishing the use of capital goods in their own farm operations. It is, therefore, conceivable that hiring-in users will have to wait for their turn for the machinery to be available. As cultivation is weather dependent and seasonal, the hiring-in users may not be able to get the machinery for use at the right time for cultivation.

Das and Bezbaruah (2020) in their study of efficiency and equity of tilling machinery rental in the Brahmaputra Valley found that suppliers in the rental markets of power tillers, despite being far fewer in number than the hirers, do not enjoy any significant market power to influence the rental rate. The probable market power of the suppliers is blunted since traditional bullocks and plough units, a substitute for hired power tillers, are still available locally. Further, there is also a risk of suppliers coming in from nearby areas in the event of relatively higher local rental rates. In other words, contestability in the local rental markets of farm machineries and equipment by owners of substitute agricultural capital goods and also suppliers of the same capital goods in nearby areas has kept the market power of suppliers in control. Even though there was an absence of any role of market power in the determination of the rental rates, the rental markets of farm machineries and equipment were not fully free from imperfections in their functioning. It was found that most of the suppliers in the rental markets of ploughing machinery are also users of the capital goods, and hence, the hiring-in users stand second in the queue to the user suppliers in accessing and using such machinery. The resulting problem for hiring-in users in getting to use the farm machineries and equipment on time seems to have had some adverse impact on their farming operations. For instance, tilling operations of hiring-in users of farm machinery were found to be somewhat less mechanized than those of the owner-users of such machinery. With respect to the use of production and productivity-enhancing practices, the owner-users of tilling machinery were found to be somewhat ahead of hiring-in users of such machinery. These observed differences in the intensity and extent of use of these practices were not found to be statistically significant. However, as per another field survey in the subsequent time period in Assam, the intensity of tilling mechanization by owner-users than hiring-in users was found to be significantly higher. Despite the presence of some imperfections of such types in the functioning of rental markets of ploughing machinery, these markets were found to be contributing to the spread of farm mechanization and related production and productivity-improving practices without a severe dent on efficiency.

Labour scarcity in the agriculture sector is a major problem in India, which limits its production, and farm mechanization has appeared to be a credible solution for this, but the poor economic condition of small and marginal farmers, the dominant section of farmers in the country, makes these diverse farm machineries unaffordable for them (Chinnappa et al. 2018). In order to facilitate farm mechanization, state and central governments have taken different initiatives to establish custom hiring service centres (CHSCs). As for instance, during 2014, the Government of Karnataka in collaboration with Shri Kshetra Dharmastala Rural Development Project

(SKDRDP) established 164 CHSCs in 25 districts of the state (Chinnappa et al. 2018). In India, the Agro Industries Corporation although had set the path for custom hiring of farm implements and machinery in an organized way in the 1960s, it was evident in the country from the 19th century itself, and the Central Research Institute for Dry Land Agriculture had been the pioneer in establishing such centres (Chinnappa et al. 2018). In the subsequent times, different state government agencies, non-governmental organizations, private companies and other entrepreneurs have established different custom hiring centres and have been operating them. There are also initiatives taken by the central government to raise the custom hiring centres in the country. For instance, through 'Sub Mission on Agricultural Mechanization', a grant assistance up to 50 per cent is provided for the establishment of custom hiring centres (NABARD 2018). Establishment of at least one custom hiring centre in every large village or gram panchayat in the case of small villages was also recommended by the Committee on Doubling of Farmers' Income (NABARD 2018). Presently, custom hiring centres have also been established under the Rashtriya Krishi Vikas Yojana (RKVY). The custom hiring centres established in different states of India are presented in Figure 6.4. As per data provided by Mechanization and Technology Division, Department of Agriculture, Co-operation and Farmers Welfare, Ministry of Agriculture and Farmers Welfare, in India, 78,117 custom hiring centres have been established (Government of India 2021c). Although custom hiring centres are functioning and initiatives have been taken to establish new centres, hiring from individual suppliers has been observed and is spreading, as such centres are limited in number and have not spread to all parts of the country. Besides, while farmers taking the services of CHSCs are realizing higher income and profit, the centres in turn are incurring losses (Chinnappa et al. 2018), and hence, the net social benefits of such centres are not very clear. In this context, it can be mentioned that if hiring from individual suppliers is facilitated effectively by the rental markets, custom hiring centres require supplementing or complementing such markets, and if such markets are non-existent or weak, custom hiring centres have to play the role of facilitating the expansion of agricultural mechanization.

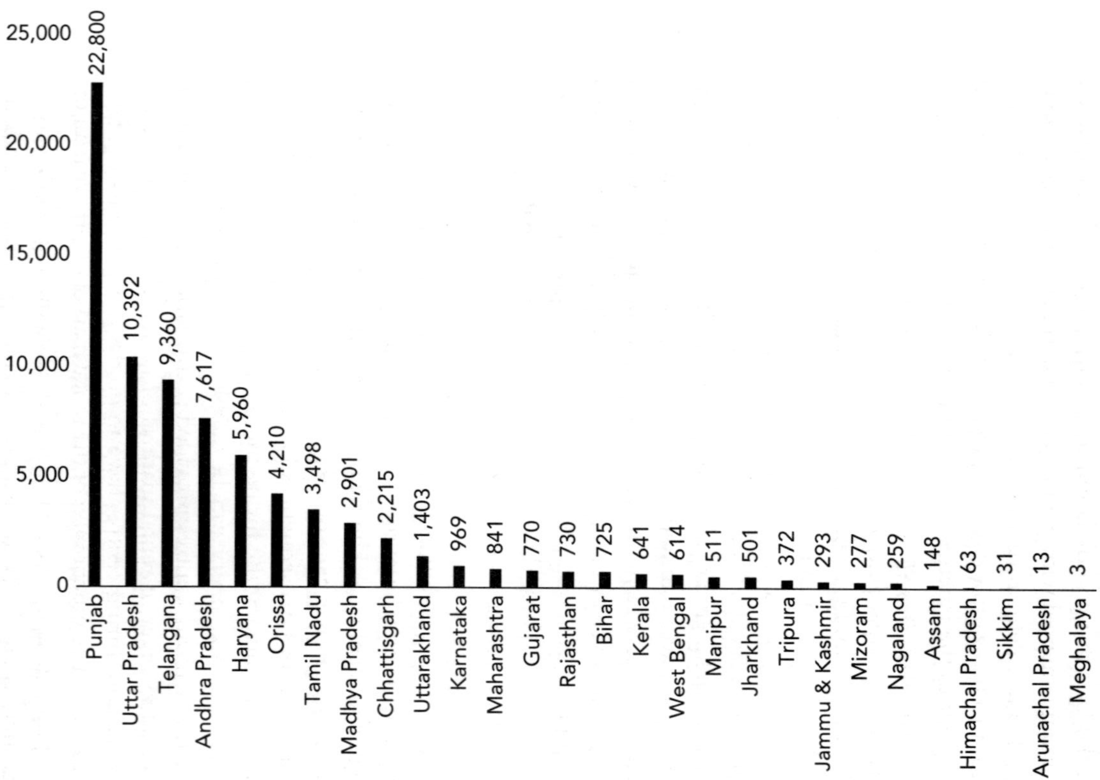

Figure 6.4 *Number of Custom Hiring Centres Established in Different Indian States*

Source: Government of India (2021c).

6.6. CONCLUSION

Despite the facts that consolidation of landholdings in India remained largely unimplemented with preponderance of small and marginal landholdings, large-scale fragmentation of landholdings and declining farm size, farm mechanization is taking place, and this can be attributed to a great extent to the emergence and functioning of the rental markets of farm machinery. As per some secondary data of the past few years, these markets are expanding over the years. Two separate micro-studies carried out in Assam in the northeastern part of India have shown that the rental markets of farm machineries and equipment are functioning extensively, and they are informal in nature. Apart from correcting factor endowments by making heavy machinery divisible, rental markets of farm machinery are facilitating farm mechanization by farmers of all size groups. More importantly, it is the small holder farms, which have benefitted more from the functioning of such markets. Apart from facilitating farm mechanization, the rental markets of farm machineries and equipment have an important role in enhancing farm production and productivity. Thus, the rental markets of farm machineries and equipment have emerged as a substitute to the long-pending consolidation of landholdings at least to some extent in India. Furthermore, in areas where rearing of bullocks is difficult, cultivation is still possible by many farmers only because of the functioning of the rental markets of ploughing machinery. The rental markets of farm machineries and equipment are, however, not free from the problem of imperfection, but no serious consequences have been reported in the existing literature. In facilitating the hiring use of farm machineries, the rental market of farm machinery can be supplemented or complemented by the custom hiring centres provided such markets are functioning effectively. However, if rental markets of farm machinery are absent or weak, custom hiring centres have to do the job of facilitating farm mechanization. The functioning of the rental market of farm machineries and equipment is not independent of the functioning of other factor markets such as credit. Non-institutional credit encourages both the own use and hiring use of farm capital goods, and institutional credit encourages the own use of farm machinery. Thus, the functioning of the rental market of farm machineries and equipment is dependent to a great extent on the credit market. As institutional credit plays a role in encouraging participation in rental markets as the suppliers, like Das (2016), more penetration of such credit can be suggested for the expansion of suppliers in the market. Increased accessibility of institutional credit will make functioning of farm machineries and equipment more efficient by raising competition among the suppliers.

REFERENCES

Agarwal, Bina. 1984. 'Tractors, Tubewells and Cropping Intensity in the Indian Punjab'. *The Journal of Development Studies* 20, no. 4: 290–302.

Benjamin, Dwayne, and L. Brandt. 1997. 'Land, Factor Markets, and Inequality in Rural China: Historical Evidence'. *Explorations in Economic History* 34, no. 4: 460–494. https://doi.org/10.1006/exeh.1997.0683 (accessed on 21 February 2022).

Birthal, Pratap Singh, and R. P. Singh. 1991. 'Land-lease Market, Resource Adjustment and Agricultural Development'. *Indian Journal of Agricultural Economics* 46, no. 3: 361–368.

Chinnappa, B., K. K. R. Patil, and H. S. Sowmya. 2018. 'Economic Impact of Custom Hiring Service Centres in Maize Cultivation: A Case Study from Karnataka'. *Indian Journal of Agricultural Economics* 73, no. 4: 478–500.

Chopra, Kusum. 1974. 'Tractrorisation and Changes in Factor Inputs: A Case Study of Punjab'. *Economic & Political Weekly* 9, no. 52: A119–A127.

Das, Anup Kumar. 2015. 'Functioning and Impact of Rental Markets of Agricultural Capital Goods in Assam'. Unpublished PhD thesis. Guwahati: Department of Economics, Gauhati University.

Das, Anup Kumar. 2016. 'Impact of Access to Credit on Rental Markets of Agricultural Capital Goods: Evidence from Assam of North-East India'. *Bangladesh Development Studies* 39, no. 1–2: 83–101.

Das, Anup Kumar. 2019. 'Rental Markets of Tilling Machinery: Its Forms and Determinants of Participation in the Brahmaputra Valley of Assam'. *Indian Journal of Agricultural Economics* 74, no. 1: 128–142.

Das, Anup Kumar, and M. P. Bezbaruah. 2017. 'Rental Markets of Agricultural Capital Goods as Substitute of Consolidation of Holdings: An Investigation in the Brahmaputra Valley of Assam'. *Journal of Land and Rural Studies* 5, no. 2: 120–139.

Das, Anup Kumar, and M. P. Bezbaruah. 2020. 'Efficiency and Imperfections of Tilling Machinery Rental Markets in the Brahmaputra Valley of Eastern India'. *Agricultural Economics Research Review* 33, no. 1: 35–44.

Dobbs, Thomas, and P. Foster. 1972. 'Incentives to Invest in New Agricultural Inputs in North India'. *Economic Development and Cultural Change* 21, no. 1: 101–117.

Dutta, Mrinal Kanti. 2007. 'Management of Groundwater Irrigation in Assam through Water Markets'. *The ICFAI Journal of Environmental Economics* 5, no. 4: 28–43.

Goswami, Binoy. 2016. 'Overcoming Farm Size Induced Constraints through Endogenous Institutional Innovations: Findings from a Field Study in Assam Plains, India'. *Economics Bulletin* 36, no. 1: 411–428.

Government of India. 2016. *All India Report on Input Survey 2011–12*. https://agcensus.nic.in/document/is2011/reports/all_india_report_2011_12.pdf (accessed on 30 August 2021).

Government of India. 2021a. *All India Report on Input Survey 2016–17*. http://agcensus.nic.in/document/is2016/air_is_16-17_210121-final_220221.pdf (accessed on 23 June 2021).

Government of India. 2021b. 'Directorate of Economics and Statistics'. https://eands.dacnet.nic.in/Cost_of_Cultivation.htm (accessed on 23 June2021).

Government of India. 2021c. 'X. 8: State Wise—Custom Hiring Centre (CHC)S Established So Far'. Mechanisation and Technology Division, Department of Agriculture, Co-operation and Farmers Welfare, Ministry of Agriculture and Farmers Welfare. https://www.tnagrisnet.tn.gov.in/dashboard/report/10_08.pdf (accessed on 25 November 2021).

Indian Journal of Agricultural Economics. 2014. 'Inter-conference Symposium of International Association of Agricultural Economists (IAAE) on Re-visiting Agriculture Policies in the Light of Globalisation Experience: The Indian Context: A Brief Report'. *Indian Journal of Agricultural Economics* 69, no. 4: 501–503.

Jodha, N. S. 1974. 'A Case of The Process of Tractorisation'. *Economic & Political Weekly* 52, no. 9: A111–A118.

Kapila, Uma. 2011. *Indian Economy Performance and Policies*. New Delhi: Academic Foundation.

Kuri, Pravat Kumar. 2003. 'Factor Market Imperfections and Explanations of Tenancy: Testing of an Econometric Model Using Evidence from Assam of Northeast India'. *Indian Journal of Agricultural Economics* 58, no. 2: 234–245.

Lin, Justin Yifu. 1995. 'Endowments, Technology, and Factor Markets: A Natural Experiment of Induced Institutional Innovation from China's Rural Reform'. *American Journal of Agricultural Economics* 77, no. 2: 231–242.

Misra, S. K., and V. K. Puri. 2008. *Indian Economy*. Mumbai: Himalaya Publishing House.

NABARD. 2018. 'Farm Sector Policy Department NABARD Head Office, Mumbai'. Sectoral Paper on Farm Mechanization. https://www.nabard.org/auth/writereaddata/file/NSP%20Farm%20Mechanisation.pdf (accessed on 20 June 2021).

Rao, C. H. Hanumantha.1972. 'Farm Mechanisation in a Labour-abundant Economy'. *Economic & Political Weekly* 7, no. 5/7: 393, 395–397, 399–400.

Rath, N. 2015. 'Declining Cattle Population: Will the Sacred Cow Finally Rest in the Temple'? *Economic & Political Weekly* 50, no. 28: 12–14.

Ray, Debraj. 2011. *Development Economics*. New Delhi: Oxford University Press.

Roy, Shyamal, and M. G. Blase. 1978. 'Farm Tractorisation, Productivity and Labour Employment: A Case Study of Indian Punjab'. *The Journal of Development Studies* 14, no. 2: 193–209.

Sharma, Krishna, and B. Goswami. 2020. 'Rental Market of Pump-sets in the Central and Western Parts of Nepal Plains'. *Asia Pacific Journal of Rural Development* 30, no. 1–2: 226–243.

Singh, G. 2006. 'Estimation of a Mechanisation Index and its Impact on Production and Economic Factors—A Case Study in India'. *Biosystems Engineering* 93, no. 1: 99–106.

Singh, J. 2006. 'Scope, Progress and Constraints of Farm Mechanization in India'. In *Status of Farm Mechanization in India*, edited by Indian Agricultural Statistics Research Institute, 48–56. Indian Council of Agricultural Research. https://www.researchgate.net/publication/266082375_STATUS_OF_FARM_MECHANIZATION_IN_INDIA_x_48_x (accessed on 25 June 2021)

Singh, K., and P. S. Rangi. 2008. 'Marketing System and Market Structure for Secondhand Tractors in Punjab'. *Agricultural Economics Research Review* 21: 30–36.

Singh, Bant, H. S. Bal, and N. Kumar. 1991. 'A Spatio-Temporal Analysis of Land-lease Market in Punjab'. *Indian Journal of Agricultural Economics* 46, no. 3: 355–360.

Vaidyanathan, A. 1986. *India's Agricultural Development in a Regional Perspective*. Calcutta: Centre for Studies in Social Sciences.

Verma, S. R. 2006. 'Impact of Agricultural Mechanization on Production, Productivity, Cropping Intensity Income Generation and Employment of Labour'. In *Status of Farm Mechanization in India*, edited by Indian Agricultural Statistics Research Institute, 133–153. Indian Council of Agricultural Research. https://citeseerx.ist.psu.edu/viewdoc/download?doi=10.1.1.511.5214&rep=rep1&type=pdf (accessed on 25 June 2021)

Chapter 7

Reviving and Remodelling the Agricultural Extension Service

Maheshwar Giri and Binoy Goswami

7.1. INTRODUCTION

In 2016, the Government of India (GoI) set out a target of doubling farmers' income by 2022. A policy paper by National Institution for Transforming India (NITI) Aayog identifies the transformative role of technology and innovation in agriculture as one of the four sources of doubling income (Chand 2017). The Three-Year Action Agenda 2017–2018 to 2019–2020, by NITI Aayog, highlights the need for a vibrant, responsive and globally competitive research systems, with adequate scientific manpower of high calibre, and a strong agricultural extension services delivery system. A dynamic extension services delivery system can strengthen the lab-to-land connection and ensure the adoption of transformative technology by farmers that may result in higher productivity and farm income (NITI Aayog 2017, 30). Given the focus of the GoI on improving farmers' income and the potential role that agricultural extension can play in it, understanding the nature and status of it becomes pertinent.

A large number of studies have assessed the status and impact of agricultural extension services in the Indian context. Glendenning et al.

(2010) assess the reasons for farmers not accessing extension and the gaps that exist in the extension approaches in India. Adhiguru et al. (2009) analyse the sources and types of information accessed by the farmers, and efficiency of sources in trial and adoption of information at the national level. Adhiguru et al. (2009) and Glendenning et al. (2010) use data from the Situation Assessment Survey (SAS), 2003, for their analysis. Sajesh and Suresh (2016) provide a discussion on the public extension services in India. There exist some state-specific studies as well. Goswami (2012) and Goswami and Bezbaruah (2017) in Assam; Reardon et al. (2011a) in Uttar Pradesh; Reardon et al. (2011b) in Madhya Pradesh; Singh et al. (2009) in Bihar; Chandrakant et al. (2017) in Maharashtra; and Lekshmi et al. (2006) in Tamil Nadu are some of those studies. On the other hand, Ramaswami et al. (2006), Singh (2005) and Sulaiman et al. (2005) examine the impact of private extension providers only. Notwithstanding the important contributions of these studies, the major limitation of them, in our view, is that they are limited in scope. The current study uses secondary data from the report (report no. 587) of the 77th round of National Sample Survey (NSS) for analyzing the current status of extension services in India. The analysis is further supplemented with the findings from the unit-level data of the SAS, 2013.

The study analyses the status of and challenges confronting the extension services at the national level. Further, it identifies the factors that affect the decision of the farmers to access extension services and also the choice of the source of extension. The study has some interesting findings. First, it has been found that a large proportion of the farmers, especially small and marginal farmers, do not access any source of extension. Second, there are regional variations in the proportions of farmers who do not access extension. Southern region has the maximum percentage of farmers who access extension. Third, non-availability and unawareness are two major reasons preventing farmers from accessing extension. Fourth, the status of public extension in the country is very disquieting. It is the least preferred source of extension. Fifth, age, sex and education of the head of the household; proportion of farmers among the family members; crop intensity; crop diversification; irrigation; farm size; awareness about minimum support price (MSP); social group; and the region to which a farmer belongs are the factors that affect the decision to access extension. These factors also influence the choice of the source of extension service.

This chapter is organized as follows. Section 7.2 presents a discussion on the existing literature. Section 7.3 elaborates on the data and methods used. Results of the empirical analysis are presented in section 7.4. Section 7.5 discusses the results. Section 7.6 summarizes the findings of the chapter and discusses the policy implications of the findings.

7.2. LITERATURE REVIEW

7.2.1. Definition of Agricultural Extension Service

The production process in agriculture requires the knowledge and information about the benefits and ways of using existing and new farm technologies, and the better ways of managing available farm inputs. Collectively, the knowledge and informational inputs in agriculture are termed as 'agriculture extension', 'agricultural extension services', 'agricultural advisory services' or simply 'extension services' (Birner and Anderson 2007, vi; Van den Ban and Hawkins 2002, 9). Besides the production aspect, extension services also include the knowledge and information on prices, market conditions, post-harvest management and adoption of safety and other standards (Ferroni and Zhou 2013). An extension services delivery mechanism aims to transfer the knowledge from scientists and researchers to farmers to help them make better decisions regarding farm activities, and also to collect farm realities to better design and implement extension strategies (Van den Ban and Hawkins 2002). Studies have shown that the research findings from the laboratory and the experiences of the progressive farmers help individual farmers achieve their farm goals more efficiently (Van den Ban and Hawkins 2002, 4–5). Birkhaeuser et al. (1991) have documented significant and positive extension results for majority of studies on the impact of the extension services on farm outcomes carried out between 1970 and 1990. Two recent reviews of the literature on extension impact have also documented positive impact of extension services (Lampach et al. 2021; Takahashi et al. 2020).

7.2.2. Objectives of Agricultural Extension

The main goal of the agricultural extension is to boost agricultural production through the transfer of technology to the farmers so that the gap between the existing productivity level and the potential level of productivity can be eliminated (Anderson and Feder 2007; Van den Ban and Hawkins 2002). The goal of increased productivity is ultimately realized at the farm level, and the role of the extension agency is to encourage farmers to adopt new knowledge to fulfil that goal. The extension agency/organization uses extension agents to pass on information about new knowledge to the farmers through various interpersonal and mass media channels. The extension agents make the farmers aware about problems related to farming and marketing, provide with a range of alternatives to overcome them, facilitate the adoption of new technology and stimulate diffusion in innovation (Van den Ban and Hawkins 2002). Alongside the information on agricultural research, extension organization also uses information from social and psychological research to design extension programmes. The flow of information is expected to occur in the reverse direction also in the form of feedback from the farmers.

7.2.3. Diffusion of Innovation in Agriculture and Role of Extension Services

In order to understand how the extension of agriculture stimulates the transfer and adoption of new technology and helps in the diffusion of innovation, it becomes pertinent to explore the process and factors that influence the diffusion of innovation in agriculture. Everett Rogers (2003, 168–218) explains the six stages through which the diffusion of innovation takes place. The first stage is the recognition of a problem or need that stimulates the scientific investigation intended to solve the problem (stage 2). The new knowledge or idea from the second stage (invention) is put into meeting the needs of an audience of 'potential adopters' in the third stage. The fourth stage is the stage of commercialization in which the product or service developed in the third stage is produced, manufactured and distributed in the marketplace. Once the product or service is in the market, in the fifth stage, the potential adopter of the technology needs to make a decision regarding the adoption of the innovation. Finally, the diffusion of the innovation in the fifth stage will result in some consequences (good or bad) to the individual or to a social system. The process of innovation and decision may not, however, always occur in a linear fashion, and the time taken in each stage may vary, and certain stages may not occur at all.

Extension services have an important role to play in each stage of the innovation–decision process. However, extension services play a crucial role in the fifth stage while imparting the new information about innovation, and helping the farmers recognize the benefits of adopting new technology and minimize the uncertainty associated with it. A farmer's decision to adopt or reject a new technology is not an instantaneous act, but, it is a process that occurs over time and consists of a series of actions (Rogers 2003). Extension supports are required over this entire process, and access to extension services enables farmers to adopt technology within a relatively shorter period.

7.2.4. Factors Affecting Farmers' Decision to Access Extension Services

A farmer's decision to access extension services involves a twofold process. In the first stage, he has to decide whether or not to access extension services. Since there are multiple sources of extension information, in the second stage, one has to decide on the sources to be accessed to. This decision has implications for the farmer's household budget and prospective income. Consequently, it becomes pertinent to examine the factors influencing a farmer's decision to access extension information from different sources.

In this context, it is important to acknowledge that farmers are heterogeneous, who have different rates of adoption of new technology. Besides the perceived attributes of the technology, the socio-economic characteristics and personality variable of the farmer, the social and political setting of which she is a part of, are some of the major factors that influence the adoption of technology by the farmers. Hence, these are also the factors that may affect the decision of the farmers about whether to access extension services (Chakravarty 2020; Rogers 2003; Ryan and Gross 1950).

7.2.5. Sources of Agricultural Extension Services

New knowledge on agriculture reaches the farmer through multiple sources. Agricultural extension workers, progressive farmers, agriculture and animal husbandry departments of the government, agricultural input selling companies, agro-vet clinics, agricultural universities/colleges and media are some of the major sources of extension services. Sources of agricultural extension can broadly be classified into two categories: interpersonal channels and mass media channels. Interpersonal channels provide opportunities for the face-to-face interaction, group work, discussion and demonstration that enable behavioural changes. Public and private extension sources provide opportunities for these activities. Mass media channels help in disseminating extension information through television (TV), radio, newspaper, Internet, etc. It is one of the cheapest ways to disseminate extension information, but its effect is mostly limited to change in knowledge base of the farmers.[1]

7.2.6. Coexistence of Private and Public Extension Services Provisioning

The changes in thinking and practice of development process over time have resulted in some fundamental changes in the way agricultural extensions are organized and financed. The idea of minimum or reduced government and market liberalization that came into vogue in the late 1980s and early 1990s, led to the downsizing of the publicly financed agricultural extension provisions in many countries (Birner and Anderson 2007, 1). The Training and Visit (T&V) programme of the 1970s was purely a public sector extension delivery system that

---

[1] For more details on the features and differences between interpersonal and mass media channels of communication, see Rogers and Shoemaker (1972, 253).

was based on the interpersonal interaction of 'contact farmer' with extension agents belonging to the public sector (Umali-Deininger 1997). Like other counties, the Indian government also invested generously in the T&V programme and continued to do so till the end of the 1990s. However, the growing emphasis on the role of state as a facilitator rather than the sole custodian of the public services during the 1990s paved the way for the private sector to enter the agricultural extension business. Besides, the poor performances of the public extension programme also catalysed the quest for this alternative approach (Umali-Deininger 1997). The number of the private extension service providers surged although that did not crowd out the public provisioning of extension services. In India, both private and public service providers coexist. In fact, the Agricultural Technology Management Agency (ATMA) model of extension delivery mechanism launched by the Indian government acknowledges the positive role of private service providers. In order to understand this coexistence, one has to examine the nature of the extension services and how the delivery of extension services is organized.

Theoretically, there should be a market for the information on extension if farmers benefit from such information (Anderson and Feder 2007). Farmers should demand information and be ready to pay for it as they do for other agricultural inputs. On the supply side, the private players should be in a position to fully cater to farmers' demands (Anderson and Feder 2004). However, traditionally, governments around the world, particularly in developing countries, have assumed the dominant role in the provision of agricultural extension services, at least at some stage of development (Anderson and Feder 2004; Umali and Schwartz 1994). The nature of the information on extension services provides an economic rationale for the dominant role of the public sector in the provisioning of extension services.

Using the economic principle of excludability and rivalry (or subtractability), the extension information can be classified as being closer to public or private goods (Anderson and Feder 2004; Umali-Deininger 1997; Umali and Schwartz 1994). The excludability principle applies when access to services can be denied to those farmers who do not pay for the information, while the rivalry principle applies when the use of information by a farmer reduces its availability to other farmers (Feldman and Serrano 2006; Kessides 1993; Musgrave and Musgrave 1989).

Anderson and Feder (2004, 43) update the conceptual framework by Umali and Schwartz (1994) and Umali-Deininger (1997), and classify agricultural extension information into two broad categories likes (a) 'agricultural information embodied in product' and (b) 'Disembodied information on agricultural practices'. Agricultural information that farmers receive indirectly upon the purchase of agricultural products are 'embodied agricultural information' (Umali-Deininger 1997, 207). It includes information related to the use and handling of production inputs (e.g., seeds, fertilizers and pesticides), equipment for farm management (e.g., telecommunication, laboratory equipment, computers and software) and technologies for post-harvest management activities (e.g., technologies related to threshing, drying, milling, storage and packaging). Since the benefits of extension are restricted only to those farmers who purchase the products, the characteristics of private goods, that is, rivalry and excludability, are satisfied. On the other hand, disembodied information on agricultural practices or 'pure agricultural information' covers all sorts of information, which can be used without the acquisition of a specific physical technology (Umali-Deininger 1997; Umali and Schwartz 1994, viii). All types of self-standing advices on cultural and production techniques, farm management, post-harvest management and community development are disembodied information. Information belonging to this category lies at different points in a continuum between private and public goods. Anderson and Feder (2004, 43) further classify this category of agricultural information into two types: (a) general and non-excludable information and (b) specialized and excludable information. Information about prices and other market conditions and cropping pattern are some of the examples of general information that is non-excludable in nature. Generally, the information that passes through mass media channels belongs to this sub-category. The information belonging to this sub-category qualifies the characteristics of public goods. The other sub-category of information is tailored information for a specific farm or farm operation. For example, the information on crops specific to a particular soil type is specialized information. This information has the characteristics of a toll good (or club good). Since the information is more farm or farmer specific, some farmers can be excluded from the access (excludability principle), but the value of the information does not diminish with one farmer's use of it (rivalry principle).[2]

Usually, the private providers should be interested in supplying agricultural information that has the characteristics of private and toll goods. However, the private firms will not supply agricultural information that qualifies as public goods. The unwillingness of the private sector to provide the component of the agricultural extension services that qualifies as public goods necessitates the presence of the public sector.

It is important to note here that the speed of diffusion also determines the degree of excludability, which has implications for the change in the nature of the information over time. Usually, when the technology is in the introductory phase, the information related to its use is of private good nature. In the long run, however, that particular information might become a common knowledge making it a public good. For example, self-pollinated seeds are private goods only in the short run but not so in the long run. A farmer who receives information about the use and handling of this variety of seed after buying the seeds will start using his self-pollinated seeds afterwards as they can be easily replicated. Although the self-pollinated seeds are highly rival in nature, the ease in replication makes it very costly for the private firms to ensure excludability. There are high chances that self-pollinated seeds acquire the characteristics of common pool goods in the long run (Umali-Deininger 1997). Only few private firms that have low overhead cost and produce high-quality common pool goods (e.g., seeds) consistently are expected to earn adequate profits from supplying replacement seeds. In India, most of the farmers use self-pollinating seeds of rice and wheat and use borrowed seeds from friends and relatives rather than buying seeds for each sowing season, making it difficult for private firms to survive on selling high-quality seeds alone (Jaffee and Srivastava 1994). Thus, the size of the market and efficiency in

---

[2] Umali and Schwartz (1994, 20) present the classifications of extension services with several examples.

operation determine the participation of the private sector in supplying common pool goods like seeds. Failing to meet these conditions, the responsibility of supplying such goods needs to be borne by the public or non-profit non-governmental sectors.

As discussed earlier, private sectors have incentives to supply private and toll goods components of extension services. However, they compare the costs incurred in and the returns received from supplying the extension information while making supply decisions. The government policies on agriculture, the agricultural extension policies in particular, influence these costs and returns of the private sector. The government policies on price, and trade, monetary and exchange rate policies influence the commodity prices that, in turn, influence the return private firms can earn by supplying agricultural information embodied in products. The government supports towards farmers through policies like minimum price support and subsides on farm inputs reduce the cost of cultivation and make paying for extension services more affordable. The research and development policies of the government in the form of tighter intellectual property rights may boost the pace of technology generation by the private sector. Likewise, the education and the extension policies of the government that make the farmers aware of new technologies determine the pace of diffusion of innovations. Given the impacts of government policies on costs and returns, the private sector decides whether to supply extension services even if they are in the form of private or toll goods. The public sector has to step in if the private sector considers providing a particular extension service as not profitable.

In developing countries, farmers have small landholding and are dispersed in remote areas. Some of the innovations are more inclined towards large farms, and even if they exist for small farms, they may be out of reach of the small farmers because of the issues of availability and affordability. Further, traditional crops mostly dominate the cropping patterns in these farms, and that makes them less likely to pay for the extension information related to these crops. All these act as barriers to the profit maximization for private firms. Under such circumstances, the public sector has to provide extension services for uplifting the welfare of the rural farmers.

7.2.7. Agricultural Extension in India

In India, formal teaching on agricultural extension started after independence with an undergraduate course at the Calcutta University in 1950. Soon after, extension activities on agriculture were incorporated as a part of the Community Development Programme under the First Five Year Plan (1951–1956). Although very less in numbers (less than 1,000 personnel), the agricultural extension workers and village-level workers were mobilized to encourage the use of improved seeds, planting and ploughing under green manure crops, proper use of commercial fertilizers, and improved agricultural and tillage practices (Chatterjee 1957; Moore 1984). As an institution, an extension centre was inaugurated at Nangloi, Delhi, in 1951, but a separate section to look after extension education was formed only in 1971 within the Indian Council of Agricultural Research (ICAR 2020, iii).

Over the past 70 years, the approach to agricultural extension in India has undergone several changes. It started with the community development approach in the 1950s that focused on state-sponsored village-level demonstration. Failing to curb the growing hunger and food shortage resulted in a shift in approach towards the linear transfer of technology in the mid-1960s. The GoI promoted the adoption of high-yielding varieties (HYVs) of seeds along with the public provisioning of irrigation, price supported and subsidized fertilizers and pesticides though various other agricultural development programmes. HYVs of rice and wheat seeds were distributed to farmers through state-level agricultural depots. These interventions led to a rise in productivity of cereals crop. However, these input-oriented strategies through HYV seeds reached its limit by the late 1970s. The extension system at that time was scarcely available, and the village-level workers who reached out to the farmers had low educational qualification and very low level of agricultural knowledge. The field staff used to be overburdened with reporting and non-extension duties, and they spent very little time in extension activities as such (Moore 1984). Under these circumstances, a major shift in the public sector extension came in 1974 with the implementation of the World Bank–sponsored T&V system, which focused on technology diffusion through the extension system (Anderson et al. 2006; Moore 1984).

T&V expanded to most of the states and improved the financial and human resource capacity of the extension system and increased the coverage and access to extension services. However, this top-down and supply-driven extension approach imposed a high investment cost and long-term recurrent costs to the government. Further, it was criticized for favouring the rich and more powerful farmers, and it benefitted only those areas with better irrigation facilities and timely availability of inputs, and places with intensive involvement of World Bank's staff (Anderson et al. 2006; Birner and Anderson 2007; ICAR 2020; Moore 1984). The stoppage of the external funding in the late and early 1990s imposed a fiscal burden on the national and state budgets that ultimately led to the abandonment of the T&V system in India (Anderson et al. 2006; Gulati et al. 2018; Moore 1984).

A qualitative change in the agricultural extension landscape occurred in the 1990s, with the growing interest in the idea of alternative extension, increased farmers' participation and greater pluralism in the extension system (Anderson et al. 2006).[3] The scepticism about the public extension system was growing for failing to meet the diverse range of demand from the farmers' community, and raising consciousness in support of the pluralistic extension system was leading the discourse. It was believed that a pluralistic extension system would share the burden of the extension services delivery. The privatization of extension services was thought as an approach to ensure competitiveness in extension service delivery, ensuring technical and allocative efficiency, leading to cost minimization, profit maximization and optimal use of resources. In addition, doubts were raised about the sustainability of the extension services if financed solely through public funds.

In 1998, the GoI introduced the ATMA as a pilot project in 28 districts of 7 states under the Innovation in Technology Dissemination (ITD) component of the World Bank–funded National Agricultural Technology Project (NATP). This was an attempt to revitalize the public sector advisory services together with the active participation

---

[3] Plurality in extension system means 'the diversity of institutional options (private, public and others) in providing and financing agricultural advisory services' (Birner et al. 2009, 342).

of other stakeholders in agriculture, including the private sector and famers' group. Following the positive feedback, the ATMA project was developed as a model and expanded to 251 rural districts in 2005 and throughout the country in 2007 (Gulati et al. 2018; Kokate et al. 2020). The introduction of the ATMA model is a major milestone in the history of agricultural extension in India. It changed the top-down approach of transferring scientific knowledge towards a more decentralized and bottom-up decision-making in extension planning and execution. Further, the focus has moved beyond mere production and productivity towards farmers' and market efficiency.

The administrative set-up of ATMA model and its functions are discussed in Box 7.1.

Box 7.1 *Agricultural Technology Management Agency*

Agricultural Technology Management Agency (ATMA) model is conceptualized as a registered society of stakeholders classified into the three tiers of the well-structured administrative set-up for integrating research and extension activities and the day-to-day management of public agricultural technology system (ATS) of the district. The governing body is the apex body that comprises the district collector/magistrate (as the chairman of the governing board—GB), project director of ATMA (the member secretary) and other high-ranking officials who head research institutions and departments in the field of agriculture and allied sectors of the district. The governing board mainly reviews and approves the strategic research and extension plan (SREP) on a regular interval. The ATMA management committee (AMC) is responsible for coordinating the research and extension activities of the district. AMC is headed by the project director who is usually the head of the department of the agriculture in the district. The other members of AMC include the line departments' heads, heads of zonal research station (ZRS), Krishi Vigyan Kendra (KVC), non-governmental organizations (NGOs) and two representatives from the farmers' organizations.

AMC is the responsible body to prepare an integrated SREP, a comprehensive document, which identifies the research and extension priorities for the district, taking consideration of the agro-ecological features and the existing technological gaps in technology generation and dissemination. AMC also prepares block action plan, which requires approval from the GB. Most important of all, the committee coordinates the execution of annual work plans among various line department, KVKs, NGOs and Farmers' Interest Groups (FIGs). The Farm Information and Advisory Centre (FIAC) carries out the implementation of SREP at block level. The FIAC coordinates with the block technology teams (BTT) that comprises the block-level technical officers of the agricultural and allied departments. It works closely with the Farmer Advisory Committee (FAC), which monitors and provides feedbacks to BTT on the formulation and implementation of block-level action plan. The bottom tier of ATMA model comprises the village level-bodies, namely farmers' organizations and FIGs, which are formed by the group of farmers interested in cultivating a specific crop or product. The village-level bodies help in organizing extension activities and provide feedbacks for research and extension activities.[4]

Source: Kokate et al. (2020, 55–59).

India now has a pluralistic agricultural extension system. Presently, the public sectors in the extension system are the state government line departments, state agricultural universities (SAUs) and the ICAR network. The ICAR leads the public system research in India and has a separate division for agricultural extension. The Division on Agricultural Extensions operates through a network of 11 agricultural technology application research institutions and a vast network of Krishi Vikas Kendra (KVKs) (Kokate et al. 2020, 43). The ICAR launched the KVK programme in 1974 to reduce the gap between the development of technologies by research institutions and their implementation at field level (Sajesh and Suresh 2016). KVKs provide need-based and skill-oriented vocational training to farmers and field-level extension workers and self-employed persons. As of July 2020, there are altogether 721 KVKs managed by mostly SAUs, followed by non-governmental organizations (NGOs), ICAR institutions, state governments, central agricultural university, public sector undertakings,

[4] For more details on the organization of the ATMA, see Kokate et al. (2020, 55–59).

deemed university, other education institutions and central university.[5] KVKs have 6–7 scientific manpower and functions as a knowledge and resource centres at the district level (Gulati et al. 2018). It is estimated that there are around 0.12 million public extension service providers in India, of which around 15 per cent of them operate at supervisory and administrative positions and are not available for field-level extension. Of the total sanctioned positions, on an average, 30 per cent remain unmanned. Overall, the ratio of extension services provided to farmers stands at around 1:1,162, meaning that there is one extension service provider for every 1,162 farmers (Ministry of Agriculture & Farmers' Welfare 2017, 43).

Private players in the Indian extension system are progressive farmers, community-based organizations, NGOs, commodity boards and association, commercial production and marketing firms (e.g., input dealers), para-extension workers, agri-clinics and agribusinesses, the corporate sector, etc. (Kokate et al. 2020, 55). Among these players, input dealers are the major source of private extension services. There are around 0.28 million input dealers in India involved in marketing of seeds, fertilizers, pesticides and farm machineries (Gulati et al. 2018, 18). The private sector mostly provides embedded advisory services, which are integrated in commercial transactions like sale of inputs or contract farming (Birner and Anderson 2007; Birner et al. 2006; Umali-Deininger 1997; Umali and Schwartz 1994). There are about 0.28 million input dealers across India involved in the marketing of seeds, fertilizers, pesticides and farm machinery. Alongside private and public extension sources, media has been the major source of extension information on agriculture.[6] The use of traditional and modern

[5] https://www.icar.org.in/content/agricultural_extension_division (accessed on 1 July 2021).

[6] The history of farm magazine in India can be traced back to 1914 when the first periodical, *Krishi Sudhar,* was published to meet the information needs of the farmers. In 1960, a press was set up within Department of Agriculture to print and disseminate extension materials, mainly leaflet, folders, wall newspapers, posters and bulletins. In 1966, All India Radio, in coordination with the Ministry of Agriculture, launched a 45-minute radio programme in the evening, to promote

information and communications technologies—ICTs (newspapers, radio, TV and Internet) has been a major source of information for farmers. The Ministry of Agriculture, in collaboration with the National Informatics Centre and ICAR with SAUs and other ICT institutions, has developed agricultural content, targeting the general needs of the farmers. These contents are disseminated through various media sources owned and operated by both private and public media channels. Though the use of mobile app for extension information is very recent, it is gaining popularity among farmers. Some of the popular apps are IFFCCO Kisan App (IFFCO), mKRISHI (TCS), Digital Mandi (BSNL), Agri market (Breivik) and others.

Some recent studies have analysed the status and impacts of extension services at the national and state levels. Adhiguru et al. (2009), using the SAS, 2003, data find that the proportion of larger farmers that accessed extension services is higher than those of small and marginal farmers. Goswami and Bezbaruah (2017) also confirm this in the context of Assam. Reardon et al. (2011a) find that only a small fraction of farmers in Uttar Pradesh use extension services. However, the situation is better in Madhya Pradesh (Reardon et al. 2011b). Goswami (2012) and Goswami and Bezbaruah (2017) evaluate the impact of extension services in the context of Assam. Singh et al. (2009) conduct an impact evaluation study in the context of Bihar and report positive impacts of extension services. Goswami (2012) finds that extension services encourage the adoption of HYV rice, but they have no impact on crop diversification and cropping intensity. Goswami and Bezbaruah (2017) report that farmers accessing extension services devote a larger part of operational holdings to horticultural crops and earn more income as compared to those who do not access extension services. The study finds public extension to be marginally more effective than private extension in terms of generation of farm income. The conflict of interest involving the private sector in providing extension services that results in higher use of inputs and costs of cultivation is rendered

the newly introduced high-yielding varieties (HYVs) of seeds. *Krishi Darshan*, a 20-minute television programme, was aired on Doordarshan in 1967.

responsible for the relatively low effectiveness of the private extension. Lekshmi et al. (2006) assess that inadequacy of skilled extension workers in Tamil Nadu may be responsible for the lower adoption rate of HYT. Sulaiman et al. (2005), Singh (2005) and Ramaswami et al. (2006) examine the impact of private extension providers. Sulaiman et al. (2005) report positive impacts of extension services provided by the Mahindra Krishi Vihar on yield and farm income. On the other hand, Ramaswami et al. (2006) and Singh (2005) evaluate the functions of processors and aggregators under contract farming as extension providers.

Studies have also highlighted the issues and challenges faced by each of the sectors involved in delivering extension services. Major issues confronting the public extension system include the general nature of the extension services that fail to meet the farmer's actual need, the limited coverage and low-level skills of the extension workers (Birner and Anderson 2007; Glendenning et al. 2010; Gulati et al. 2018; Kokate et al. 2020; Ministry of Agriculture & Farmers' Welfare 2017). The private sector's challenges include its limited coverage that comprises only the farmers who can afford to pay for services. This sector is either not present or present in a limited manner in remote areas. Farmers' bargaining power vis-à-vis the private sector is usually limited. Like the extension workers in the public sector, private extension providers are also under- or unqualified (Birner and Anderson 2007; Glendenning et al. 2010; Kokate et al. 2020; Nandi and Nedumaran 2019). The media sector has its own limitations. Very often, extension services provided through the media fail to bring about a behavioural change in the farmers. The media sector may also struggle to expand its services to remote areas (Rogers and Shoemaker 1971; Van den Ban and Hawkins 2002).

It transpires from the aforementioned discussion that although there exist some important studies on extension services, they are limited in scope. Particularly, the studies at the national level examine only a few dimensions of the subject under consideration. The present study attempts to present a comprehensive analysis of the issues confronting the Indian agricultural extension services.

7.3. DATA AND METHOD

7.3.1. Description of Data

We use secondary data from the report (report no. 587) of the 77th round of National Sample Survey (NSS) for analysing the current status of extension services in India. This analysis is further supplemented by the findings from the unit-level data extracted from the SAS of agricultural households, carried out by the NSSO in 2013. The econometric analysis presented in this chapter is entirely based on unit-level data from the SAS, 2013.

From 4,529 sample villages, the SAS, 2013, covered 35,200 farm households. Each sample household featured twice across two visits. The survey collected details about farm households, farming practices and preferences, availability of resources, access to credit, awareness about MSP and access to technical advice along with other aspects of farming.

The survey has a separate section on access to technical advice, which presents information about a farmer's access and adoption of extension services from eight different sources, namely agricultural extension workers, Krishi Vigyan Kendra (KVK), agricultural university/college, private commercial agents, progressive farmers, veterinary department, NGOs and radio/TV/newspaper/Internet. Following the NSSO classifications, we have categorized these sources into three groups: private, public and the media.[7] These classifications are based on the channels through which the extension information flows from the sources to receiver.

A total of 30,521 farm households from all the Indian states responded to the queries in the section on access to technical advice. However, we limit our analysis to 19 major states belonging to five

---

[7] Public extension sources: extension agents/workers, Krishi Vigyan Kendra, agricultural universities and colleges, veterinary department; Private extension sources: private commercial agents (e.g., input dealers), progressive farmers and NGOs; media source: radio/TV/newspaper/Internet.

different agro-ecological regions: southern region (Andhra Pradesh, Karnataka, Kerala, Tamil Nadu and Telangana); western region (Gujarat, Maharashtra and Rajasthan); northern region (Bihar, Haryana, Himachal Pradesh, Jharkhand, Punjab and Uttar Pradesh); central region (Madhya Pradesh and Chhattisgarh) and eastern region (Assam, Odisha and West Bengal). Thus, a total of 19,900 rural agricultural households belonging to the aforementioned regions have been considered for the purpose of this study.

7.3.2. Methods Used

We start our analysis with an exploration of the status of the extension service through tabular analysis. Thereafter, an econometric analysis is undertaken to identify the factors that affect farmers' decision to access the extension service as well as the choice of the source of extension. The probit model is used to identify the factors influencing the decision about whether to access extension services. The dependent variable is a dummy variable that takes the value of 1 if the household accessed the extension service from at least one of the extension sources, and 0 if otherwise. On the other hand, a multinomial logit model is used to identify the factors responsible for the choice of sources of extension services (private, public and media). In order to apply multinomial logit regression, we require mutually exclusive categories of options. This assumption gets violated in the case of those households that accessed extension services from two or more sources. Thus, to overcome this problem, we consider only those households that accessed only one of three sources as defined earlier. Consequently, we have identified 5,922 households for the multinomial logit model. The explanatory variables included in both the regression models feature various socio-economic and farm characteristics of the households. These variables have been identified from the relevant literature (Anderson and Feder 2004; Chakravarty 2020; Cook et al. 2021; Goswami and Bezbaruah 2017; Lampach et al. 2021; Ryan and Gross 1950; Takahashi et al. 2020). Table 7.1 presents definitions of the explanatory variables along with their expected signs.

Table 7.1 *Independent Variables Used in Probit and Multinomial Logit Regression Models*

Explanatory Variables	Description	Expected Sign
Age	Age of the household head	–
Age square	Square of age of the household head	–
Education of HH head	Four dummy variables were considered: literate–non-formal/below primary, below secondary/secondary and above. Illiterate is considered as a base category	–
Gender of household head	Dummy: 1 = female-headed HH	–
Farmers as a proportion of total family size	Number of family members engaged in farming/total family members	+/–
Cropping intensity	Cropping intensity = gross cropped area/net cropped area; measured using visit 1 and visit 2 survey data	+
Crop diversification	Crop diversification measured using Herfindahl Index for the whole agriculture year $H = S_1^2 + S_2^2 + \ldots + S_N^2$, where S_i is the share of *i*th crop in the total cropped area	–

Share of gross irrigated area to gross cropped area	Gross irrigated area/gross cropped area	+
Cultivation as the principal income source	Cultivation is the largest source of household income	+
Farm expenses per hectare	Expenses on seeds, fertilizers, chemicals and manure/total farm expenses	+
Land ownership per capita (in ha)	Total land owned by household/total family members	+
Awareness about MSP for at least one crop	Dummy: 1 if household is aware about MSP for at least one crop	+

Source: The authors.

7.4. RESULTS OF EMPIRICAL ANALYSIS

7.4.1. Status of Extension Service: Farm Size and Access to Extension

The 77th round of the NSS shows that while 48.7 per cent of the agricultural households accessed technical advices from any source during the first round of visit (July–December 2018), the corresponding figure for the second round of visit (January–June 2019) of the survey was 42.2 per cent. Progressive farmers and input dealers are the major sources of technical advice or extension service. The percentages of households accessing these two sources during January–June 2019 are 20.3 per cent and 19.1 per cent, respectively. The other important sources are electronic media, print media and veterinary departments. Only a negligible portion of households accesses public sources like government extension workers and KVK.

Table 7.2 presents the proportions of agricultural households accessing extension services across states in India. The percentages of households accessing technical advice in the southern states, especially in Andhra

Table 7.2 *Percentage of Agricultural Households across States Accessing Technical Advice/Extension Service*

States (1)	Percentage (%) of Agricultural Households (2)
Andhra Pradesh	65.2
Karnataka	46.2
Kerala	61.9
Tamil Nadu	62.8
Telangana	48.0
Gujarat	45.2
Maharashtra	46.6
Rajasthan	23.5
Bihar	41.5
Haryana	63.0
Himachal Pradesh	58.8

Jharkhand	22.0
Punjab	44.7
Uttar Pradesh	50.2
Madhya Pradesh	48.5
Chhattisgarh	17.4
Assam	18.6
Odisha	26.4
West Bengal	40.7
All India	42.2

Source: Table 9, NSS report no. 587, January–June 2019.

Pradesh, Kerala and Tamil Nadu, are relatively higher. Among the states in the western part of the country, Rajasthan has the lowest proportion of agricultural households that accessed extension service from any source (23.5%). The relevant figures for the other two states in the western region, namely Gujarat and Maharashtra, are slightly higher than that at the national level. In northern India, Haryana and Himachal Pradesh have relatively higher percentages of households accessing any source of extension service. On the other hand, only half of the agricultural households in Uttar Pradesh accessed technical advice. The percentages of households accessing extension services in Bihar and Punjab are around that at the national level. Among the states in the central part of India, while the percentage of households that accessed any source of technical advice is more than that at the national level in Madhya Pradesh, the opposite is the case in Chhattisgarh. Table 7.2 further shows that only a small proportion of agricultural households in eastern India, especially in Assam and Odisha, accessed technical advice.[8]

[8] Our analysis, based on unit-level data from SAS, 2013, shows that the proportions of farmers accessing only private extension are higher than those accessing only public extension in all the regions. However, the difference is the lowest in the southern region. Further, the southern region has the highest proportion of farmers (45.81%) that access more than one source of extension. Central region has the highest and the lowest percentages of farmers accessing only private extension (22.44%) and only public extension (5.45%), respectively. To save space, we do not report the results here.

Table 7.3 shows the proportions of farmers across size classes of operational holdings that do not access any source as well as the proportions of farmers that access different sources of extension services based on unit-level data from the SAS, 2013. While the report of the 77th round of NSS (report number 587) gives the percentages of households that access any technical advice separately for two rounds of visit, we combine both the rounds of SAS, 2013, to calculate the figures in Table 7.3. As per our estimate, about 42 per cent of the farmers did not access any source of extension services in 2013.[9] The proportions of farmers that do not access extension service are higher among the landless (70.83%), marginal (49.36%) and small farmers (38.34%), and they decline as the land size increases. It may be noted that marginal and small farmers constituted about 77 per cent of the sample farmers. The fact that more than half of these farmers did not access any source of extension services is worrisome.

In terms of the sources of extension services (Table 7.3), on the whole, 13.81 per cent of farmers access only private sources, followed by only the media (10.06%) and only public extension (6.07%). In other words, the proportion of farmers accessing only public extension is the lowest. On the other hand, 28.18 per cent of the farmers access more than one source of extension services. The proportions of farmers accessing more than one source increase as the land size class increases. A comparison of the farmers accessing only public and only private extension suggests that except for the landless class, the proportions of farmers accessing the former are lower as compared to those accessing the latter in all land size classes.

[9] If a farm household accessed extension services in any one of the two or in both visits, we consider that household as one which accessed extension service while analysing the unit-level data from SAS, 2013. If we consider only visit 1, the proportion of farmers that did not access extension services at all is higher (54%) as compared to both the visits combined (42%). The lower proportion of farmers not accessing any sources of extension as derived from the combined data of visits 1 and 2 implies that some farmers did not access extension in visit 1 but accessed it in visit 2. This is also the reason why the percentage of farmers (58%) accessing any source of extension service in 2013 (Table 7.3) is higher than those in the two separate visits during 2018–2019 (i.e., the 77th round of NSS).

Table 7.3 *Percentage Share of Farm Households Accessing Extension Sources across Size Classes of Operational Holding (Visit 1 and Visit 2 Combined, 2013)*

		Access to extension sources (*N* = 19,900)					
Land Size Classes of Operational Holdings (in hectare)[a] (1)	% Share in Total Sample Farmers (2)	Do not Access Any Source (3)	Only Private (4)	Only Public (5)	Only Media (6)	More than One Source (7)	Total (8)
Landless (≤0.002)	0.12	70.83	4.17	4.17	4.17	16.67	100
Marginal (0.002–1.000)	47.15	49.36	13.77	6.00	10.09	20.78	100
Small (1.000–2.000)	29.91	38.34	13.56	6.24	10.48	31.39	100
Semi-medium (2.000–4.000)	17.99	32.81	14.13	5.86	9.33	37.87	100
Medium (4.000–10.000)	5.14	26.78	14.37	6.35	10.36	42.13	100
Large (>10.000)	0.68	24.44	16.30	7.41	7.41	44.44	100
Overall farmers	100	41.89	13.81	6.07	10.06	28.18	100

Source: Authors' calculation based on unit level data from Situation Assessment Survey of Agricultural Households, 2013.
Note: [a] Land size classes are along the lines as adopted in National Sample Survey Office (2015, p. 12)

Table 7.4 shows the purpose for which the agricultural households accessed technical advice from various sources. An overwhelming majority of the households accessed various sources of extension service for advice on issues related to cultivation. Only for animal

Table 7.4 *Percentage Distribution of Agricultural Households Accessing Technical Advice for Different Purposes from Various Sources*

Sources (1)	Percentage of Households Accessing Technical Advice for		
	Cultivation (2)	Animal Farming (3)	Fishery (4)
Progressive farmers	96.7	2.7	0.7
Input dealers	97.4	1.8	0.7
Government extension agents/ ATMA	93.0	6.2	0.7
Krishi Vigyan Kendra	94.7	0.5	4.8
Agricultural university/colleges	95.3	3.1	1.6
Private commercial agents	93.9	4.7	1.4
Veterinary departments	1.7	98.1	0.2
Cooperatives/diary cooperatives	23.5	73.5	3.0
Farmer producer organizations	87.2	10.1	2.8
Private processors	81.8	16.3	2.0
Agri-clinics and agribusiness centres	90.1	8.9	1.0
NGOs	68.6	25.5	5.9
Kisan call centres	92.3	5.2	2.5
Print media	89.7	7.9	2.4
Radio/TV/other electronic media	86.5	10.9	2.6
Smartphone apps-based information	81.5	15.0	3.4

Source: Table 9, p. A-450, NSS report no. 587, January–June 2019.

farming, veterinary departments and cooperatives/diary cooperatives are main sources of accessing technical advice. A sizable proportion of households accessed NGOs also for technical advice regarding animal farming, followed by private processors and electronic media. On the other hand, proportions of households accessing any source of extension service for fishery are negligible.

Within cultivation, households sought information/advice mainly with regard to improved seed/variety, fertilizer application and plant protection. Healthcare, breeding and feeding of animals are the main issues for which agricultural households accessed extension services. In the case of fishery, the few households that accessed technical advice did so mainly on the marketing and management aspect.

7.4.2. Reasons for Not Accessing Extension Services

A substantial portion of the farmers feels that they do not require extension services. However, figures in Table 7.5 reveal that unawareness and non-availability are major reasons for not accessing extension services from a source. For example, 45.44 per cent and 32.97 per cent of those who do not access extension from KVK state non-availability and unawareness, respectively, as the reasons for not accessing information from this source. The corresponding figures in the case of extension agents are 39.51 per cent and 37.74 per cent, respectively. The situation is the same in the case of other sources of public, private and media extension.

7.4.3. Private Extension Providers and Conflict of Interest

Goswami and Bezbaruah (2017) find that farmers in Assam who consult private extension sources, like input dealers and traders, apply higher doses of inputs like chemical fertilizers and pesticides relative to those who consult only public extension sources. This, according to them, suggests the presence of conflict of interest involving the private providers of extension services, especially sources like the ones mentioned earlier. Input dealers and traders may encourage the farmers to use more—at times, probably more than what is required—of the inputs that they sell.

Table 7.5 *Reasons Behind Not Accessing Extension Services*

Source (1)		Reasons for Not Accessing				
		Not Required (2)	Not Aware (3)	Not Available (4)	Others (5)	Total (6)
Public	Krishi Vigyan Kendra (KVK)	19.53	32.97	45.44	2.06	100
	Extension agent	20.28	37.74	39.51	2.46	100
	Veterinary department	27.33	28.86	40.61	3.20	100
	Agricultural university/college	19.15	30.70	48.20	1.95	100
Private	Progressive farmer	29.39	31.70	34.33	4.57	100
	Private commercial agents	22.96	33.53	41.27	2.24	100
	NGO	20.37	32.35	44.94	2.34	100
Media	Radio/TV/newspaper/Internet	27.86	33.24	33.54	5.36	100

Source: Same as in Table 7.3.

The findings from SAS, 2013, data, however, show (Table 7.6) only marginal difference between the average per hectare expenditures on different inputs incurred by farmers who consult only private extension sources and those by farmers that consult only public sources. While the average per hectare expenditure on all inputs by famers accessing only public sources is ₹37,417, the same is ₹37,695 for farmers accessing only private sources. In the case of purchased inputs such as seeds, fertilizers and plant protection chemicals, the average per hectare expenditure by farmers accessing only public sources is only marginally lower than that of farmers accessing only private extension services. Table 7.6 further shows that while the average per hectare expenses by the farmers who do not access any source of extension is the lowest, the same is the highest for the farmers accessing more than one source. Given the findings from Table 7.6, it can be concluded that there may be an association between the expenses on inputs and access to extension, as well as the number of sources consulted. Further, the aggregate level (at the national level) analysis does not suggest the presence of conflict of interest involving the private providers of extension services. However, analysis at the state level across different land size classes and for specific source of public and private extension services may reveal a different picture, which is beyond the scope of the current chapter.

7.4.4. Factors Affecting the Decision to Access and Choice of Sources of Extension Services

A probit model has been estimated to identify the factors that affect farmers' decision of whether to access an extension service. The results of the estimated model are presented in Table 7.7. The coefficients of the variables, namely 'gender of the head of the household', 'age of the head of the household', 'farmers as a proportion of total family size' and 'share of gross irrigated area to gross cropped area', are significant at the 10 per cent level of significance. The negative coefficient of the dummy for the gender of the household's head implies that a female-headed household is less likely to access extension services. The variable 'age of the head of the household' has a positive coefficient that suggests that the older farmers are more likely to access extension services. With regard to the variable 'farmers as a proportion of total family size', the

Table 7.6 *Mean Expenditure per Hectare (₹/ha) on Different Farm Inputs*

Farm Inputs (1)	No Extension (2)	Only Public (3)	Only Private (4)	Only Media (5)	More than One Source (6)	Overall (7)
Seeds	3,738.93	3,849.50	3,920.89	3,449.81	4,042.11	3,827.12
Fertilizers	6,950.93	7,270.20	7,821.71	8,149.33	8,547.62	7,660.94
Manure	1,067.80	1,264.01	1,070.54	1,396.78	1,647.41	1,276.40
Plant protection chemicals	1,845.80	2,131.59	2,335.49	2,122.31	2,770.41	2,219.08
Diesel and electricity	1,926.50	1,873.02	2,398.75	1,960.30	2,207.60	2,071.07
Human labour	6,701.45	9,713.52	8,515.92	10,562.05	11,678.46	8,925.36
Animal labour	429.80	601.04	428.10	500.93	534.76	476.70
Overall inputs	32,657.05	37,417.77	37,695.56	36,512.22	42,193.80	36,716.52

Source: Same as in Table 7.3.

Table 7.7 *Results of the Probit Model*

Dependent variable: 1 = Access to at least one extension source; 0 otherwise	
Explanatory Variables (1)	Coefficients/Values (2)
Dummy: 1 = female headed HH	−0.0769[a] (0.0360)
Age of HH head	0.0102[a] (0.00434)
Square of age of household age	−0.0000760 (0.0000404)
Education of HH head (Base: Illiterate)	
Literate: non-formal	0.265[b] (0.101)
Formal: below primary	0.170[c] (0.0316)
Formal: below secondary	0.206[c] (0.0245)
Formal: secondary and above	0.270[c] (0.0263)
Farmers as a proportion of total family size	0.0970[a] (0.0399)
Cropping intensity	−0.212[c] (0.0338)
Crop diversification (HFI)	−0.629[c] (0.0655)
Share of gross irrigated area to gross cropped area	0.0594[a] (0.0266)
Dummy: 1 = cultivation as principal income source	0.0384 (0.0232)
Per hectare cultivation expenditure (₹/ha)	0.0000006 (0.00000032)
Operational holding (measured in ha)	0.0681[c] (0.00779)
Dummy: 1 = aware about MSP for at least one crop	0.314[c] (0.0227)
Social Group (Base: General)	
Scheduled Tribes	−0.187[c] (0.0340)
Scheduled Castes	−0.0859[b] (0.0319)
Other Backward Castes	−0.0179 (0.0226)
Locational dummies (base: southern region)	
Western region	−0.528[c] (0.0359)

(Table 7.7 Continued)

(Table 7.7 Continued)

Dependent variable: 1 = Access to at least one extension source; 0 otherwise	
Explanatory Variables (1)	**Coefficients/Values (2)**
Northern region	−0.660[c] (0.0306)
Central region	−0.400[c] (0.0418)
Eastern region	−0.397[c] (0.0329)
Constant	0.571[c] (0.142)
Observations	19,736
Log pseudo-likelihood	−12,579.267
Wald chi² [22]	1,504.09
Prob > chi²	0.000[c]
Pseudo R^2	0.06

Source: The authors.
Note: Robust standard errors within ( ); degree of freedom within [ ]; and $^{a}p < 0.10$, $^{b}p < 0.05$ and $^{c}p < 0.01$.

positive coefficient implies that the higher is the proportion of farmers out of total family members, the larger is the chance that the household shall consult extension sources. On the other hand, the positive coefficient of the variable 'share of gross irrigated area to gross cropped area' suggests that the households with higher shares of irrigated land in cropped area are more likely to access extension services.

The variable showing the level of education has four dummies with 'illiterate' as the base category. While the coefficient of the dummy for 'literate: non-formal' is positive and significant at the 5 per cent level, the coefficients of the other three dummies: 'Formal: below primary', 'Formal: below secondary' and 'Formal: secondary and above' are positive and significant at the 1 per cent level of significance. The results related to education imply that literate farmers are more likely to access extension services.

The variables 'cropping intensity' and 'crop diversification (HHI)' have negative coefficients that are significant at the 1 per cent level of significance. The negative coefficient of 'cropping intensity' implies that farmers who cultivate the land more intensively are less likely to access extension services. On the other hand, farmers cultivating a diversified portfolio of crops are more likely to access extension services.

The coefficient of 'operational holdings' and that of the dummy for 'awareness about MSP for at least one crop' are significant and positive at the 1 percent level of significance. The positive coefficient of farm size in terms of operational holdings indicates that large farmers are more likely to consult extension sources. Figures in Table 7.3 also indicate this result. Further, the farmers who are aware of the MSP provided by the government are likely to access extension services relative to those who are not aware of the same.

In terms of social group where the base category is general, the coefficients of dummies for Scheduled Tribes (ST) and Scheduled Castes (SC) are negative and significant at the 1 per cent and 5 per cent levels of significance, respectively. In other words, ST and SC farmers are less likely to access extension services relative to general category farmers. Finally, all the locational dummies are negative and significant at the 1 per cent level of significance. The result with respect to locational dummies indicates that famers in all other regions are less likely to access extension services relative to farmers in the southern regions.

Table 7.8 presents the results of the multinomial logit model that identify the factors affecting farmers' choice of sources of extension services. The coefficient of the variable 'age of the head of the household' is positive and significant at the 10 per cent level of significance for public extension. This implies that relatively older farmers are likely to access information from public sources as compared to only media as source of extension. However, the negative and significant (at the 10% level of significance) coefficient of 'square of the age of the head of the household' indicates that beyond a certain level as the farmer's age further increases, the likelihood of consulting public extension relative to the media declines.

The coefficients of three education dummies, namely 'formal: below primary', 'formal: below secondary' and 'formal: secondary and above', are negative and significant in the case of private extension. In

Table 7.8 *Results of Multinomial Logit Model*

Explanatory Variables (1)	Only Private Extension (2)	Only Public Extension (3)
Dummy: 1 = female headed HH	−0.168 (0.125)	0.0814 (0.140)
Age of HH head	−0.00202 (0.0146)	0.0458[a] (0.0188)
Square of age of household age	−0.000194 (0.000135)	−0.000406[a] (0.000172)
Education of HH head (base: illiterate)		
Literate: non-formal	0.0826 (0.319)	−0.139 (0.402)
Formal: below primary	−0.472[c] (0.106)	−0.228 (0.132)
Formal: below secondary	−0.556[c] (0.0857)	0.0410 (0.100)
Formal: secondary and above	−0.994[c] (0.0900)	−0.328[b] (0.108)
Farmers as a proportion of total family size	0.485[c] (0.139)	0.756[c] (0.158)
Cropping intensity	−0.226[a] (0.114)	−0.0864 (0.131)
Crop diversification measured using HFI	−0.255 (0.224)	0.0604 (0.257)
Share of gross irrigated area to gross cropped area	1.157[c] (0.0903)	0.423[c] (0.104)
Dummy: 1 = cultivation as principal income source	0.181[a] (0.0765)	−0.139 (0.0863)
Per hectare cultivation expenditure (₹/ha)	0.00000085 (0.0000007)	0.0000002 (0.0000009)
Operational holding (measured in ha)	−0.000088 (0.000426)	−0.00087 (0.00052)

Dummy: 1 = aware about MSP for at least one crop	−0.367[c] (0.074)	−0.12 (0.085)
Social Group (base: general)		
Scheduled Tribes	−0.108 (0.123)	0.114 (0.131)
Scheduled Castes	0.622[c] (0.111)	0.277[a] (0.131)
Other Backward Castes	0.311[c] (0.0758)	−0.0566 (0.0889)
Agricultural and ecological region (base: southern region)		
Western region	1.24[c] (0.13)	0.62[c] (0.14)
Northern region	0.41[c] (0.10)	−0.33[b] (0.11)
Central region	1.39[c] (0.14)	0.16 (0.16)
Eastern region	0.55[c] (0.11)	0.01 (0.15)
Constant	0.11 (0.48)	−1.97[b] (0.60)
Observation	5922	
Log pseudo-likelihood	−5738.35	
Wald chi^2 [44]	818.07	
Prob > chi^2	0.000[c]	
Pseudo R^2	0.08	

Source: The authors.

Note: Robust standard errors in (); degree of freedom within []; and $^{a}p < 0.10$, $^{b}p < 0.05$ and $^{c}p < 0.01$.

the case of public extension, the coefficient of only one dummy, that is, 'formal: secondary and above', is significant and negative. This result implies that educated farmers with formal education prefer the media (base category) to private and public extension.

Households with a higher share of family members as farmers prefer private and public extension services to the media services. The coefficients of the variable are positive and significant at the 1 per cent level for both private and public extension services. The results of the model also suggest that the farm households with higher cropping intensity are more likely to access extension from media than that from private sources. Furthermore, the farm households with larger shares of irrigated land in total cropped land prefer to access extension from private and public sources rather than that from the media. The coefficient of the dummy variable 'cultivation as principal income source' is positive and significant at the 10 per cent level of significance for private extension. This result suggests that households where the main source of income is cultivation prefer private sources to the media to access extension services. On the other hand, awareness about MSP makes a farm household less likely to access extension from private sources relative to the media. The coefficient of the dummy for 'awareness about MSP for at least one crop' is negative and significant at 1 per cent in the case of private extension. In terms of social group, farmers belonging to Schedule Castes and Other Backward Castes are more likely to access extension services from private sources rather than that from the media as compared to the general category farmers. The coefficients of the dummies for these two social groups are positive and significant at the 1 per cent level of significance. Farmers from Schedule Castes also prefer public sources of extension to the media as compared to the general category farmers. The results for locational dummies suggest that farmers in all other regions prefer private sources to the media as compared to those in the southern region. All the locational dummies are positive and significant at the 1 per cent level of significance for private extension. On the other hand, while farmers in the western region prefer public sources of extension to the media as compared to those in the southern region, the opposite is the case in the northern region.

7.5. DISCUSSION OF RESULTS

The analysis of data does not present a very encouraging picture of the state of agricultural extension services in India. As Table 7.3 shows, only 58 per cent of the farmers accessed extension services in 2013. In fact, if only one visit is considered instead of both the visits together, the figure will be even lower. The data from the 77th round of NSS also shows the dismal state of extension services even in 2018–2019. Except for some states in the southern and the northern regions of India, the percentage of farmers not accessing extension services is very high in all other states (Table 7.2). The field-level studies by Reardon et al. (2011a) in Uttar Pradesh from the northern region and Goswami and Bezbaruah (2017) in Assam from the Eastern region confirm our aggregate-level analysis. Lower access to extension poses a big challenge in the diffusion of technology in agriculture that in turn may limit the realization of the potential benefits of efforts to increase productivity and farm income.

The problem of not accessing extension service becomes compounded when we look at the composition of those who do not access extension by land size classes of their operational holdings. Table 7.3 reveals that substantial portions of landless, marginal and small farmers do not access extension services. Given that an overwhelming majority of Indian farmers are small and marginal farmers (75% in the sample of the data set used in this chapter), their lower access to extension services makes technology diffusion more challenging, which has far-reaching implications.

The phenomenon of non-access to extension services has two sides, namely the demand side and the supply side. Farmers may not demand extension if they think it is not required or useful. Table 7.5 shows that a substantial portion of farmers think that they do not need extension services from any source. Farmers may or may not need extension services based on the crops that they grow and also the information they receive from the sources. If the crops grown are traditional ones, and the information provided is not effective, it is natural that demand for information will be less. On the supply side, non-availability of any source of extension service is also a major reason of non-accessing extension service (Table 7.5). Besides, a sizable proportion of farmers are not aware about extension information. Therefore, efforts to increase the awareness level of the farmers about extension services are important alongside the improved availability of better extension services.

While the provision of extension through private sources is demand-driven, public extension is usually supply-led. However, the condition of the public extension is very disquieting. Table 7.3 shows that the proportion of Indian farmers who consult only public sources is a meagre 6.07 per cent.

Figures in Table 7.9 provide an explanation of the disappointing state of public extension. Overall, there is only one extension official against as many as 1,162 operational holdings. The ratio of extension official to operational holdings is the highest in the southern region. India has a very high ratio of extension workers to farmers (1:1,162), and about 30 per cent of the sanctioned positions have remained vacant (Ministry of Agriculture & Farmers' Welfare 2017). These numbers clearly establish that the public extension network is grossly inadequate, and the extension workers are overburdened (Glendenning et al. 2010; Goswami and Bezbaruah 2017; Gulati et al. 2018; Kokate et al. 2020; Ministry of Agriculture & Farmers' Welfare 2017). Furthermore, those who work as extension staff are not well qualified and skilled, and they lack adequate training on updated extension methods and communication skills. Goswami and Bezbaruah (2017) report in their study that a sizable portion of the surveyed farmers in Assam believe that the information provided by village-level extension workers on basic items like seeds and fertilizers is not useful. These staff rarely make field visits because of the lack of operational fund (Birner and Anderson 2007; Glendenning et al. 2010). Even when they visit the farmers, they discriminate against small farmers (Ramachandran 1974). Goswami and Bezbaruah (2017), in fact, suggest a nexus between the big farmers and the extension workers, which, however, may be due to the numerous constraints that the extension workers face.

In addition, concerns are being raised about the incentives these extension staff receive. Further, the bureaucratic procedures in the

Table 7.9 *Manpower in Agricultural Extension across Agro-ecological Regions and States*

Agro-ecological Regions (1)	Operational Holdings Per extension Official across Region (2)	States (3)	Operational Holdings Per Extension Official across States (4)
Southern region	1,830	Andhra Pradesh	3,162
		Karnataka	2,428
		Kerala	1,737
		Tamil Nadu	976
		Telangana	NA
Western region	1,029	Gujarat	1,395
		Maharashtra	869
		Rajasthan	1,254
Northern region	1,397	Bihar	1,583
		Haryana	536
		Himachal Pradesh	886
		Jharkhand	656
		Punjab	753
		Uttar Pradesh	1,798
Central region	836	Madhya Pradesh	823
		Chhattisgarh	869
Eastern region	1,139	Assam	979
		Odisha	1,230
		West Bengal	1,156
Across India			1,162

Source: Computed based on data from the Ministry of Agriculture and Farmers' Welfare (2017, 72).

public extension system provide lesser flexibility for extension staff to work as per local demand. Often, the highly centralized bureaucratic structure is blamed for creating a barrier in coordination between the research wing and extension wing. There is also evidence of both these wings often competing for budget allocation (Anderson and Feder 2007; Glendenning et al. 2010). In terms of dealing with the farmers, public extension staff are often criticized for treating farmers as a state subject rather than clients or customers. Famers who are poor, female and belonging to marginalized communities often find it difficult in accessing public extension services (Glendenning et al. 2010). Just like in the public extension system, the extension staff in the private extension services are not well qualified, unskilled and may not be up to date with new knowledge of extension activities. They are criticized for working in the commercial interest of the private companies, promoting the use of purchased inputs like chemical fertilizers and pesticides (Glendenning et al. 2010; Goswami and Bezbaruah 2017). In the case of the progressive farmers, they may be reluctant to disseminate the paid technologies and knowledge to their fellow farmers (Glendenning et al. 2010).

As for the decision whether to access extension services, the estimated probit model suggests that a female-headed household is less likely to access extension services. Existing literature also suggests that female-headed households find it difficult to access extension services (Glendenning et al. 2010). Given the important role that women play in Indian agriculture, agricultural technology must reach women. This is especially the case when the participation of women in agriculture is increasing (Ministry of Finance 2018). The results also confirm the importance of farmer's education. Farmers with formal education are more likely to access education. In fact, the coefficient of the dummy for successive higher level of formal education is higher, which implies that the chance of accessing extension increases as the level of education of the farmer also increases. Educated farmers are likely to be more willing to adopt new technology, and hence, their informational requirement is high (Rogers 2003). Another variable that is significant with a positive coefficient is 'share of gross irrigated area to gross cropped area'. Irrigation allows farmers to cultivate a diversified portfolio of crop, which increases their likelihood of accessing extension services. That is also the reason that the variable 'crop diversification' has a positive impact on the probability of accessing extension services (Goswami 2018). The only surprising result from the probit model is the negative coefficient of 'cropping intensity'. Goswami (2012) and Saud (2021) show that access to extension services does not have any impact on cropping intensity. This could be the case when the extension service providers offer only basic information related to the application of inputs like seed and fertilizer. In fact, when a farmer cultivates land intensively, and gains sufficient knowledge about the application of basic inputs, her dependence on basic information decreases. The results also suggest that large farmers are more likely to consult extension sources. Das and Das (2018) also report a similar finding. Further, the farmers who are aware of the MSP provided by the government are likely to access extension services. These farmers may receive information on MSP through the extension workers as well as the media, which increases the probability of these farmers accessing other information also besides that on MSP. In terms of social groups, results indicate that SC and ST farmers are less likely to access extension services relative to general category farmers. Krishna et al. (2019) also find that SC and ST farmers have a lower probability of accessing the public extension services mainly due to their poorer resource endowment. Finally, the result with respect to locational dummies indicates that famers in all other regions are less likely to access extension services relative to farmers in the southern region. It is interesting to note that despite having the highest number of operational holdings per extension officials, the proportions of farmers accessing public extension services in some of the southern states are relatively higher. Thus, it may not be only a function of availability, and there may be other factors that encourage farmers in these states to access extension services. This requires further investigation.

With regard to the choice of source of extension, it is interesting to note that beyond a certain level of the farmer's age, the likelihood of consulting public extension relative to the media declines. Given the poor state of public extension as discussed earlier, this finding is not surprising. The results of the multinomial logit also show that educated farmers with formal education prefer the media to private and public extension. Farmers who have reading capabilities may be interested on a varied nature of information that they can access from the media. Further, farm households with higher shares of irrigated land in total cropped land prefer to access extension from private and public sources. Application of inputs with irrigation may require a demonstration by knowledgeable persons, which is not possible if information is accessed through the media. Our results further show that households, wherein cultivation is the main source of income, prefer private sources to the media to access extension services. Given the limitation of media as a source of extension and the sorry state of public extension, the dependence of such households on private extension is not surprising. Awareness about MSP makes a farm household more likely to access extension from the media relative to private sources for the reason discussed earlier. In terms of social group, SC farmers are more likely to access extension services from private and public sources rather than that from media as compared to the general category farmers. The relatively lower level of literacy among the SC population may be the reason why these farmers prefer to access extension through interpersonal sources rather than through the media. The results for locational dummies suggest that farmers in all other regions prefer private sources to the media as compared to those in the southern region. As discussed earlier, it is difficult to ascribe the preference of farmers from a specific region to certain factors and hence requires further investigation.

7.6. CONCLUSION AND POLICY IMPLICATIONS

This chapter discusses the evolution of the agricultural extension and its status in India. Our analysis, based on data from the 77th round of NSS and SAS, 2013, reveals that notwithstanding regional variations, a substantial proportion of farmers do not access any source of extension. In terms of sources, public extension is the least preferred one.

The estimated probit model identifies age, sex and education of the head of the household, proportion of farmers among the family members, crop intensity, crop diversification, irrigation, farm size, awareness about MSP, social group and the region to which a farmer belongs as the factors that affect the decision to access extension. These factors also influence the choice of the source of the extension service.

Given the numerous problems confronting the Indian agricultural extension service, there are multiple dimensions that require immediate attention. The first of those interventions could be in the public extension service. Since private extension is likely to provide only the information that is rival and excludable in nature, the presence of public extension is essential in order to improve the coverage of extension services. Public extension in India, however, requires improvements in many areas. Strengthening and expanding the network of public extension services and improving the quantity and quality of manpower in the public extension sector through enhanced budgetary allocations are two areas of urgent policy action. Our results show that female-headed households and SC and ST farmers are less likely to access extension services. The mechanism of providing extension services, therefore, needs to be more inclusive.

A serious problem that the current extension service delivery system suffers from is that a substantial portion of small and marginal farmers do not access extension services. As discussed earlier, non-availability and unawareness are two major reasons for not accessing extension services. Hence, besides expanding the network of extension services to improve availability, farmers also need to be made aware about the need and availability of extension services. One possible way to reach out to more farmers, especially the small and marginal farmers, is to organize the farmers into groups through field management committees and such similar institutions. If the farmers are organized into groups, it will be easier for the extension workers also to reach out to more farmers with less efforts and costs. Encouraging the use of ICT can also improve the reach of the extension service providers.

Another way to improve the delivery of and access to extension services is to link extension with agribusiness. Farmers producing a similar portfolio of crops may be encouraged to organize themselves into producers' organization and link themselves with agribusiness. If the farmers are organized into producers' organization, the organization on behalf of the individual farmers, can easily reach out to various sources of extension providers. Alternatively, agribusinesses, both private and public, can be encouraged to develop complete supply chains wherein they provide extension services to the individual or group of farmers at the back end.

A state-level study has shown that the information provided through the current extension system, especially the public extension, is very limited in scope (Goswami and Bezbaruah 2017). With the change in the cropping pattern, the extension requirements of the farmers are bound to change. Hence, the extension service delivery mechanism has to evolve over time by keeping in mind the changing need of the farmers. Extension workers should be trained to provide crop-specific information rather than a general set of information. It has also been observed that animal farming can be a major driver of farmers' income (Chandrasekhar and Mehrotra 2016). Hence, besides crops, extension service delivery mechanism should be well equipped to provide information on animal husbandry and other dimensions of rural livelihood so that the objective of increasing farmers' income can indeed be realized.

REFERENCES

Adhiguru, P., P. S. Birthal, and G. K. Kumar. 2009, June. 'Strengthening Pluralistic Agricultural Information Delivery Systems in India'. *Agricultural Economics Research Review* 22: 71–79.

Anderson, J. R., and G. Feder. 2004. 'Agricultural Extension: Good Intentions and Hard Realities'. *World Bank Research Observer* 19, no. 1: 41–60.

———. 2007. 'Agricultural Extension'. In *Handbook of Agricultural Economics*, Vol. 3, edited by R. E. Evenson and P. Pingali, 2343–2378. Amsterdam: North Holland.

Anderson, J. R., G. Feder, and S. Ganguly. 2006. 'The Rise and Fall of Training and Visit Extension: An Asian Mini-drama with an African Epilogue'. World Bank Policy Research Working Paper No. 3928. Washington, DC: World Bank.

Birkhaeuser, D., R. E. Evenson, and G. Feder. 1991. 'The Economic Impact of Agricultural Extension: A Review'. *Economic Development and Cultural Change* 39, no. 3: 607–650.

Birner, R., and J. R. Anderson. 2007. 'How to Make Agricultural Extension Demand-driven? The Case of India's Agricultural Extension Policy'. IFPRI Discussion Paper No. 00729. New York, NY: IFPRI.

Birner, R., K. E. Davis, J. L. Pender, E. Nkonya, P. Anandjayasekeram, J. Ekboir, A. N. Mbabu et al. 2006. 'From "Best Practice" to "Best Fit": A Framework for Designing and Analyzing Pluralistic Agricultural Advisory Services Worldwide'. DSGD Discussion Paper No. 37. Washington, DC: IFPRI.

Birner, R., K. Davis, J. Pender, E. Nkonya, P. Anandajayasekeram, J. Ekboir, A. Mbabu et al. 2009. 'From Best Practice to Best Fit: A Framework for Designing and Analyzing Pluralistic Agricultural Advisory Services Worldwide'. *The Journal of Agricultural Education and Extension* 15, no. 4: 341–355.

Chakravarty, A. 2020. 'Information Seeking by Agricultural Households in India: Determinants of Access and Choice of Sources'. Working Paper No. 499. Thiruvananthapuram: Centre for Development Studies.

Chand, R. 2017. 'Doubling Farmers' Income: Rationale, Strategy, Prospects and Action Plan'. NITI Policy Paper No. 1/2017. New Delhi: National Institution for Transforming India.

Chandrakant, A. S., S. Ghosh, and R. B. Singandhupe. 2017. 'Agricultural Information Needs and their Fulfillment as Perceived by the Farmers in Changing Agricultural Scenario in Maharashtra'. *Indian Journal of Extension Education* 53, no. 2: 11–17.

Chandrasekhar, S., and N. Mehrotra. 2016, 30 April. 'What Would It Take? Doubling Farmers' Incomes by 2022'. *Economic & Political Weekly*. https://www.epw.in/journal/2016/18/commentary/doubling-farmers-incomes-2022.html (accessed on 21 February 2022).

Chatterjee, B. 1957. 'Rural Community Development in India'. *Civilisations* 7, no. 2: 187–198.

Cook, B. R., P. Satizábal, and J. Curnow. 2021. 'Humanising Agricultural Extension: A Review'. *World Development* 140: 1–19.

Das, B., and A. Das. 2018. 'Technology Adoption in Indian Agriculture and Its Determinants : An Inter-state Analysis'. In *Indian Agriculture after the Green Revolution*, edited by B. Goswami, M. P. Bezbaruah, and R. Mandal, 112–129. Abingdon: Routledge.

Feldman, A. M., and R. Serrano, eds. 2006. *Welfare Economics and Social Choice Theory. Welfare Economics and Social Choice Theory*. New York, NY: Springer.

Ferroni, Macro and Y. Zhou. 2013. 'Review of Agricultural Extension in India'. In *India 2040 Transforming Indian Agriculture Productivity, Markets and Institutions*, edited by Marco Ferroni, 187–237. New Delhi: SAGE Publications.

Glendenning, C. J., S. C. Babu, and K. Asenso-Okyere. 2010. 'Review of Agricultural Extension in India'. IFPRI Discussion Paper No. 00689. Washington, DC: IFPRI.

Goswami, B. 2012. Economic Implication of Tenancy: A Study in Assam's Agrarian Set-up. Unpublished PhD Thesis. Guwahati: Department of Economics, Gauhati University.

———. 2018. 'Rental Market of Agricultural Land: Changing Context and Need for Tenancy Reform'. In *Indian Agriculture after The Green Revolution: Changes and Challenges*, edited by B. Goswami, M. P. Bezbaruah, and R. Mandal, 29–45. Abingdon: Routledge.

Goswami, B., and R. J. Bezbaruah. 2017. 'Comparing Public and Private Agricultural Extension Services : Insights from the Brahmaputra Valley of Assam'. *Review of Rural Affairs* 52, no. 52: 72–80.

Gulati, A., P. Sharma, A. Samantara, and P. Terway. 2018. *Agriculture Extension System in India—Review of Current Status, Trends and the Way Forward*. New Delhi: Indian Council for Research on International Economic Relations.

Indian Council of Agricultural Research. 2020. *Handbook of Agricultural Extension*. New Delhi: Indian Council of Agricultural Research.

Jaffee, S., and J. Srivastava. 1994. 'The Roles of the Private and Public Sectors in Enhancing the Performance of Seed Systems'. *The World Bank Research Observer* 9, no. 1: 97–117.

Kessides, C. 1993. 'Institutional Options for the Provision of Infrastructure'. World Bank Discussion Papers No. 212. Washington, DC: The World Bank.

Kokate, K. D., M. Chander, P. K. Rathod, and S. Sarkar. 2020. 'Agricultural Extension Approaches in India'. In *Handbook of Agricultural Extension*, 32–71. New Delhi: Indian Council of Agricultural Research.

Krishna, V. V., L. M. Aravalath, and S. Vikraman. 2019. 'Does Caste Determine Farmer Access to Quality Information'? *PLoS ONE* 14, no. 1: 1–22.

Lampach, N., N. Van Phu, and N. To-The. 2021. 'The Effect of Agricultural Extension Programs on Technical Efficiency of Crop Farms in Low and Middle-Income Countries'. *SSRN Electronic Journal*. https://papers.ssrn.com/sol3/papers.cfm?abstract_id=3208034 (accessed 16 July 2021).

Lekshmi, P. S. S., K. Chandrakandan, and N. Balasubramani. 2006. 'Yield Gap Analysis among Rice Growers in North Eastern Zone of Tamil Nadu'. In *Agriculture Situation in India*, 729–733. http://eprints.cmfri.org.in/7958/1/swathileshmi_yield_gap-729-733.pdf (accessed on 21 February 2022).

Ministry of Agriculture & Farmers' Welfare. 2017. *Report of the Committee on Doubling Farmers' Income. Volume XI: Empowering the Farmers through Extension and Knowledge Dissemination*. New Delhi: Ministry of Agriculture & Farmers' Welfare. https://agricoop.gov.in/sites/default/files/DFI%20Volume%2011.pdf (accessed on 21 February 2022).

Ministry of Finance. 2018. *Economic Survey 2017–18*. New Delhi: Ministry of Finance.

Moore, M. 1984. 'Institutional Development, the World Bank, and India's New Agricultural Extension Programme'. *The Journal of Development Studies* 20, no. 4: 303–317.

Musgrave, R. A., and P. B. Musgrave, eds. 1989. *Public Finance in Theory and Practice*. Singapore: McGraw-Hill.

Nandi, R., and S. Nedumaran. 2019. 'Agriculture Extension System in India: A Meta-analysis'. *Research Journal of Agricultural Sciences* 10, no. 3: 473–479.

National Sample Survey Office. 2015. *Household Ownership and Operational Holdings in India*. Kolkata: National Sample Survey Office.

NITI Aayog. 2017. *India: Three Year Action Agenda 2017–18 to 2019–20*. New Delhi: NITI Aayog.

Ramachandran, P. K. 1974. A Multivariate Study on Information Source Utilization of Big, Medium and Small Farmers. Unpublished PhD Thesis. New Delhi: Faculty of Post-Graduate School, Indian Agricultural Research Institute.

Ramaswami, B., P. S. Birthal, and P. K. Joshi. 2006. 'Efficiency and Distribution in Contract Farming: The Case of Indian Poultry Growers'. MTID Discussion Paper, No. 91. New Delhi: IFPRI.

Reardon, T., B. Minten, M. P. Mehta, S. Das Gupta, S. Rajendran, and S. Singh. 2011a. *Agri-services in Uttar Pradesh for Inclusive Rural Growth: Baseline Survey Findings and Implications*. Report Submitted to USAID. New Delhi: USAID.

Reardon, T., B. Minten, M. P. Mehta, S. Das Gupta, S. Rajendran, S. Singh, A. Sarawgi, and B. Beohar. 2011b. *Agri-services in Madhya Pradesh for Inclusive Rural Growth: Baseline Survey Findings and Implications*. Report Submitted to USAID. New Delhi: USAID.

Rogers, E. M., ed. 2003. *Diffusion of Innovations*. New York, NY: Free Press.

Rogers, E. M., and F. F. Shoemaker, eds. 1971. *Communication of Innovations: A Cross-cultural Approach*. New York, NY: Free Press.

Ryan, B., and N. Gross. 1950. 'Acceptance and Diffusion of Hybrid Corn Seed in Two Iowa Communities'. *Iowa Agriculture and Home Economics Experiment Station Research Bulletin* 29, no. 372: 663–708.

Sajesh, V. K., and A. Suresh. 2016. 'Public-sector Agricultural Extension in India: A Note'. *Review of Agrarian Studies* 6, no. 1: 116–131.

Saud, J. 2021. 'Cropping Intensity, Its Determinants and Farmers' Income with Special Reference to the Brahmaputra Valley in Northeast India'. *Acta Scientific Agriculture* 5, no. 6: 49–58.

Singh, K. M., M. S. Meena, and A. K. Jha. 2009. 'Impact Assessment of Agricultural Extension Reforms in Bihar'. *Indian Research Journal of Extension Education* 9, no. 2: 110–114.

Singh, S. 2005. 'Contract Farming for Agricultural Development: Review of Theory and Practice with Special Reference to India'. Working Papers No. 2. New Delhi: Center for Trade and Development.

Sulaiman, R., A. Hall, and N. Suresh. 2005. 'Effectiveness of Private Sector Extension in India and Lessons for the New Extension Policy Agenda'. Network Paper No. 141. London: Agricultural Research and Extension Network.

Takahashi, K., R. Muraoka, and K. Otsuka. 2020. 'Technology Adoption, Impact, and Extension in Developing Countries' Agriculture: A Review of the Recent Literature'. *Agricultural Economics* 51, no. 1: 31–45.

Umali-Deininger, Dina. 1997. 'Public and Private Agricultural Extension: Partners or Rivals'? *World Bank Research Observer* 12, no. 2: 203–224.

Umali, D. L., and L. Schwartz. 1994. 'Public and Private Agricultural Extension: Beyond Traditional Frontiers'. World Bank Discussion Papers No. 236. Washington, DC: The World Bank.

Van den Ban, A. W., and H. S. Hawkins, eds. 2002. *Agricultural Extension*. New Delhi: CBS Publishers.

Chapter 8

Agricultural Credit in India

The Dominance of Informal Sources

Abhijit Sharma and Prasenjit Bujar Baruah

8.1. INTRODUCTION

One of the characteristics of the agricultural sector is that it needs investment in the initial period of production and gets the return after harvesting. Small and marginal farmers have low level of income, so they have lower savings. They need more capital than they can generate through savings. Thus, access to adequate and affordable credit is the precondition for agricultural development. Das and Bezbaruah (2020) report that access to credit has a positive impact on cropping intensity, crop diversification and agricultural production. Credit is not a primary factor of production. But access to other factors is linked to their access to credit. Farm households need credit for different purposes. First, they need credit for capital investment, that is, for investment in agricultural capital goods, such as tractors, power tillers, construction of guard wall around the paddy ground and building irrigation infrastructure. The absence of credit facilities may adversely affect the adoption of new technology in agriculture (Samah et al. 2009). Although credit for fixed investment is necessary for the growth of agriculture, the credit for working capital expenditure and consumption purposes is more important for the small and marginal farmers. Rapid commercialization of agriculture has increased the need for credit, especially for working capital. Farmers also need credit for spending on working capital like expenditure on labour wage and to purchase different inputs like chemical fertilizer or HYV seeds. The cost of cultivation in India has increased in the post-reform period due to an increase in input cost such as cost of fertilizers, irrigation charges, machine labour and seeds (Bezbaruah and Hassan 2018). Along with expenditure on agriculture for productive purposes, they also need credit for consumption purposes. Credit for consumption purposes is needed to link the gap between the cultivating and harvesting period. They also need credit to smoothen the consumption expenditure if there is crop failure. Thus, the absence of crop insurance also increases the demand for credit for consumption purposes. Moreover, fluctuation in wage rate between the lean season and harvesting season also increases the demand for consumption loan. The seasonality of agricultural production and low income of the farmers make demand for credit more important. Besides the aforementioned points, loan is also taken for social ceremonies such as wedding, birth and death rituals.

In India, at the onset of the Green Revolution, the financial needs of the farms have also increased. The government, along with providing subsidized inputs and marketing facilities to the agricultural sector, also introduced policies for easier financial access by the farm households. Such policies include the nationalization of commercial banks, establishment of regional rural banks and establishment of National Bank for Agriculture and Rural Development (NABARD). As a result of such policies, there was an expansion in rural branches of commercial banks, and credit penetration in rural areas also increased. During the post-liberalization period, reforms took place in the financial sector along with other sectors in India. One of the important key reforms in the banking sector was the recognition of profitability as an important performance of the banks, resulting in the recognition of loan defaults. As a result, provision of credit to the agricultural and rural sectors was adversely affected due to loan defaults and poor recovery (Bezbaruah 2018). Along with the reduction in credit penetration in the rural areas, there was also a reduction in government support to the agricultural sector in the form of reduction in fertilizer and electricity subsidy.

All these factors had increased the cost of cultivation. It contributed towards reduction in farmers' income. There was an increase in farmers' suicide rate during the post-reform period up to 2005. It was hypothesized that one of the common causes of farmers' suicide throughout the country was their indebtedness (Bezbaruah and Hassan 2018). The indebtedness was not only to the moneylenders but also to other informal and formal sources like banks. All these factors have inspired us to investigate into different aspects of agricultural credit in India.

This chapter consists of five sections. Section 8.2 tries to analyse agricultural credit penetration in India. Section 8.3 discusses the causes behind the dominance of informal sources of credit in agriculture. Section 8.4 discusses about the government policies and programmes to expand institutional credit to the agricultural sector in India. Section 8.5 is concludes the chapter with a discussion on policy implications.

8.2. AGRICULTURAL CREDIT PENETRATION IN INDIA

In order to understand the penetration of agricultural credit and its impact on rural development, it is important to know the extent of indebtedness of the agricultural households. A household is identified as indebted if it has outstanding loan. Table 8.1 presents the indebtedness of farm households across different states in India. At the all-India level, 50.2 per cent of the farm households had access to credit during 2019. Moreover, there is widespread variation across the states regarding indebtedness of farm households. While, in Andhra Pradesh, more than 93 per cent of the farm households are indebted, in Nagaland, only 6.0 per cent of the farm households are indebted. While a larger percentage of the farm households are indebted in the southern states, indebtedness is very low in the north-eastern and hilly states. Although the percentage of agricultural households indebted at the all-India level fluctuates around 50 per cent during the past three decades, the fluctuation is higher among some states. For example, in Uttar Pradesh, only 7.2 per cent of the agricultural households had an outstanding loan during 2003, which increased to 43.8 per cent during 2013, and then it marginally declined to 41.9 per cent. On the other hand, the percentage of indebted households in Nagaland, Mizoram and Sikkim had declined significantly during this period. Along with the extent of indebtedness,

Table 8.1 *Percentage Distribution of Indebted Agricultural Households across Different States over the Years*

State	2003 (%)	2013 (%)	2019 (%)
Andhra Pradesh	82	92.9	93.2
Arunachal Pradesh	5.9	19.1	12.5
Assam	18.1	17.5	31.0
Bihar	33	42.5	39.7
Chhattisgarh	40.2	37.2	31.2
Gujarat	51.9	42.6	42.5
Haryana	53.1	42.3	47.5
Himachal Pradesh	33.4	27.9	29.2
Jammu and Kashmir	31.8	30.7	31.9
Jharkhand	20.9	28.9	25.3
Karnataka	61.6	77.3	67.6
Kerala	64.4	77.7	69.9
Madhya Pradesh	50.8	45.7	48.4
Maharashtra	54.8	57.3	54.0
Manipur	24.8	23.9	20.6
Meghalaya	4.1	2.4	9.1
Mizoram	23.6	6.2	8.0
Nagaland	36.5	2.5	6.0
Odisha	47.8	57.5	61.2
Punjab	65.4	53.2	54.4
Rajasthan	52.4	61.8	60.3
Sikkim	38.8	14.3	10.6
Tamil Nadu	74.5	82.5	65.1
Telangana	–	89.1	91.7
Tripura	49.2	22.9	47.7
Uttarakhand	40.2	50.8	46.6
Uttar Pradesh	7.2	43.8	41.9
West Bengal	50.1	51.5	50.8
Group of Union Territories	50.8	37.2	27.5
All India	48.6	51.9	50.2

Sources: GOI (2005, 2014, 2021).

it will be informative to have some idea about the outstanding amount of loan per household. In the year 2019, the outstanding amount of loan per farm household was ₹47,000 at the all-India level (refer to Figure 8.1). Regarding outstanding amount of loan also, there is wide a variation across the states. The outstanding amount of loan per household in Andhra Pradesh is as high as ₹245,554, while it is only ₹1,750 in Nagaland. Outstanding loan per farm household is higher among the southern states and very low among the north-eastern states.

Discussion on agricultural credit would be incomplete without examining the sources of credit. The sources of agricultural credit may be broadly classified into two sources, that is, the formal financial institutions and informal sources. In India, formal financial institutions (FFIs) include cooperative credit societies, commercial banks, regional rural banks and other term lending institutions. In addition, occasionally, the government also provides credit to the agricultural sector. Informal sources of credit include indigenous moneylenders, landlords, traders and businessman, and friends and relatives. Nevertheless, a large segment of the farm households is dependent on the informal sources of credit. As a result of different measures taken by the government for financial inclusion of the agricultural sector, the shares of FFIs have increased in the total credit taken by the farm households over the years. The share of FFIs has increased from 10.2 per cent in 1951 to 66.3 per cent in 1991. However, there is a decline in it in the post-reform period. The percentage share of FFIs declined to 61.1 per cent during 2002, and then, it improved to 69.6 per cent during 2019 (see Table 8.2). Among the informal sources, the importance of landlords has declined significantly. However, the indigenous moneylenders are still a dominant source of agricultural credit in India. It is found that even after 60 years of planning, the informal sector is still a dominant source. More than 30 per cent of the agricultural credit comes from this source. Koker and Jentzsch (2013) clearly show that an increase in access to credit from FFIs need not necessarily lead to a decline in credit from the informal source.

The informal sources of credit itself are heterogeneous in nature (Sharma 2010). The informal sources could be broadly categorized into two major groups: (a) the first group is in which credit is extended

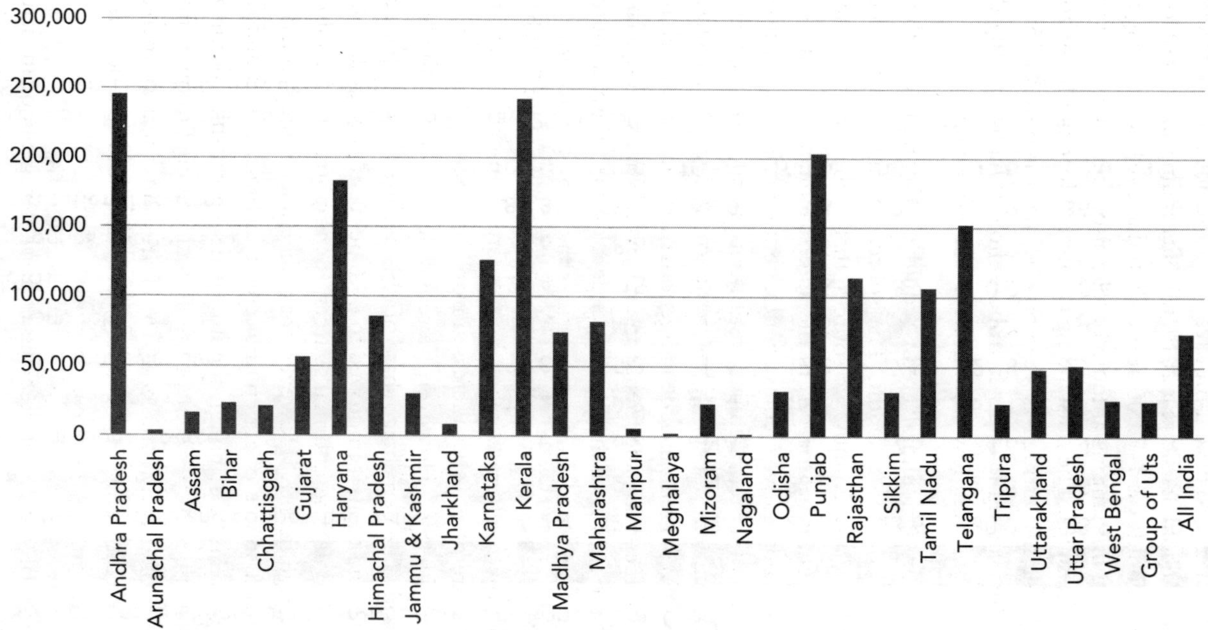

Figure 8.1 *Average Size of Outstanding Loan per Agricultural Household in India during 2019*

Source: GOI (2021).

Table 8.2 *Percentage Share of Different Sources in Agricultural Credit in India*

Source	1951	1961	1971	1981	1991	2003	2013	2019
Cooperative societies and cooperative banks	6.2	12.5	NA	27.6	23.6	30.2	28.9	10.7
Commercial banks	4.0	2.2	NA	23.8	35.2	26.3	30.7	52.6
Other institutional sources	0	6.2	NA	4.8	7.5	4.6	4.4	6.3
Institutional sources	**10.2**	**20.9**	**32.0**	**56.2**	**66.3**	**61.1**	**64.0**	**69.6**
Indigenous moneylenders	39.8	25.3	NA	17.2	17.5	26.8	29.6	20.5
Friends and relatives	NA	NA	NA	11.5	4.6	6.2	4.3	5.7
Landlords	21.4	15	NA	3.6	3.7	0.9	0.4	0.7
Other non-institutional sources	28.6	38.8	NA	11.5	7.9	5.0	1.7	3.8
Non-institutional sources	**89.8**	**79.1**	**68.0**	**43.8**	**33.7**	**38.9**	**36.0**	**30.7**
Overall	**100.0**	**100.0**	**100.0**	**100.0**	**100.0**	**100.0**	**100.0**	**100.0**

Sources: 1951–1991: Calculated from Hoda and Terway (2015); 2003–2019: compiled and calculated from different rounds of NSS All India Debt and Investment Survey.

by entities (whether individuals or institutions) to other entities and (b) credit is extended to the members of a close group only or group finance. The first group could be subdivided into three more subgroups: (a) the first major subgroup is the direct but intermittent lending by individuals or institutions with a temporary surplus fund. This group could also be net borrowers. Friends and relatives fall under this category. The credit serves as an insurance, and there is an element of reciprocity in such relationship, and the loans are usually interest free. (b) The second subgroup is the lending by lenders whose main activity lies in markets other than credit, but who tie credit transactions to transactions in other markets. For example, traders who trade in agricultural commodities and provide short-term credit to the farmers for various purposes. (c) The third subgroup is lending by individuals or institutions specializing in lending, either on the basis of their own funds or on the basis of intermittent funds. Some traditional institutions are also specializing in credit (like the Dong Committees in the Bodo areas in Assam and the Namghar Committees in Assam).

Under the second major group, group finance forms the bulk of the credit. Having carried out a primary investigation in Assam, Sharma (2010) found that there were some groups known as Xonchoi Xamities or Xamabais or simply Goots. Xonchois function like mini banks. These institutions gathered savings from their members and lent out to the members as well as to the non-members. A larger proportion of Xonchois have managed to develop linkages with banks and post offices (Sharma and Mathews 2010). Further, Sharma (2010) found another system of group finance, which can be termed as rotating savings and credit associations. 'Marups' in Manipur are a classic example. All of them are in the informal sector. However, of late, semi-formal institutions, like the self-help groups (SHGs) and the groups promoted by microfinance institutions, have also emerged as an alternative source of credit for agricultural and rural households. Table 8.2 shows that even after six decades of first All India Debt and Investment Survey, the informal sources have 30.7 per cent share in the total amount of agricultural credit in India, and that of moneylenders is 20.5 per cent. However, it does not mean that only 30.7 per cent of the agricultural households are dependent on informal sources of credit. In reality, relatively better-off households borrow from the formal sources of credit, and the average size of loans from such sources are relatively large (Sharma 2010). The relatively poor households are more dependent on the informal sources of credit. They frequently borrow and the sizes of loans are relatively small. So, it may be concluded that more farm households are dependent on the informal sources of credit. Furthermore, it is found that the households with smaller size of landholding are more dependent on the informal sources of credit. For example, households with less than 0.01 hectare of landholding take 28 per cent loans from the formal sources, while households with 4.01 to 10 hectares of land borrow more than 80 per cent of their loan from the formal sources of credit (GOI 2021).

It is already discussed that in the post-reform period, the share of banks has declined in the total credit to the agricultural and rural households. It has made the farmers dependent on the commission agents, and the dependence on the commission agents has reduced their choice regarding the sale of agricultural products (Chand 2012). Further, some of the supermarket chains are also involved in contract farming with the objective to procure fresh agricultural products. They provide credit and other inputs to the farmers, and their outputs are purchased by such supermarket chains directly (Sutradhar 2018).

Another dimension of agricultural credit is the utilization of credit. Table 8.3 clearly shows that 57.5 per cent of the credit taken by the agricultural households is for expenditure on farm business. As many as 25.9 per cent of the loan was for capital expenditure in the farm sector. The capital expenditure in farm business covers the amount of money spent to purchase land or land rights, purchase of animals, new purchases or major repairing of farm machinery or equipment, and new construction, repairing and addition to farm infrastructure. On the other hand, the revenue expenditure on farm business covers expenditure on seeds, manure, wages to the labourers, fodder, rent to the landlord, land revenue, payment made for irrigation; and hiring charge of pumps, tractors or other machineries. Some studies show that credit from FFIs plays an important role in the case of procurement of farm capital goods or farm asset creation, while non-institutional sources play a major role in the case of credit for current expenditure on farm business (Das 2016; Khaund 2002). A total of 11 per cent of the borrowings made by the agricultural households was meant for housing.

Table 8.3 *Percentage Distribution of Loan Spent for Different Purposes by the Agricultural Households during 2019*

Purpose of Loan	Percentage Share
Capital expenditure in farm business	25.9
Revenue expenditure in farm business	31.6
Expenditure on farm business	57.5
Expenditure in non-farm business	3.9
Housing	11.2
Marriage and ceremonies	6.4
Education and medical	5.4
Other consumption expenditure	9.4
Others	6.2
Overall	100.0

Source: GOI (2021).

Expenditure on housing covers the expenditure meant for the purchase of residential plots, construction of new building for residential purpose and repairing of exiting residential buildings.

It is found that the percentage of loan taken by the agricultural households for productive purposes increases along with an increase in the size of their landholding. Households with less than 0.01 hectare of land spent only 6.8 per cent of their loan on farm business, while households with more than 10 hectares of land invested around 83 per cent of their loan on farm business (NSS 2021). The percentage of loans taken for consumption purposes such as marriage and ceremonies, education and medical expenditure is higher among the households with smaller land size.

8.3. DOMINANCE OF THE INFORMAL SECTOR IN AGRICULTURAL CREDIT

The above-mentioned analysis shows that, nonetheless, the informal sources of credit are playing a dominant role in agricultural lending in India.

This section tries to analyse the factors responsible for such a situation. The Indian credit market is characterized by risk and uncertainty. Agriculture in India is a risky activity as it is highly dependent on monsoon. It raises the probability of involuntary risk of credit default (Mohan 2004). Involuntary risk means the probability of default of a loan when the borrowers do not have the capacity to repay it. So, the FFIs hesitate to lend to the farmers. Moreover, farmers are also afraid to borrow as it may lead to indebtedness (Kuri and Laha 2018). As stated from the above-mentioned discussion, a lot of credit needs of farmers are associated with household expenditure, particularly in their low-income months, and, hence, given the scarcity of such credit in the formal system, farmers often substitute the credit for investment for meeting these needs. This is also helped by a weak enforcement through a weak legal machinery, and the judicial procedure being costly in terms of both money and time. This lax legal machinery also encourages wilful default, more particularly, for the subsidized loans being rolled out by the government, as these are 'perceived' to be doles rolled out by the government and need not have to be repaid.

Both the problems of voluntary and involuntary defaults take place, as credit markets suffer from the twin problems of information asymmetry and moral hazard. In other words, lenders that is, the FFIs, do not have information (and find it very difficult to extract it) about the nature of borrowers (information asymmetry) and after disbursing the credit, find it very difficult to ensure that the loans are used for the purpose intended (moral hazard). Due to these reasons, financial institutions demand collateral to mitigate these risks while advancing loans to the farmers. However, the small and marginal farmers, and agricultural labourers, do not have suitable assets to provide the collateral. Moreover, given the poor state of land records, the titles are also not very clear. This results in the exclusion of the small and marginal farmers from the FFIs. They are therefore mostly dependent on the informal lending. On the other hand, large farmers by their access to tangible assets are therefore more accessible to the FFIs. Informal sources do not suffer from the twin problems cited earlier for the FFIs. Informal sources, like moneylenders and the informal groups mentioned earlier, provide credit to those who are known to them. Generally, their clients belong to the same village. In fact, each indigenous moneylender has a fixed group of borrowers with whom he dealt in (Aleem 1990). There is a long-run relationship between the moneylenders and the borrowers. Even if the moneylender lends to a new borrower, the size of the loan happens to be relatively small due to the risk of default. However, with the passage of time, the loan size increases (Ray 2008). The traders lend money to the farmers on the condition that the farmers have to sell their products to the former at a predetermined price just after harvesting (Siamwalla et al. 1990). As the traders have better information about harvesting, there is no chance that the farmer can violate the contract. This is a classic case of interlocked markets between credit and commodities. Moreover, the repayment terms of the informal sources are also flexible based on the cash flows of the borrowers. Moreover, to reduce the risk further, informal lenders take collateral in different forms like labour of the borrower and his family members or assets like jewellery and cattle. Informal money-lenders also accept such physical collateral, which has no value for him but is valuable for the borrowers due to some emotional and cultural attachment (Ray 2008). Sometimes, farm households borrow from the moneylenders for a very short period of time. They put their land as collateral to the moneylenders. The moneylenders get no return from the land, but they accept it so that the borrower cannot borrow from other sources. Sometimes, the ownership of land and other physical assets (offered as collateral) is transferred to the informal lender, as the farmers are unable to repay the loan on time. This is one of the causes of increased inequality in the rural areas. The FFIs cannot exercise these options and hence is in a disadvantaged position. Therefore, despite the strong focus on providing credit to the agricultural and rural households through the banks, the importance of informal moneylenders is still there. Even in those countries, where government efforts to provide rural credit is strong, the informal credit sector flourishes. The informal moneylenders also borrow from the formal sources to lend to their clients. A Study conducted in Philippines shows that a large number of traders and businessmen borrowed from the banks to provide loans to the farmers (Umali 1990 cited in Ray 2008).

The objection against the indigenous moneylenders is that they exploit the cultivators through high interest rate. So, there is the demand for regulating the interest rate. However, this issue is not so simple because the relationship between the moneylenders and the farm households in the developing countries is not a one-way relationship. For example, many a times, the moneylenders are also the landlords. The poor farmers and their family members generally work on their (landlord's) land or home. So, if the interest rate is regulated by the government by fixing a ceiling on it, the moneylenders may increase the rent on land or may make the farmers to work on the agricultural field for a longer time or give them lower wages. Similarly, the village traders give loan to the farmers for their working capital requirement with the condition that the farmer has to sell his/her output to the trader after harvesting. The trader may lend to the farmer at a lower rate of interest than an indigenous money lender (whose only objective is to earn interest). But the price the trader offers to the farmer is also lower than the market price. According to Ray (2008), all of the above fall in the category of interlinked markets among credit, commodities, land, labour, etc.

Given the above, there is an increasing trend to utilize the strength of the informal sector to provide credit to the agricultural and rural households. This is done by providing credit to the informal money lenders, so that they can on-lend to the farm households. It is expected that it would expand supply of credit by expanding the base of the informal lenders as well as encouraging new players to enter the market. This in turn would reduce the interest rate due to increased supply and competition. But it is equally possible that the competition among the moneylenders may increase the cost of loan, and the interest rate may increase. Similarly, as the lending capacity of the moneylenders increases, the inefficient moneylenders may shut down their business, which will create a monopoly of a few lenders, and the interest on loan will be increased (Ray 2008).

8.4. DIFFERENT GOVERNMENT POLICIES TO PROVIDE AGRICULTURAL CREDIT IN INDIA

During the post-Second World War era, the governments across the developing countries took different policies to provide easier credit to the agricultural sector (Markose et al. 2020; Ozili 2020). India was not an exception towards it. Up to 1969, cooperatives were the only institutions to provide credit to the farm sector. The rural credit cooperative institutions made a significant stride in delivering credit for agricultural and rural development (Satyasai and Badatya 2000). The aim of the cooperative movement was to save the poor farmers from the moneylenders who were notorious for charging exorbitant rates of interest and oppressive practices (Satyasai and Badatya 2000). The All-India Credit Review Committee, 1969, considering the larger credit needs of this sector, advocated for the participation of the commercial banks. At that time, the percentage of rural and agricultural credit in the total credit of the commercial banks was only 3.3 per cent, and the credit deposit ratio in the rural area was 37.6 per cent only, contrary to overall credit deposit ratio of 71.9 per cent (Shah et al. 2007). This indicated that the rural funds were shifted to the urban areas by the commercial banks. The rural credit review committee appointed by the Reserve Bank of India (RBI), submitted its report in July 1969, which advocated for active participation of commercial banks in agricultural credit. Fourteen largest scheduled commercial banks of India were nationalized in 1969. Later, in 1980, the other six were also nationalized. After nationalization, the expansion of the bank branches was skewed in favour of the previously unbanked areas (Shah et al. 2007). After nationalization, the priority sector of rural areas, agricultural sector and weaker sections were defined with 40 per cent of mandatory credit and interest concession (Dasgupta 2001). Along with the branch expansion, the credit outstanding by these commercial banks to the rural sector also increased. However, by the end of the 1980s, due to the twin problems related to credit markets (which have been discussed earlier), there were huge loan defaults of the banks, leading to questions of their viability (Shah et al. 2007).

Meanwhile, in 1975, the working group on rural bank under the chairmanship of M. Narashimhan suggested for the establishment of government-owned, regionally based and rurally oriented banks, combining the advantages of cooperatives and commercial banks, to supplement the existing institutional credit agencies and to supplant them to be known as Regional Rural Banks (RRBs). The main objective of RRBs was to develop the rural economy by providing credit and other financial services to the weaker sections, particularly small and marginal farmers, agricultural labourers, rural artisans and small entrepreneurs. (Uddin 2003). The RRBs also suffered from the loan defaults because of the problems cited earlier. Later, in 1982, the NABARD was established as an apex body for financing agricultural and rural development by a special act of parliament.

During the 1990s, along with the economic reform in the other sectors, reform in the financial sector also began. The Narashimhan Committee, on financial sector reform, was against using the credit system for redistributive objective and argued that 'directed credit programme should be phased out' (Shah et al. 2007). The post-reform trend in the Indian Banking system was exactly opposite to that of the post-nationalization period. The share of agriculture in total bank credit fell from 19 per cent in 1990 to 11 per cent in March 2005 (Shah et al. 2007). Thus, the attempt to provide credit to the rural sector through bank nationalization could not succeed. Instead, in recent years, the rural poor tended to depend on the informal moneylenders once again.

Most of the programmes rolled out during the nationalization phase were 'supply led rather than demand led' (Dasgupta 2001). The focus was on providing more and more credit without understanding the demand. Meeting the credit target was the goal of the bureaucratic machinery put into place. The result has been poor with very little achievement in terms of providing credit on a sustainable manner to the poor farmers. The poor infrastructure and manpower in the rural branches also discouraged the banks from fulfilling their desired objectives in a vigorous manner.

As has been seen earlier, informal sources do not suffer as the FFIs in providing credit sustainably to the farmers. This is because it could manage the twin problems and also because of its flexibility. It was therefore felt that integrating the features of the informal sector with the formal sector could help obviate the problem. The result was the microfinance programme, which was rolled out in India in a big way with the FFIs (which included banks, NBFCs, NGOs, etc.) taking the lead. NABARD started the SHG programme inspired by the Bangladesh Grameen Bank experience of Bangladesh. Under this programme, facilitated by NABARD, banks took the lead in rolling the

SHG Bank Linage Programme (SBLP) across the country. Similarly, Small Industries Development Bank of India (SIDBI) also started a microcredit programme where microfinance institutions (MFIs) consisting mostly of non-banking finance companies (NBFCs) or NGOs took the lead. By the second decade of the 21st century, some of these MFIs (mostly in the NBFCs space) converted into small finance banks and also universal banks like Bandhan. By 2020, the Gross Loan Portfolio Outstanding of all the microcredit players excluding the banks comes to ₹1,461,060 million, covering 30.7 million borrowers (MFIN 2021). Of late, there have been allegations that MFIs provide loans beyond the absorption capacity of the borrowers, and there has been protests by them in some states like Assam of not repaying back those loans. The Government of Assam has also come out with a debt waiver scheme (an election promise by the ruling party) to obviate the problems of the borrowers. However, debt waiver schemes punish the good borrower and incentivize the bad borrowers. Numerous studies have shown the poor effects of debt waivers on the rural credit markets (Chakraborty and Gupta 2017; Gine and Kanz 2017; Hoda and Terway 2015).

On the other hand, the SHG movement spearheaded by NABARD and the banks, better known as the SHG Bank Linked programme or the SBLP in short, has ₹1,032,897.1 million loan outstanding against 5.78 million SHGs as on March 2021 (NBARD, n.d.).

Both of the programmes show much higher success with good repayment records as compared to the earlier supply-led credit programmes.

8.4.1. Agricultural Debt Waiver

The farm loan waiver programme was adopted in 1990 for the first time. Another national loan waiver scheme, the Agricultural Debt Waiver and Debt Relief Scheme (ADWDRS) was introduced in May 2008 to address the problem of indebtedness and difficulties faced by the farmers. Under this programme, there was the provision of complete loan waiver for the small and marginal farmers with landholdings up to 2 hectares. There was also provision of one-time relief of 25 per cent debt relief for the large farmers (with landholdings more than 2 hectares), provided they repay the balance 75 per cent of the eligible amount. This programme was expected to cover 36.9 million small and marginal farmers and 6 million other farmers. In the latter years also, some of the state governments announced such loan waiver programmes.

The aforementioned policy is widely criticized by the agricultural economists. Basically, farm loan waiver is a political decision taken prior to the elections. First, it has deteriorated the health of the public sector banks by increasing their non-performing assets. It is found that the repayment of agricultural loan in India had drastically reduced during those days. After the first loan waiver programme in 1990, it took several years for the banks to recover their losses (Hoda and Terway 2015). At the same time, it had encouraged the borrowers not to repay their loans, which ultimately affected the advancing of credit to the agricultural sector. The ultimate victims were those who were regularly paying their loan instalment. Further, it generates expectations among the farmers regarding such schemes in future. Moreover, such a programme covers those farmers who have access to credit from FFIs. But a large segment of literature states that the economically weaker section of the farmers is still dependent on the informal sources of credit. Thus, the poorest of the poor farmers are not covered by this programme, and only relatively better-off farmers get the benefit.

During 2006, a rehabilitation package for the farmers in the farmers' suicide-prone districts of India was announced. This programme included an element of partial debt waiver for the farmers. This debt relief included waiving off cumulative interest overdue on loans up to 1 July 2006. Moreover, the loans were rescheduled for three to five years by issuing fresh loans. Although the programme was a partial debt waiver, its effect on the rural credit markets was not so devastating, as it was linked to investment in agriculture.

8.5. CONCLUSION AND POLICY IMPLICATIONS

The above-mentioned analysis shows that even after seven decades of planning, agricultural credit is a major problem in India. Although the government has introduced various policies and programmes for financial inclusion of the farm households, a larger percentage of them are dependent on the informal sources of credit and do not have access to credit from FFIs. A large section of the small and marginal farmers is excluded from the FFIs. There are still a large number of landless tenants in India, and their tenancy is mostly informal. So, the tenants are not covered by the credit programme of the FFIs. Goswami (2018) advocates for the registration of the tenants in order to help them to have access to agricultural credit.

Indian agriculture mainly depends on monsoon. Bad weather may lead to crop failure, and crop failure may lead to indebtedness of the farmers. Since they are aware of the risks in agriculture, they sometimes hesitate to borrow from the FFIs. On the other hand, banks are also discouraged to lend to the agricultural sector because of the factors highlighted earlier. Since the rural credit markets are interlinked with the risks associated with agriculture, some economists have suggested that crop loans should be linked to crop insurance so that neither the bank nor the farmers suffer due to crop failure (Bezbaruah and Hasan 2018). Kuri and Laha (2018) also advocate for policies incorporating credit–insurance mix to facilitate the growth of credit and insurance markets for agricultural development.

As has been clearly brought out, rural credit markets are interlocked with commodities, labour and land markets. It is also clear that there is a major problem of information asymmetry and moral hazard associated with these markets. In addition, the fact that money is fungible and can be used for any purpose makes it extremely challenging to deliver rural credit by FFIs. It is therefore imperative to expand options where local intermediaries are integrated in the delivery of credit. The MFIs and SBLP is a case that needs to be accelerated further. There is a need to explore credit linkages with local intermediaries like the primary agricultural cooperative (PAC) societies and farmer's producer companies (FPCs). An extensive institutional capacity building of these institutions needs to be initiated so that they can perform these roles effectively.

However, agriculture being extremely risky, mitigation of risks through insurance cover, using technology for price discovery, weather forecasting and information on soil quality needs to be integrated with the credit lines. In addition, asset creation, like land development, irrigation facilities, use of larger machinery like tractors, is critical for improved productivity, and there is a great need to develop the long-term credit delivery structure so as to supplant the short-term credit needs discussed earlier.

Only such a comprehensive mechanism could ensure that agricultural credit is provided sustainably so that the vision of doubling farmer's income is achieved.

REFERENCES

Aleem, I. 1990. 'Imperfect Information, Screening, and the Costs of Informal Lending: A Study of a Rural Credit Market in Pakistan'. *The World Bank Economic Review* 4, no. 3: 329–350. https://documents1.worldbank.org/curated/en/543971468759317437/pdf/%20multi-page.pdf (accessed on 19 December 2021).

Bezbaruah M. P. 2018. 'The Way Forward'. In *Indian Agriculture after the Green Revolution: Changes and Challenges*, edited by B. Goswami, M. P. Bezbaruah, and R. Mandal, 216–226. New York, NY: Routledge.

Bezbaruah, M. P., and M. Hassan 2018. 'Indian Agriculture through the Turn of the Century: Gathering Stress and Farmers'. In *Indian Agriculture after the Green Revolution: Changes and Challenges*, edited by B. Goswami, M. P. Bezbaruah, and R. Mandal, 152–167. New York, NY: Routledge.

Chakraborty, T., and A. Gupta. 2017. *Loan Repayment Behaviour of Farmers of Farmers: Analysing Indian Households*. https://home.iitk.ac.in/~tanika/files/research/BorrowingBehaviorAT.pdf (accessed on 20 May 2021).

Chand, R. 2012. 'Development Policies and Agricultural Markets'. *Economic & Political Weekly* 47, no. 52: 53–62.

Das, A. K. 2016. 'Impact of Access to Credit on Rental Markets of Agricultural Capital Goods: Evidence from Assam of North-East India'. *Bangladesh Development Studies*, 39, no. 1–2: 83–101.

Das, A. K., and M. P. Bezbaruah. 2020. 'Efficiency and Imperfections of Tilling Machinery Rental Markets in the Brahmaputra Valley of Eastern India'. *Agricultural Economics Research Review* 33, no. 1: 35–44.

Dasgupta, R. 2001. 'An Informal Journey through Self Help Groups'. *Indian Journal of Agricultural Economics* 56, no. 3: 370–386.

Gine, X., and M. Kanz. 2017. 'The Economic Effects of a Borrower Bailout: Evidence from an Emerging Market'. *The Review of Financial Studies* 31, no. 5: 1752–1783.

GOI (Government of India). 2005. *Situation Assessment Survey of Farmers: Indebtedness of Farmer Households, 2003*. Report No. 498, NSS 59th Round. Ministry of Statistics and Programme Implementation, Government of

India. https://www.thehinducentre.com/resources/article36690521.ece/binary/498_final.pdf (accessed on 21 February 2022).

———. 2014. 'Key Indicators of Situation of Agricultural Households in India, 2013, NSS 70th Round. Ministry of Statistics and Programme Implementation, Government of India'. http://www.indiaenvironmentportal.org.in/content/403847/key-indicators-of-situation-of-agricultural-households-in-india-january-december-2013/ (accessed on 21 February 2022)

———. 2021. *Situation Assessment of Agricultural Households and Land and Livestock Holdings of Households in Rural India, 2019*. NSS Report No. 587, NSS 77th Round. Ministry of Statistics and Programme Implementation, Government of India. https://www.mospi.gov.in/documents/213904/301563//Report_587m1631267040957.pdf/3793650e-8cf1-7872-ae90-51470c8d211c (accessed on 1 December 2021).

Goswami, B. 2018. 'Rental Market of Agricultural Land: Changing Context and Need for Tenancy Reform'. In *Indian Agriculture after the Green Revolution: Changes and Challenges*, edited by B. Goswami, M. P. Bezbaruah, and R. Mandal, 29–44. New York, NY: Routledge.

Hoda, A., and P. Terway. 2015. 'Credit Policy for Agriculture in India: An Evaluation'. Working Paper No. 302, Indian Council for Research on International Economic Relations. https://icrier.org/pdf/Working_Paper_302.pdf (accessed on 2 June 2021).

Khaund, S. 2002. 'Agricultural Investment and the Role of Financial Institutions: A Study with Special Reference to the Central Brahmaputra Valley Zone'. Unpublished PhD Thesis. Guwahati: Department of Economics, Gauhati University.

Koker, L. D., and N. Jentzsch. 2013. 'Financial Inclusion and Financial Integrity: Aligned Incentives?' *World Development* 44, no. C: 267–280.

Kuri, P. K., and A. Laha. 2018. 'Implications of Credit-Insurance Interlinked Contracts: An Evaluation of Crop Insurance Schemes in India'. In *Indian Agriculture after the Green Revolution: Changes and Challenges*, edited by B. Goswami, M. P. Bezbaruah, and R. Mandal, 63–77. New York, NY: Routledge.

Markose, S. M., T. Arun, and P. K. Ozili 2020. 'Financial Inclusion, at What Cost? Quantification of Economic Viability of a Supply Side Roll Out'. https://papers.ssrn.com/sol3/papers.cfm?abstract_id=3548997 (accessed on 13 May 2021).

MFIN. 2021. *Micrometer, Issue 37*. https://mfinindia.org/Resources/micrometer (accessed on 18 December 2021).

Mohan, R. 2004. 'Agricultural Credit in India: Status, Issues and Future Agenda'. Reserve Bank of India Bulletin. http://www.rakeshmohan.com/docs/AgricreditBulletin.pdf (accessed on 20 June 2021).

National Bank for Agriculture and Rural Development (NBARD). n.d. 'National Bank for Agriculture and Rural Development: Fostering Rural Prosperity'. https://www.nabard.org/about-departments.aspx?id=5&cid=477 (accessed on 28 July 2021).

Ozili, P. K. 2020. 'Financial Inclusion Research around the World: A Review'. In *Forum for Social Economics*. https://www.researchgate.net/publication/338432774_Financial_inclusion_research_around_the_world_A_review (accessed on 15 May 2021).

Ray, D. 2008. *Development Economics*. New Delhi: Oxford University Press.

Samah, B. A., H. A. M. Shaffril, M. S. Hassan, M. A. Hassan, and N. Ismail. 2009. 'Contribution of Information and Communication Technology in Increasing Agro-Based Entrepreneurs Productivity in Malaysia'. *Journal of Agriculture and Social Sciences* 5, no. 3: 93–98.

Satyasai, K. J. S., and K. C. Badatya. 2000. 'Restructuring Rural Credit Co-operative Institutions'. *Economic & Political Weekly* 35, no. 5: 307–330.

Shah, M., R. Rao, and P. S. V. Shankar. 2007. 'Rural Credit in 20th Century India: Overview of History and Perspectives'. *Economic & Political Weekly* 42, no. 15: 1351–1364.

Sharma, A. 2010. 'Rural Financial Markets of Assam: A Spatio-economic Analysis'. Unpublished PhD Thesis. Guwahati: Department of Economics, Gauhati University.

Sharma, A., and B. Mathews. 2010. 'On an Informal Frontier: The ASCAs of Lower Assam'. In *Financial Promise for the Poor: How Groups Build Micro Savings*, edited by K. Wilson, M. Harper, and M. Griffith, 39–50. Boston, MA: Kumarian Press.

Siamwalla, A., C. Pinthong, N. Poapongsakom, P. Satsanguan, P. Nettayarak, W. Mingmaneenakin, and Y. Tubpun 1990. 'The Thai Rural Credit System and Elements of a Theory: Public Subsidies, Private Information and Segmented Markets'. *The World Bank Economic Review* 4, no. 3: 271–296. https://documents1.worldbank.org/curated/en/543971468759317437/pdf/%20multi-page.pdf (accessed on 19 December 2021).

Sutradhar, R. 2018. 'Transforming Agricultural Marketing in India'. In *Indian Agriculture after the Green Revolution: Changes and Challenges*, edited by B. Goswami, M. P. Bezbaruah, and R. Mandal, 78–95. New York, NY: Routledge.

Uddin, N. 2003. *Regional Rural Banks and Development*. New Delhi: A Mittal Publication.

Umali, D. 1990. 'The Structure and Price Performance of the Philippine Rice Marketing System'. PhD Dissertation. Stanford, CA: Stanford University.

Chapter 9

Agricultural Risks and Crop Insurance Market in India

Sumit Ghosh

9.1. INTRODUCTION

Agricultural production and farm income in India are very often affected by various risks such as weather risks arising from floods, droughts, cyclone and hailstorm; biological risks due to pest attack and plant diseases; and market risks in the form of fluctuations of input/factor and output prices. The resulting instability of farm output and income often affects a farmer's well-being. For mitigating market risk, especially that of post-harvest output price slump, several mechanisms have come into operation over the years. The minimum support price (MSP) constitutes one such mechanism, which is to safeguard the farmers if there is a fall in the prices of crops after harvest than the cost incurred. The MSP was announced for the first time in 1966–1967 for wheat to provide safety net to the farmers. The MSP regime then has been expanded to many crops. But even after so many years of operation, the MSP has achieved limited success in addressing the price risks. Besides such government-initiated policy measures, the market system itself has come up with some other arrangements for the mitigation of farmers' risk of uncertainty of output price. Contract farming and future trading[1] are some such arrangements that can provide some insurance against price fluctuations. But these mechanisms do not cover all crops and/or all farmers.

As for a farmer's production risk, which arises from vagaries of weather and biological occurrences of pest attacks and plant diseases, there are few market-provided mechanisms in operations in India. Ideally, a crop insurance market could provide farmers the opportunity for hedging against the risk of such production losses. Theoretically, farmers covered under crop insurance would be compensated in the event of crop loss through indemnification. Thus, crop insurance transfers agricultural risks from the insured farmers to the insurers, which may be a private or a public sector operator. Notwithstanding the various initiatives of the Government of India since the late 1970s to make crop insurance available for farmers, such insurance coverage has remained thin and scanty.

In the absence of the insurance market, a farmer is often left to adopt steps to insure him/herself. In the literature, self-insurance is defined as the practice of using and depleting one's own wealth and assets (either movable or immovable) to smooth uncertain shocks in income. Stocks of cash or accumulated savings, and grain stocks (although grain is not perfectly durable), can work as self-insurance. This is the most important mechanism for consumption smoothing other than market credit and inter-family lending, the sale and purchase of assets. Agricultural households hold many different forms of wealth, including land, capital goods such as pump sets and tractors, livestock, jewellery and stock of food grains. Self-insurance relates to using these assets as buffer stocks. A farmer accumulates stocks during periods of affluence and depletes these reserves to finance consumption expenditure during bad years. It is obvious that self-insurance can be quite costly in terms of asset/wealth holding of the farmer. The process may even be unsustainable if a farmer is exposed to adverse states in successive periods. From

---

[1] Contract farming involves agricultural production being carried out on the basis of an agreement between the farm producers and buyers. It involves the buyer specifying the quality required and prices, with the farmer agreeing to deliver at a future date. Future trading enables the farmers to deliver the crop at a specified price at some future date.

the perspective of long-term well-being of the farmers, it is therefore desirable that formal insurance coverage is made available to them. In view of inadequacies of formal insurance for the farmers in India, it is pertinent to examine the operation of existing mechanisms for the purpose and to design more effective policies.

The chapter is organized into six sections. Section 9.2 discusses the idea and theoretical concepts of insurance in general, what determines the demand for and supply of insurance, and the information problems associated with the insurance market. Section 9.3 discusses the risks in agriculture, and the problems and issues of crop insurance in particular. Section 9.4 analyses the various government-initiated crop insurance schemes in India till date and their efficacy and penetration. A ground-level investigation regarding farmers' demand for crop insurance and willingness to buy such products is discussed in section 9.5. Section 9.6 is the final section, which gives the concluding comments and policy implications.

9.2. ECONOMICS OF INSURANCE

The basis of insurance business is that most of the people do not like to take risks (called risk-averse people), and people who shy away from taking risks are prepared to pay a price (premium) to take care of the uncertain events. Besides that, a standard situation for the insurance market to exist is that the insurers have a fair knowledge about the risks involved, a large number of similarly susceptible risky individuals, the independence of risk, that is, not all who are insured should fall in the adverse situation at the same time and individuals cannot have control over the occurrence of the risky event, nor they, after being insured, should be able to influence the compensation amount. In such conditions, insurance exists, and the premium is determined by the forces of demand and supply (Ahsan et al. 1982).

9.2.1. Demand for Insurance

A frequently asked question is: Why does demand for insurance arise? As stated earlier, risk-averse people are better off paying premium to insurers who take care of the uncertain prospects. There is a theorem concerning the demand for insurance. The theorem states that if fair insurance is available, a risk-averse person would insure fully, that is, the person would go for full coverage of his risk (Hands 2004, 162–163). A fair insurance is insurance at a premium, which leaves the insurance provider with zero expected profit.

In real life, completely fair insurance is unlikely to be available. After all, an insuring firm is required to cover its administrative expenditures to remain in business. Yet if insurance is available at not-too-'unfair' price, most people would buy full or partial insurance cover. Only those whose risk aversion is very close to zero, that is, those who are very nearly risk neutral, may opt out of the insurance market.

Like any other commodity, demand for insurance coverage decreases with the increase in its price, namely premium, and increases with the increase in expected loss. The demand for insurance coverage increases with the increase in risk aversion of the individuals (Duncun and Myers 2000).

9.2.2. Supply of Insurance

Insurance is not provided for all kinds of risks to which people are exposed. An insurer sells assurance that if its clients fall into an adverse state, it will compensate for the damage from the adverse consequences. The price it charges for this is known as the premium. The insurance business runs on the principle that there will be many buyers of its product, namely the assurance, and the compensation it will be required to pay will be only few. Thus, at a reasonable low price, many agents, who are exposed to the risk damage due to adverse state of nature, can insure themselves, and the insurers can also make a profit out of it as the entire premium collection is generally not required to compensate the actual damage of those unfortunate agents who actually face the adverse consequences. It is worth noting that the supply of insurance may not be available on its own if two conditions are not fulfilled. The first condition is that there is a large number of agents or individuals who are exposed to the particular risk. In other words, the risk is repeated in the case of many possible agents. The second one is that risk of getting into a damage by any particular agent is not related to the risk of getting into trouble by the other agents. This is known as independence of the risk. Let me illustrate why insurance may not be easily available when the risks are not independent. For instance, in the case of a flood or pest attack, all the farmers in a particular locality may be adversely affected. Hence, if all the farmers were insured, the insurer will have to pay out to all of them. Consequently, its payout will be in excess of its premium collection. The insurer may offer the insurance at a higher premium. But at such a higher premium, there may not be takers of the insurance. In contrast, a farmer's crop failure due to a problem with the seeds it used, assuming that all farmers are not getting the seeds from the same source, is an example of an independent and repeated risk. Hence, the insurer may not have a difficulty in insuring such a crop failure. Thus, in real life, we see that insurance supply is relatively easily available when the risk is independent and repeated, and it is less easily available in a situation where the risks are isolated and are interrelated. The supply of insurance coverage increases with an increase in the premium and decreases with an increase in cost and risk aversion of insurance firms.

9.2.3. The Information Problem and Market Failure

There are two problems associated with the insurance market because of asymmetric information, and therefore, the insurance business is often exposed to market failure. These two problems are adverse selection and moral hazard, which prevent the insurance providers from offering fair insurance. Adverse selection is a situation when one party, usually the seller of insurance, has less information about the potential insured regarding the risk position of the buyer (the insured). The potential insured individuals have a fair knowledge about their own risk position, but the insurers having no accessibility of such information cannot differentiate among customers, leading to adverse selection, that is, only high-risk individuals will buy insurance policies, and hence, insurers incur heavy losses.

Moral hazard occurs when the individuals have an incentive to engage in more risky behaviour because he or she is insured. A risk-averse individual will purchase full-coverage insurance at actuarially fair rates. With such full-coverage insurance, the individual is no worse off if an accident happens than if it does not happen. But if accident prevention entails some cost, there is no incentive for the fully covered individual to engage in any accident prevention. In the case of crop insurance, an insured farmer tends to take less care and preventive measures to minimize the damage of his/her crop or engage in more risky activities at the expense of the insurance provider, leading to moral hazard. Formally, moral hazard occurs when the probability of a bad state of nature β is a function of the level of care or safety taken by the individual (Hands 2004, 164), that is,

$$\beta = \beta\ (\alpha) \qquad \text{with } d\beta/d\alpha < 0$$

where α is the amount of care or prevention taken by the individual. Moral hazard implies that

$$\delta\alpha/\delta C < 0$$

where C is the amount of coverage. That is, an increase in the amount of insurance coverage will reduce the amount of care—α—taken by the individual. Asymmetric information and hidden information can affect any market, but the insurance market is typically prone to these hazards.

One approach to mitigating moral hazard is to require the insured to share some of the loss. Loss sharing can occur through co-payments under which insurance companies pay only a part of the total loss, and the insured bears the rest of the cost. Another measure is deductibles through which the insured bears all of the cost of any loss up to some maximum amount before the insurance company provides an indemnity for the rest of the loss (Smith and Glauber 2012).

9.3. AGRICULTURAL RISKS AND THEORETICAL PERSPECTIVE OF CROP INSURANCE

Agriculture is susceptible to various risks arising from variations in weather, fluctuations of input and/or output prices, pest attack and plant diseases, etc. However, of all the risk factors affecting crop production, weather is typically the most significant (Miranda and Vedenov 2001). To induce the farmers to make investment in agriculture, their agricultural risks must be shifted. For the safeguard of farmers' income in the adverse situation, they must be covered under crop insurance programmes. Though crop insurance does not reduce the risk of crop failure and thus is not preventive in nature, certainly, it is curative, by helping the farmer to recoup the losses through indemnity payment (Swain 2013).

Theoretically, the supply of insurance against crop failure is not easy to be available. The risk of crop failure is one situation where none of the mentioned criteria for supply of insurance is satisfied. Agricultural risks or risk of crop loss tend to be correlated across the insureds, crops and geographic regions, leading to catastrophic risk. From an insurance perspective, a catastrophe can be defined as an infrequent event that has undesirable outcomes for a sizeable subset of the insured population (Duncun and Myers 2000), that is, events like floods, droughts and hailstorms, which create a huge damage to all in a particular region. The supply of insurance will be available if risk pooling is possible. But most of the agricultural risks are not independent in nature, which cannot be pooled, and the market is unlikely to naturally ensure the supply of crop insurance. The systematic nature of agricultural risks goes against the working of the 'law of large numbers' on which premium and indemnity calculations are based (Nair 2010).

Private insurance markets are good at handling independent risks, that is, risks that are not correlated across insureds. By pooling the independent risk faced by a large number of individuals, insurers can eliminate aggregate risks. But insuring, catastrophic risk is not easy. Agricultural risks are correlated in nature. When risks are correlated, they cannot be eliminated through pooling, and insurers must bear some of the cost of the risk (Doherty and Dionne 1993). Because of the systematic risk, insurers cannot diversify their risk across space and would have to hold large reserves in the event of a large crop loss. Although insurance companies can diversify their risks through the use of re-insurance, catastrophic losses are, by their nature, large, and so an insurance company trying to diversify such risks may find it costly to develop enough number of different markets that are large and diverse enough to offer any real risk-pooling benefits (Duncun and Myers 2000). Again, even insurers who re-insure their catastrophic risks are not fully protected because of deductibles and co-payments that are part of re-insurance agreements. Furthermore, re-insurance firms face adverse selections and the same problems and costs that make it difficult for individual insurance companies to diversify their own catastrophic risks. This leads to high re-insurance premium and limited private re-insurance capacity. Ultimately, re-insurance firms face many of the same problems and costs as smaller primary insurers (Skees and Barnett 1999).

The agricultural insurance market also faces the problem of adverse selection and moral hazard. Higher premium rates discourage majority participation, and only high-risk individuals purchase the insurance, leading to adverse selection. An insured farmer hardly takes care in preventing the loss or takes more risk at the expense of the insurance provider because he or she would be indemnified if he/she faces uncertain events that result in damage. The asymmetric information and hidden action on the part of the insured party discourage private participation in the crop insurance market. As related to demand, the ability to behave with moral hazard would increase participation. However, when viewed at the market level, moral hazard can reduce participation from those who think that they are paying for the recurring losses incurred by others (Coble and Barnett 2013).

Adverse selection, moral hazard and correlated risks are not problems unique to crop insurance. Other lines of insurance face similar problems, yet private market exists. However, the costs of addressing these problems for crop insurance appear to be sufficiently large to make crop insurance too expensive for private insurers. Therefore, for crop insurance to be made available, government intervention in the form of subsidy is an imperative.

9.4. CROP INSURANCE IN INDIA: EARLIER GOVERNMENT INITIATIVES TO LATEST DEVELOPMENTS

Soon after the independence, the necessity of introducing a crop insurance scheme in the country was felt. In this context, the government examined the feasibility of introducing crop and cattle insurance in the country. The first ever crop insurance scheme was launched in Gujarat, during 1972–1978. The scheme covered the H-4 cotton variety initially, while other crops were also brought under its coverage gradually. The scheme was implemented in Andhra Pradesh, Gujarat, Karnataka, Maharashtra, Tamil Nadu and West Bengal. It continued until 1978–1979 and covered only 3,110 farmers for a premium of ₹454,000 against claims of ₹3.788 million (Raju and Chand 2007).

9.4.1. Pilot Crop Insurance Scheme 1979

In 1976, an expert committee headed by V. M. Dandekar looked into issues and modalities of crop insurance in India (Dandekar 1976). The committee submitted its report to the General Insurance Company (GIC) in May 1976. Based on the recommendations of the report a Pilot Crop Insurance Scheme (PCIS) came into effect in 1979, which was based on 'area approach' for making insurance coverage available against a decline in crop yield below the threshold level. The scheme covered cereals, millets, oilseeds, cotton, potato and chickpea, and it was confined to only loanee farmers on a voluntary basis. The premium paid was shared between the General Insurance Corporation of India and state governments in the ratio of 2:1. This was implemented in 12 states till 1984–1985 and covered 623,000 farmers for a premium of ₹19.501 million against claims of ₹15.568 million in the entire period (Raju and Chand 2008).

9.4.2. Comprehensive Crop Insurance Scheme 1985–1999

The Comprehensive Crop Insurance Scheme (CCIS) was linked to short-term credit and implemented based on the 'homogenous area approach'. Till *kharif* 1999, the scheme was adopted in 15 states and 2 union territories (UTs). Both PCIS and CCIS were confined only to the loanee farmers. While PCIS was on a voluntary basis, the CCIS was compulsory for loanee farmers in the participating states/UTs. CCIS was implemented till *kharif* 1999, and it covered 76.3 million farmers for a premium of ₹4.04 billion against claims of 23.03 billion. More than half (58%) of the total indemnities under CCIS were paid to groundnut farmers of Gujarat alone. The other participating states, which contributed 84 per cent of the premium during 1985–1999 received only 42 per cent of the total claims. The claim–premium ratio was nearly 20.74 for Gujarat, while it was only about 5.72 at the all-India level (Raju and Chand 2008).

9.4.3. National Agricultural Insurance Scheme 1999

The National Agricultural Insurance Scheme (NAIS) was introduced in the country from the *rabi* season of 1999–2000. The Agricultural Insurance Company of India took over the implementation of NAIS. This scheme was available to both loanees and non-loanees. It covered all food grains, oilseeds and annual horticultural/commercial crops for which past yield data are available for an adequate number of years. Among the annual commercial and horticultural crops, sugar cane, potato, cotton, ginger, onion, turmeric, chillies, coriander, cumin, jute, tapioca, banana and pineapple were covered under the scheme. The scheme was based on both 'area approach' for widespread calamities and 'individual approach' for localized calamities such as hailstorm, landslide, cyclone and floods.

Under NAIS, for the whole time period of operation, from 1999 to 2015, more than 240 million of farmers had been covered. Among the states, Maharashtra had the highest number of farmers covered, followed by Madhya Pradesh, Andhra Pradesh, Uttar Pradesh, Gujarat and Karnataka.

The scheme was demand-driven, and claims were based on the occurrence of natural calamities. The Government of India had constituted a joint group to study the NAIS and to suggest improvements. Based on the suggestions received, the crop insurance scheme, Modified National Agricultural Insurance Scheme (MNAIS) was implemented on a pilot basis in 50 districts from 2010–2011 to 2013–2014 and implemented full-fledged from *rabi* 2013–2014 to 2015–2016. The major improvements made in MNAIS were actuarial premium, with subsidy in premium ranging up to 75 per cent to farmers, unit area of insurance reduced to village–village panchayat level, indemnity for preventing sowing/planting risk and for post-harvest losses due to cyclone in coastal areas, on account of payment up to 25 per cent of likely claims as immediate relief (Mukesh and Pandey 2019).

9.4.4. Weather-based Crop Insurance Scheme 2003

This scheme launched in the year 2003 was based on weather parameters, with an aim to provide protection to the insured farmers from the financial loss on account of anticipated crop loss, resulting from variations in weather. Crop loss due to vagaries of weather (i.e., excess or deficit rainfall, aberrations in sunshine, temperature and humidity, etc.) could be covered on the basis of weather index. The scheme operates on the concept of area approach, whereby each reference unit area is linked a reference weather station (RWS). The scheme was made mandatory for the loanee famers and optional for the non-loanee farmers.

But even after government's effort to make weather insurance successful, there have been major constraints in its implementation. The variations in weather parameters are high in a country like India, and basis risk (deviation of individual losses from the average) can only be minimized if the claims structure for such products is worked out at smaller units (Nair 2010). Weather data are often recorded at taluka level, which may result in the actual impact of adverse weather condition at the farm location being significantly different from that recorded by the RWS. The poor density of weather stations and lack of weather data have been major impediments in the spread of the product. Again, the necessity of installing large numbers of weather stations results in high costs, making it difficult for the insurers to operate such products. The success of such a weather insurance product depends on establishing accurate correlation between productivity levels and weather variations. It is very complex to estimate the correlation arising out of the interactive nature of agricultural inputs (Nair 2010). In addition, for the increase in penetration levels, the famers need to be made aware of the availability of such products and of claims structures, which are highly technical and complicated.

By merging the MNAIS and Weather-Based Crop Insurance Scheme (WBCIS with some fine-tuning, the National Crop Insurance Programme (NCIP) was formulated and approved for its implementation with effect from *rabi* 2013–2014 season. Hence, all the pilot-based schemes that were being operated till then were launched as a full-fledged component under the umbrella scheme NCIP with some improvements, and NAIS was discontinued. Again, all state/UTs were given options to implement either NAIS or MNAIS for the year 2014–2015 and 2015–2016.

9.4.5. Pradhan Mantri Fasal Bima Yojana 2016

Keeping the increase in premium rates in view, farmers' share in premium, capping on premium rate reduction in sum insured and lower coverage, NCIP/NAIS has been reviewed and a new scheme, namely the Pradhan Mantri Fasal Bima Yojana (PMFBY) was launched in the country in the year 2016. This flagship scheme was introduced to provide for financial support to the farmers suffering crop loss arising from uncertain events. More importance is given on increasing farmers' income than increasing farm production. The main objective of this initiative is to double the farmers' income by 2022. All farmers, including sharecroppers and tenant farmers, are eligible for coverage under the scheme. Loanee farmers would be covered compulsorily, while the scheme is optional for the non-loanee farmers. The premium rates for food crops and oilseeds (FCOS) are fixed at 2 per cent of the sum insured or actuarial rate, whichever is less, for the *kharif* season and 1.5 per cent for the *rabi* season. For commercial/horticulture crops, a premium rate of 5 per cent is fixed to be paid by the farmer. The central government and the state government will equally share the difference between the premium rate and the rate of insurance payable by farmers as premium subsidy.

The scheme is implemented on an 'area approach' basis. The area approach treats all farmers in a defined area as identical in terms of risks and losses and, therefore, paying identical premium receiving identical claim amount. However, losses due to localized perils (hailstorm, landslide) and post-harvest losses due to specified perils (cyclone, cyclonic rain, unseasonal rains) are assessed at the affected insured field of the individual insured farmer. The unit of insurance is village–village panchayat. Farmers are eligible for indemnity claims up to a maximum of 25 per cent of the sum insured, if a majority of farmers in a notified area are prevented from sowing the insured crops due to adverse weather conditions.

9.4.6. Performance of *the Pradhan Mantri Fasal Bima Yojana* across States

The performance of any crop insurance scheme is evaluated through various insurance-specific variables such as the number of farmers insured, area insured, beneficiary ratio and claim–premium ratio. The number of farmers insured under PMFBY has increased for all major states during 2016–2017 to 2019–2020 as presented in Table 9.1. States such as Andhra Pradesh, Chhattisgarh, Jharkhand and Odisha have recorded more than 400 per cent increase in the coverage of farmers from *rabi* 2016–2017 to *rabi* 2019–2020. There is an increase by more

Table 9.1 *Farmers Insured under PMFBY from Rabi 2016–2017 to Rabi 2019–2020*

States	Farmers Insured		Percentage Change in the Numbers of Farmers Insured
	Year 2016–2017	Year 2019–2020	
Andhra Pradesh	1,005,181	5,630,792	460.1
Assam	8,516	1,178,614	13,739.9
Bihar	2,713,178	5,017,345	84.9
Chhattisgarh	1,542,449	8,570,925	455.6
Gujarat	1,975,139	8,430,792	326.8
Haryana	1,336,028	5,817,386	335.4
Himachal Pradesh	260,565	832,390	219.4
Jharkhand	8,77,754	4,461,254	403.1
Karnataka	2,611,964	8,395,447	221.4
Kerala	18,415	67,305	265.4
Madhya Pradesh	6,667,721	27,953,594	319.2
Maharashtra	11,793,372	50,349,075	326.9
Odisha	1,820,236	10,597,611	482.2
Uttar Pradesh	6,751,422	23,493,928	247.9
West Bengal	4,130,164	13,294,047	221.8

Source: Department of Agriculture, Cooperation and Farmers Welfare.

300 per cent in farmers' coverage in states such as Gujarat, Haryana, Madhya Pradesh and Maharashtra. In Bihar, though, increase in the number of farmers insured is lower than the rest of the major states. In Assam, the number of farmers insured has increased by 13,739 per cent from 8,516 to 1,178,614 during this period.

Table 9.2 presents the area insured under PMFBY during rabi 2016–2017 to rabi 2019–2020 for major states. The highest crop area has been insured in Madhya Pradesh, followed by Rajasthan, Maharashtra, Uttar Pradesh and Gujarat. As in the case of farmers insured, coverage in terms of area insured in Bihar was registered as lower than that

Table 9.2 *Area Insured under PMFBY for Major States during Rabi 2016–2017 to Rabi 2019–2020*

States	Area Insured (in Million ha)		Percentage Change in Area Insured
	2016–2017	2019–2020	
Andhra Pradesh	78,588.3	404,266.4	414
Assam	431.2	68,855.9	15,868
Bihar	246,524.9	460,883.4	86
Chhattisgarh	241,459.8	906,806.9	275
Gujarat	284,156.7	1,112,344.4	291
Haryana	208,457.5	828,342.7	297
Jharkhand	37,376.4	193,697.4	418
Karnataka	286,198.0	821,521.4	187
Kerala	1,296.1	5,574.2	330
Madhya Pradesh	124,574.9	4,722,683.5	3,691
Maharashtra	72,278.1	2,863,220.8	3,861
Odisha	131,871.1	599,371.4	354
Rajasthan	1,013,787.9	3,788,455.7	273
Uttar Pradesh	581,959.1	1,973,275.8	239
West Bengal	202,304.7	544,300.0	169

Source: Department of Agriculture, Cooperation and Farmers Welfare.

of the other states. On the other hand, the area insured has increased significantly during the said period for the state of Assam.

Table 9.3 presents the beneficiary ratio for major states during *rabi* 2016–2017 to *rabi* 2019–2020 under PMFBY. Beneficiary ratio is the ratio of the total number of farmers benefitted to the total number of farmers insured under the crop insurance scheme. There is an increase in this insurance variable for almost all the major states, except Gujarat and Uttar Pradesh. The all-India level beneficiary ratio stands at 0.31 in 2019–2020 as compared to that in 2016–2017, which was 0.20. There

Table 9.3 *Beneficiary Ratio under PMFBY for Major States during Rabi 2016–2017 to Rabi 2019–2020*

	Beneficiary Ratio	
States	2016–2017	2019–2020
Andhra Pradesh	0.12	0.32
Assam	0	0.008
Bihar	0.05	0.08
Chhattisgarh	0.09	0.33
Gujarat	0.34	0.30
Haryana	0.16	0.25
Himachal Pradesh	0.08	0.23
Jharkhand	0.05	0.06
Karnataka	0.27	0.45
Kerala	0.12	0.24
Madhya Pradesh	0.14	0.26
Maharashtra	0.26	0.47
Odisha	0.09	0.26
Uttar Pradesh	0.16	0.14
West Bengal	0.12	0.18
All India	0.20	0.31

Source: Author's calculation based on data taken from Department of Agriculture, Cooperation and Farmers Welfare.

is an insignificant increase in beneficiary ratio for states such as Bihar, Jharkhand and Assam.

Table 9.4 presents the claim–premium ratio for major states under PMFBY cumulative up to *rabi* 2019–2020. Claim–premium ratio is the ratio of the total claims paid by the insurer to the total premium received by them. For Andhra Pradesh, the claim–premium ratio being 0.96 implies that 96 per cent of the total premium collected was used for payment of claim by the insureds. Claim–premium ratio is greater than 1 for states such as Chhattisgarh, Haryana, Kerala and Odisha, implying insurance suppliers had to pay more than what they received as premium. Claim–premium greater than 1 implies the existence of adverse selection.

Table 9.4 *Claim–Premium Ratio for Major States under PMFBY (2019–2020)*

States	Claim–Premium Ratio
Andhra Pradesh	0.96
Assam	0.02
Bihar	0.30
Chhattisgarh	1.45
Gujarat	0.43
Haryana	1.05
Jharkhand	0.08
Karnataka	0.89
Kerala	1.11
Madhya Pradesh	0.95
Maharashtra	0.89
Odisha	1.0
Rajasthan	0.82
Uttar Pradesh	0.48
West Bengal	0.57
All India	0.83

Source: Author's calculation based on data taken Department of Agriculture, Cooperation and Farmers Welfare.

Although the important insurance-specific indicators such as the number of farmers insured, area insured and beneficiary ratio have increased during 2016–2017 to 2019–2020, the scheme is still unable to attract and meet the expectations of the farmers. As many as seven states, including agriculturally important states such as Andhra Pradesh, Bihar, Punjab and West Bengal, have opted out of the PMFBY scheme in recent times due to low claim ratio. Gujarat has also exited the scheme temporarily.

There is a provision in the scheme that those loanee farmers who do not want to avail and be covered by the scheme have to give it in writing. But most of the farmers are unaware about this provision, and the premium amount gets deducted mandatorily from their bank account. Besides that, the district- and state-level grievance redressal forums set up under the PMFBY could not resolve the complaints of farmers. The Parliamentary Standing Committee attached to the Ministry of Agriculture recommended to set up toll-free number for queries regarding the PMFBY scheme.

Delay in claim settlement is one of the issues on the part of the farmers with the PMFBY. If farmers suffer crop damage in one of the sowing seasons, then they cannot earn any surplus for that particular season, resulting in short of cash to sow for the next season. Crop insurance can be useful if the claims are paid to farmers before sowing for the next season begins. To address this problem, the government announced that it would impose a penalty of 12 per cent interest rate per annum on insurance companies, which delay payments beyond 10 days of prescribed cut-off date for payment of claims.

Another issue from the supply side regarding the PMFBY is that the insurance companies did not set up offices at the tehsil level, which was to be done as per guidelines of the scheme. Moreover, the insurance companies are cutting exposure to the PMFBY as the companies are facing losses due to high claim–premium ratio. Public sector insurance firms, such as New India Assurance, United India Insurance, National Insurance and Oriental Insurance, have reduced their exposure to government's flagship scheme. Private sector insurers—ICICI Lombard General Insurance and TATA AIG—had already exited from PMFBY due to huge losses they faced.

Thus, the flagship crop insurance scheme, which was launched with an aim to stabilize and double farm income, has met limited success. In light of this, the government has announced a number of changes and tweaks in the scheme, which include penalizing insurance companies in the case of delayed claim settlements, imposing enrolment targets on insurers, increasing awareness of the programme, which requires insurance companies to spend 0.5 per cent of the revenue earned in gross premium on advertisement and publicity of the scheme and increasing the risks that can be covered under the scheme. Farmers will now get coverage for hailstorms, crop fires, damage from animals and rainstorms. Again, farmers will now get 72 hours instead of 48 hours to inform state governments about the crop damage.

9.5. FARMERS' WILLINGNESS AND DEMAND FOR CROP INSURANCE: A GROUND-LEVEL INVESTIGATION

Although the government has initiated various crop insurance schemes, the latest being the PMFBY, the coverage of these schemes has not been expanded to the desired level. This situation begs the question whether such insurance coverage has remained low due to demand-side factors or supply-side factors. For seeking an answer to this question, a field survey was carried out in two pockets of the Brahmaputra Valley of Assam.

The study has been conducted in Kamrup (R) and Darrang districts of the Brahmaputra Valley in Assam. Farmers of these valleys are more exposed to risks as irrigation facilities have not been expanded to the desired level, and therefore, they heavily depend on weather. Heavy rainfall leads to frequent floods that damage crop and make agricultural activities more uncertain.

Kamrup district falls under the lower Brahmaputra Valley zone. The major portion of the geographical area of Kamrup district is put to agricultural uses. The frequent occurrence of floods adversely affects crops in the district. Darrang district is situated at the central part of Assam and on the northern side of the mighty Brahmaputra River. The soil of this district is very fertile for cultivation, and the main crops are paddy, rice, oilseeds, sugarcane and jute. The district is also rich with a sizeable production of vegetables.

The study is based on a sample household drawn from six villages of two districts, namely Darrang district and Kamrup (R) district of the Brahmaputra Valley in Assam. The total number of sample farm households drawn is 80 out of 405 farm households in 6 villages. In Darrang, three villages have been selected—Bihudia, Janaram Chowka and Bechimari. From Kamrup (r), three villages were selected, namely Singimari, Paschimdhuli and Kalita Para. These villages have been selected purposively with the due consideration of representing diversity of physical and sociocultural conditions of farmers. The household data have been collected through field survey.

From the field survey, it has been found that the prominent cause of crop loss and loss of income on the part of the sample farm households is pest attack. As a mitigation measure, the sample farm households were found to be heavily dependent on self-insurance in the form of savings. Besides savings, some others borrow from moneylenders and sell their movable assets to provide for their loss of income due to crop failure.

It was found from the field survey that none of the sample farmers have ever bought crop insurance. Nor were any of them aware of the various crop insurance schemes promoted by the government. This finding is in line with the national-level data provided by the National Statistical Office, 2021 (GOI 2021, 79), where it is found that the reason for not purchasing insurance products by the farmers is mainly because they are not aware about crop insurance products. But once the provisions of the PMFBY were explained to them, 68 per cent expressed willingness to buy. Another 10 per cent responded that they would buy crop insurance if there was a provision of some cash back (as proposed by the National Institution for Transforming India (NITI) Aayog to return 75 per cent of the premium paid by the farmers under the PMFBY if they do not file claims for crop damages for four to six consecutive seasons).

This shows that there is no dearth of demand for crop insurance among farmers, and it is the supply-side issues that are the impediments in increasing the coverage and penetration of crop insurance. For this, awareness must be created among the farmers about the prevailing crop insurance schemes and other necessary measures to reach out the farmers.

9.6. CONCLUDING COMMENTS AND POLICY IMPLICATIONS

Despite various schemes launched from time to time in the country, the coverage and penetration of such schemes have remained scanty and thin. Coverage in terms of farmers insured, crop insured and area insured has been low. Although the latest implemented scheme (PMFBY) was launched with high ambitious aim of contributing significantly to the government's target of doubling farmers' income by 2022, the scheme so far has not been able to serve the desired expectation. This requires renewed efforts by the government in terms of designing appropriate product and mechanism. The fundamental issue in the design of a crop insurance product is for the insurers to decide whether to cover all the risks or only certain specific risks. An insurance product, which covers all perils, is known as yield insurance, and under such insurance scheme, an insured farmer is entitled to get indemnified if the yield is below a certain guaranteed level for any reason. On the other hand, insurance schemes, which cover only certain specific risks, will provide a safeguard to an insured farmer for that specified risk. In India, the schemes so far implemented and the one which is in operation presently cover all the risks, and this makes way for insured farmers to affect the indemnity amount (case of moral hazard). Therefore, it is necessary to provide measures to reduce the extent of moral hazard.

Crop insurance schemes in India are based on 'area approach'. But for the success of a crop insurance product, loss assessment should be made on an individual basis. Though assessment of loss on an individual basis is costly, to reduce basis risk, such an approach should be considered. There is a need to promote private sector companies' participation in agricultural insurance. Although private insurance companies will be unable to compete with government-supported and subsidized insurance, there can be private–public partnership in providing agricultural insurance. This may increase the coverage and viability of insurance schemes. Under the area-based schemes, damage is addressed on the basis of crop-cutting experiences (CCE). They are conducted for all notified crops to assess the crop yield and the extent of crop failure. The time gap between conducting CCE and settlement of claims is long. Using remote sensing technology could reduce this time gap.

The lack of awareness regarding the available crop insurance products is the most prominent issue, which has reduced the viability of crop insurance schemes in India. For the success and viability of crop insurance, farmers need to be made aware about such insurance products available. Therefore, measures should be taken to create awareness about crop insurance among farmers. The government and corporate agencies may engage grassroots-level non-governmental organizations (NGOs) for spreading awareness besides using media like radio and television. Besides that, the complexity in documentation needs to be reduced so that it becomes easy for the buyers to avail such products.

REFERENCES

Ahsan, S. M., A. Ali, and N. Kurian. 1982. 'Toward a Theory of Agricultural Insurance'. *American Journal of Agricultural Economics* 64, no. 3: 520–529.

Coble, K.H. and B.J. Barnett 2013. 'Why Do We Subsidize Crop Insurance?'. *American Journal of Agricultural Economics*, Vol. 95, No. 2: 498–504

Dandekar, V.M. 1976. 'Crop Insurance in India: A Review, 1976-77 to 1984-85'. *Economic and Political Weekly*, Vol. 20, No. 25/26: A46–A59

Doherty, N., and G. Dionee. 1993. 'Insurance with Undiversifiable Risk: Contract Structures and Organizational Form of Insurance Firms'. *Journal of Risk and Uncertainty* 6: 187–203.

Duncun, J., and R. J. Myers. 2000. 'Crop Insurance under Catastrophic Risk'. *American Journal of Agricultural Economics* 82, no. 4: 842–855.

GOI (Government of India). 2021. 'Situation Assessment of Agricultural Households and Land and Holdings of Households in Rural India, 2019, NSS 77th Round'. Ministry of Statistics and Programme Implementation, Government of India. https://www.mospi.gov.in/documents/213904/301563//Report_587m1631267040957.pdf/ (accessed on 21 February 2022).

Hands, D. W. 2004. *Introductory Mathematical Economics*. New York, NY: Oxford University Press.

Miranda, M., and Dmitry V. Vedenov. 2001. 'Innovations in Agricultural and Natural Disaster Insurance'. *American Journal of Agricultural Economics* 83, no. 3: 650–655.

Mukesh, and K. Pandey. 2019. 'Assessment of Crop Insurance in India through 4Cs: Cost, Coverage, Compensation and Crop Loss'. *Indian Journal of Agricultural Economics* 74, no. 2: 256–266.

Nair, R. 2010. 'Crop Insurance in India: Changes and Challenges'. *Economic & Political Weekly* 45, no. 6: 19–22.

Raju, S. S., and R. Chand 2007. 'Progress and Problems in Agricultural Insurance'. *Economic & Political Weekly* 42, no. 2: 1905–1908.

———. 2008. 'Agricultural Insurance in India: Problems and Prospects'. Working Paper No. 8, National Centre for Agricultural Economics and Policy Research. https://www.rfilc.org/wp-content/uploads/2020/08/Agricultural-Insurance-in-India-Problems-and-Prospects.pdf (accessed on 21 February 2022).

Skees, J. R., and B. J. Barnett. 1999. 'Conceptual and Practical Considerations for Sharing Catastrophic/Systematic Risks'. *Review Agricultural Economics* 21: 424–441.

Smith, V. H., and J. W. Glauber. 2012. 'Agricultural insurance in Developed Countries: Where Have We Been and Where Are We Going?' *Applied Economic Perspectives and Policy* 34, no. 3: 363–390.

Swain, M. 2013. 'Agricultural Risk and Efficiency of Crop Insurance Schemes in Odisha'. In *Agrarian Crisis in India: The Way Forward*, edited by G. V. Ramanjaneyulu. New Delhi: Academic Foundation.

Chapter 10

Challenges of Post-harvest Management of Farm Output

Amiya Sarma and Binod Goswami

10.1. INTRODUCTION

In recent times, a remarkable shift in the demand pattern of food items has been observed in India, wherein per capita consumption of as well as expenditure on staple foods like cereals and pulses has drastically declined, and the demand for products such as fruits, vegetables and livestock items has received a boost (Kannan 2014). According to the *Annual Report, 2018*, Ministry of Food Processing industry, Government of India, business of organic packaged food, naturally healthy beverages and Ayurveda-based juices has significantly expanded in terms of value. Food items such as noodles, jam, sauces, chocolates and cheese have also acquired high demand. Such trends in consumer preferences manifest people's increasing attention towards nutritious foods and foods which can be conveniently stored for some time. Easy access to supply, changed tastes and preferences and change in relative prices have intensified the consumption diversification effect, which may be partly attributed to this structural shift in consumption–demand pattern (Kumar 1998; Murthy 2000; Radhakrishna and Ravi 1992).

Concomitantly, increase in per capita income, owing to economic growth (Meenakshi 1996), increasing urbanization and modernization of agriculture, has created significant impacts on the change in demand pattern of food items. These changes in demand pattern are also visible in the rural areas of the country. Mechanization of agricultural activities and improvement in infrastructure facilities have reduced physical energy requirements of the rural people, which has contributed to the decline in cereal consumption (Rao 2000).

With the change in consumption pattern towards horticultural products such as fruits, vegetables and livestock products, the necessity of post-harvest treatment of these products has increased manifold as such products are highly perishable and prone to loss in terms of both quantity and quality. It is to be noted that India suffers from a significant post-harvest losses of her fruit and vegetable production because of the absence of a well-functioning post-harvest system, resulting in a large gap between the gross production and net availability of these products. A study by Jha et al. (2015) conducted on post-harvest loss of a few agricultural and horticultural crops and some livestock products in India found that the losses in selected fruits were to the extent of 6.70–15.88 per cent, the losses in vegetables varied from 4.58 to 12.44 per cent, losses in inland and marine fisheries were found to be 5.23 per cent and 10.52 per cent, respectively. While the assessed loss in the milk sector was 0.92 per cent, the losses in poultry and meat were 6.74 per cent and 2.71 per cent, respectively. Minimization of such losses is critical since it can expand the supply of the products without utilizing additional inputs like land into the production process. Again, processing of these products adds value and, at the same time, enhances the shelf life of the products, giving the producers sufficient time for marketing. India is one of the largest producers of fruits, vegetables, milk and livestock products in the world. But only a nominal amount of them are processed. As per a report of the Confederation of Indian Industry (2019), India processes merely 2 per cent of fruits and vegetables, 21 per cent of meat, 6 per cent of poultry, 23 per cent of marine and 35 per cent of milk products. It is, thus, evident that India has ample scope to embark upon initiatives towards putting in place an efficient post-harvest management system for farm products. As part this system, the rate of product processing has to be increased to add value to these products, minimize losses and ensure remunerative prices to the producers.

As per Agricultural Census (2015), more than 86 per cent of the farmers in India are small and marginal farmers.[1] These farmers have not received commensurate benefits from this changed demand pattern (Boss and Pradhan 2020) as they are not able to put their produce efficiently in the post-harvest value chain after harvesting. Commonly, the post-harvest value chain comprises four critical stages, namely harvesting and primary processing, storage, processing and marketing. As agricultural produce passes through these phases, a value is added to them, but at the same time, losses also occur either quantitatively or qualitatively, or both, due to several internal and external factors. Empirical studies have recognized several internal factors of post-harvest loss of agricultural produce. Significant ones include inadequate harvesting practices and technology, lack of proper processing and grading, insufficient infrastructure for storage and crop protection, transportation bottlenecks, access to the market and also lack of skills of the farmers in post-harvest handling. Additionally, lack of coordination and interlinkages among various post-harvest phases are also significant aspects of loss. Among external factors, climate and socio-economic conditions are major contributors of post-harvest loss of agricultural produce worldwide. Thus, it is very essential to avert post-harvest losses as far as possible or else minimize it. Loss reduction measures may directly influence the farmers' income by increasing the volumes and quantity of produce they sell. An efficient post-harvest management system may reduce post-harvest loss extensively.

Post-harvest management can be defined as methods and techniques applied to reduce the post-harvest loss and to increase the shelf life of the product. In a broader sense, it also includes some crucial issues such

[1] According to Agricultural Census (2015–2016), Government of India, marginal farmers are those who cultivate agricultural land up to 1 hectare, and small farmers are those who cultivate agricultural land of more than 1 hectare and up to 2 hectares (GOI 2020).

as enabling the farmers to choose the right time and location for selling, enhancing quality of their products, foster product differentiation and discover better prices.

In view of the above-mentioned discussion, this chapter presents a brief discussion on various stages of post-harvest management of agricultural produce in section 10.2. Section 10.3 is an assessment of the status of post-harvest management of farm products in India. Discussion on the necessity of reforms in the farm sector and an evaluation of the marketing system of agri-products in India through the Agricultural Produce Market Committees (APMCs) are incorporated in section 10.4. The chapter is summarized in section 10.5.

10.2. STAGES OF POST-HARVEST MANAGEMENT SYSTEM

Agricultural products, after harvesting, pass through various stages of post-harvest operations, handling and storage before sending for selling in the market. Product losses may occur in each of these stages either in qualitative or in quantitative term. Quality losses refer to the reduction in nutrient/caloric content, acceptability and edibility of a product, whereas quantity losses indicate to the loss in the amount of the product. The pattern of post-harvest loss in developed and developing countries is not similar. While quality losses are more common in developed countries, developing countries generally face the problem of quantity losses (Hodges et al. 2011; Kader 2002). These losses mostly occur during the early and middle phases of the supply chain (FAO 2011). Inadequate capacity of the farmers, deficient infrastructure and market inefficiencies are three core inefficiencies in the post-harvest value chain in developing countries like India, leading to post-harvest losses of agricultural products.[2]

The range of activities of post-harvest management of agricultural produce lies between harvesting and marketing. All the actions encompassing to reduce post-harvest loss and increasing shelf life of agricultural produce and measures for better price discovery either at farmers or organizational level between these two phases constitute

[2] For more details on post-harvest management system, see Ganesh et al. (2016).

the post-harvest management system. Different phases of an ideal post-harvest management system of agricultural produce may be discussed as follows:

10.2.1. Harvesting

In the post-harvest value chain harvesting is the first important phase where mature crops are gathered from the fields and processed so that they become either edible or ready for entering into subsequent phases of the food value chain. There is a greater possibility of crop loss in this phase unless the activities required to be performed are not carried out with maximum efficiency. Maturity index,[3] harvesting methods and weather play an important role in the harvesting phase of crops.

10.2.1.1. Maturity Index

The quality and shelf life of agricultural and horticultural commodities critically depend on harvesting on maturity. There are two types of maturity indicators of agricultural produce—physiological maturity and commercial maturity. Physiological maturity refers to the attainment of full development stage just prior to ripening and attainment of full growth in the case of non-climacteric fruits, which do not ripen further after harvesting. Commercial maturity refers to the stage at which growth and development is optimum for specific uses. In fact, it is the stage of marketing and final consumption of the products.

Physiological maturity of food products is determined by indices such as number of days, visual appearance, shape, size, colour, texture, lenticels number, specific gravity, soluble solids, starch content, sugar–acid ratio and oil contents. Based on these indicators, experienced farmers harvest their products at proper time, which enhances quality and shelf life of the products. It also helps attaining adequate time required to channelize the products through the post-harvest supply chain. Crops harvested either premature or too late, on the other hand,

[3] Maturity index for a commodity is a measurement that can be used to determine whether a particular commodity is mature.

suffer from post-harvest physiological disorders and diseases, leading to losses in both quality and quantity, which in turn reduce return to the farmers. However, some commodities do not exhibit these maturity indices (Kaya 2014), resulting in untimely harvesting, reduced post-harvest life and monetary losses.

10.2.1.2. Methods of Harvesting

The methods of harvesting significantly affect the post-harvest quality of agricultural produce. Agricultural produce may be harvested manually or mechanically. Harvesting methods vary from country to country as well as commodity to commodity. In developed countries, the most expensive and sophisticated farm machineries are used for harvesting, whereas in developing countries like India, farmers generally adopt largely labour-intensive conventional harvesting methods. Further, some commodities like tomato and potato can be harvested mechanically, but fruits like mango are harvested manually. Since most of the agricultural produce are perishable in nature, utmost care is required to be taken while choosing the method of harvesting; otherwise, there is the possibility of huge losses of quality and quantity.

10.2.1.3. Weather

Weather plays a key role at the time of harvest. Harvesting decision of farmers is greatly affected by it. Many a times, farmers have to postpone harvesting decision due to bad weather as it affects the operations and functionality of harvesting machines or human labour and usually increases the moisture content of the harvested product. On the other hand, the postponement of harvesting decision increases the possibility of crop loss in the field. Although it is an external factor, it can be avoided to some extent by adopting proper planning at the pre-harvesting phase.

10.2.2. Processing

Processing of agricultural produce is one of the vital phases of post-harvest value chain as it minimizes wastage and losses of agricultural produce, handles the glut and stabilizes farm price by utilizing the excess produce in the process of value addition to provide additional income to the farmers. Depending on the type and extent of value addition, agricultural food processing can be categorized as primary and secondary processing. Primary processing relates to the conversion of raw commodity into products that are ready for consumption. Milling of rice, sugar, edible oil and flour are examples of primary processing. The key activities of primary processing include threshing, drying, grading, sorting, etc.

10.2.2.1. Threshing

Cereals like paddy, wheat and pulses are required to be threshed to separate the grains from the husk and plant. This may be done either manually or mechanically using machines such as threshers, shellers or combine harvesters. Though there is greater risk of grain damage in mechanical threshing than manual threshing, mechanical threshing is preferred as losses due to spillage are lesser in the process.

10.2.2.2. Winnowing and Cleaning

Threshing is followed by winnowing or cleaning. In this phase, the grains are cleaned up by blowing the chaff away from it. It is also used to remove insects, weevils, debris or other pests form the stored grains. However, losses may occur in this process as some amount of the edible grain passes into chaff.

10.2.2.3. Drying

Drying is another method of processing of agricultural produce. This process is essential to wipe off the moisture content of the grain so that those can be made ready for storage, selling or consumption. If the grain is not dried to a recommended level, the possibility of fungal damage arises during storage. In addition, loss may occur during drying because of pest infestation, rodents, birds, etc., particularly in situations where the grain is dried in the open. This is a common phenomenon in developing countries like India.

10.2.2.4. Grading

For bidding a better price, grading of agricultural produce is crucial. The process of grading involves inspection, assessment and sorting of the products with respect to freshness, quality, legal compliance and sale value. Products like fruits and vegetables are generally graded based on physical features such as size, shape, weight, colour, specific gravity and freedom from diseases. Grading is often carried out manually, in which products are inspected and sorted. Sometimes, grading and sorting may also be carried out using specific machinery. Presently, electronic grading systems are becoming popular in the horticultural sector. Causes of post-harvest losses in this stage are lack of specific standard as well as poor enforcement of standard, lack of skill, awareness and financial resources.

10.2.3. Storage

Storage of agricultural produce occupies a significant place in the post-harvest management system. It involves keeping and preserving agricultural produce since harvesting till those are sent for selling to reach the ultimate consumer. Since most of the agricultural produce, particularly vegetables and fruits, are perishable in nature, proper storage is required for them to prevent post-harvest losses in between the time of harvesting and reaching the end consumers. Generally, the harvesting season for most of the commodities is very short, while their consumption is spread all through the year. This necessitates the availability of proper storage infrastructure to ensure the availability of food grains throughout the year. Further, storage facilities are also essential to hold the surplus stock for use during a crisis situation. Proper storage is also important to discard distress sale by small and marginal farmers who lack proper storage facilities for harvested agricultural produce (Bhoi and Dadhich 2019) and ensure that farmers get remunerative price for their produce.

During storage, the agricultural produce suffers from both qualitative and quantitative losses. Qualitative losses occur in terms of reduction in nutritional conditions resulting from insect attacks, changes in appearance and chemical properties, contamination of mycotoxins,[4] residue, etc. Quantitative losses are mostly caused by insect infestation, rodents, birds and by changes in temperature, moisture content, etc. In addition, at high temperature, perishable farm products deteriorate in both quantity and quality. As such, proper storages, especially cold storage facilities, are extremely important to store such products till disposal in the market.

10.2.4. Marketing

In the entire chain of post-harvest management of agricultural output, the marketing component occupies the most significant place. A well-functioning marketing system is crucial as the prospect of income and profit depends on it. The marketing system provides farmers the platform through which they can sell their farm output to get reasonable income, which again in turn incentivizes them to produce further. At the same time, marketing facilities are extremely important to encourage farmers to expand their scale of production, introduce modern farm practices and contribute to the overall development of their economies. Contrarily, farmers may face difficulties in selling their farm products in the absence of a well-structured marketing system, which acts as a cause of post-harvest losses and deterioration of product quality (Kasso and Bekele 2018). Obviously, it reduces the prospect of getting income and profit from farming. As such, the existence of a well-structured marketing mechanism is the key requisite for selling off farm produce, ensuring sufficient income to the farmers to keep them engaged in farming practices.

The link through which a farm product is sent from its farmers to the market to reach the ultimate consumers may be considered as the marketing channel of that product. In this channel, there may or may not be intermediary agents in between the farmers and the end consumers. A hypothetical marketing channel for a product may be represented as:

---

[4] Mycotoxins are naturally produced toxins by certain moulds. They may develop in different crops and foodstuffs under warm and humid conditions.

Farmer ⇒ Pre-harvest Contractor ⇒ Wholesaler ⇒ Retailer ⇒ Consumer

In this hypothetical marketing channel, there exist three different types of intermediaries (pre-harvest contractors, wholesalers and retailers) in between farmers and consumers. Some portion of the price paid by the end consumers is appropriated by these intermediaries, and only the remaining amount is received by the actual farmers of the product. If the farmer can directly sell their products to the consumers, then the entire amount paid by the consumers for the product is received by the farmers themselves. In this case, price received by the farmers and, hence, their profit is relatively higher. On the other hand, with intermediaries in the marketing channel, farmers receive relatively lesser amounts of the price paid by the consumers. Clearly, farmer's price and profit go on declining with an increase in the number of intermediary agents in the marketing channel.

It is now clear from the aforementioned discussion that a marketing channel without intermediaries, that is, the channel where the farmers can sell directly to the end consumers, ensures the highest price and profit to the farmers. Thus, this channel may be regarded as the best marketing channel. But in actual practice, farmers do not have direct access to the market and end consumes, and, hence, they have to rely on the marketing agents for selling their products. In such situations, those marketing channels are considered better where numbers of intermediary agents are less, and, therefore, the gap between the price that consumers pay and the price that the farmers receive is the minimum. For comparison of efficacy of different marketing channels, the concept of 'price spread' can be applied.

Price spread indicates to the difference between the net price received by the farmer and the price paid by the end consumer for a particular product (Kakaty and Borah 2011). A higher price spread results in a lower share of the farmers in the price paid by end consumers, and thus, it reveals a greater degree of exploitation of the farmers. A marketing channel for a product involving many intermediaries definitely has a higher price spread, and efficacy of such marketing channels are relatively less. On the other hand, the marketing channels with none or less intermediaries have lower price spread, which ensures a higher share of the farmers in consumers' rupee. Clearly, the efficacy of such a marketing channel is relatively higher from the farmer's perspective and is always desirable. The following hypothetical example helps us understand the efficacy of different marketing channels with the help of price spread.

Let us suppose that a banana farmer has two marketing channels through which he can sell his output.

Channel I: Farmer ⇒ Wholesaler ⇒ Retailer ⇒ Consumer
Channel II: Farmer ⇒ Retailer ⇒ Consumer

Let us suppose that consumers purchase per dozen of bananas at ₹30. In the first marketing channel, the farmer sells per dozen of bananas to the wholesaler at ₹20, and the wholesaler sells to the retailer at ₹25. The retailer purchases at ₹25 and sells to the consumers at ₹30 per dozen. Thus, the price spread (difference between the consumer price and price received by the farmer) is ₹ (30–20) = ₹10 (33.33 per cent) per dozen. The farmer's share in consumer's rupee is 66.67 per cent.

On the other hand, in the second marketing channel, the farmer sells to the retailer at ₹25 per dozen and the retailer sells to the end consumers at ₹30 per dozen. Hence, the price spread here is ₹ (30–25) = ₹5 (16.67%) per dozen. The farmer's share in consumer's rupee in this case is 83.33 per cent.

Obviously, the price spread in channel I is higher than in Channel II, and, therefore, the farmer receives a lesser price if he uses Channel I to sell his products. This is because Channel I has relatively more marketing intermediaries than in Channel II. From this simple example, it is now clear that the existence of many marketing intermediaries in the marketing channels leads to a higher price spread reducing farmer's profit and share in consumer's rupee, and vice versa.

Although a marketing channel with none or less intermediary agents is always desirable, farmers often find it difficult to find such a link for channelizing their products to the market. A number of factors actually restrict the farmers to reach the market without relying on market intermediaries/middlemen. For instance, lack of (cold) storage facilities, not so improved transportation network, asymmetry in market information and unorganized farmers are some of the factors acting as hindrances against the farmers in directly accessing the markets. Such factors are generally found in relatively higher degrees in the developing countries like India. For minimizing the influence of marketing agents and for protecting the farmers from the exploitation by middlemen, the government has a critical role to play in addressing the problems of marketing, thereby helping the farmers to access the market easily without depending heavily on the market intermediaries.

10.3. STATUS OF POST-HARVEST MANAGEMENT OF FOOD PRODUCTS IN INDIA

India is the second largest producer of food products after China. As per a report by the Ministry of Food Processing, Government of India (2019), it is the largest producer of food items such as milk, pulses, ginger, chickpeas, banana, guava, papaya and mango, as well as the second largest producer of wheat, rice, potato, cashew nut, groundnut, garlic, dry onion, pumpkin, gourd, green peas and cauliflower. Most of these products are perishable requiring post-harvest management to add value, on the one hand, and to increase the shelf life of the products, on the other. But the percentage of these products going through proper post-harvest management processes is very less in India. According to the Ministry of Food Processing, Government of India, only 10 per cent of agricultural commodities were processed in 2018. This is only an example of improper treatment that food products receive after harvesting continuously over the years as a result of which the country suffers from huge post-harvest losses in different food items every year. In 2012, India produced 257 million tons of food grains, 75 million tons of fruits and 149 million tons of vegetables. Among these, there was 10 per cent post-harvest losses in durables (pulses, cereals and oilseeds), 20 per cent in semi-perishables (onion, potato, tapioca) and around 25 per cent in livestock products such as meat, milk, eggs and fish (Hegazy 2013). Generally, losses in food products are observed during harvesting and post-harvest processing such as threshing, drying, storage, transportation and marketing (Jha et al. 2015).

Indian farmers mostly depend on conventional harvesting techniques and primary processing (carried out mostly through milling of products such as rice, sugarcane, oilseeds and wheat) activities due to the lack of awareness, access and limited ability to pay for scientific processes (Ganesh et al. 2016). This leads to a huge quantity of crop loss at the harvesting and primary processing phases. The extent of loss for selected crops at harvesting and primary processing phases in India is presented in Table 10.1.

It is to be understood that only primary processing adds lower value to the products. For better value addition, secondary processing is extremely important, which covers processing of high-value products such as fruits and vegetables, dairy and bakery items and chocolates. However, a shift in the value chain towards processed food products can improve the level of economic status of the farmers by reducing food losses and enhancing food as well as processed food exports.

Next to processing, the products need storage facilities so as to keep them safe until transported to different markets. Indian farmers retain about 60–70 per cent of food grains produced for self-consumption or meeting their other financial requirements. The remaining part is generally stored adopting some conventional storage structures made from locally available material. The grains are also stored at the trader's level and urban organizational storage level for the central pool by the Food Corporation of India (FCI) and state government agencies (SGAs). The Food Corporation of India is the single largest entity with a storage capacity of 26.62 million tons of food grains. Apart from this, there is Central Warehousing Corporation (CWC) and State Warehousing Corporations (SWCs), which provide storage facilities for nearly 120 farm and industrial products in India. The total warehousing capacity available in India in the public and private sectors is about 108.75 million tons. However, this amount is very less in comparison to overall production of food grains of 255.36 million tons (Jain et al. 2015). India produces a huge quantity of vegetables and fruits. They are perishable in nature and require sophisticated cold storage facilities to prevent loss during glut. But the present available cold storage facilities are mostly meant for storing a single commodity such as potato, apple, grapes, orange, pomegranates and flowers, which remain inadequate to store all commodities requiring such facilities (Ganesh et al. 2016). Thus, storage facilities through warehouses and cold storages are much less as compared to its demand. Due to the

Table 10.1 *Percentage of Crop Loss in India at Times of Harvesting and Primary Processing*

Crop Variety	Crop	Harvesting		Collection		Threshing		Winnowing		Drying	
		2012	2015	2012	2015	2012	2015	2012	2015	2012	2015
Cereals	Paddy	1.2	2.08	0.74	0.37	1.15	1.44	0.36	0.50	0.23	0.10
	Wheat	1.69	1.43	0.56	0.56	1.62	1.43	0.48	0.40	0.04	0.07
	Maize	0.5	1.42	0.19	0.42	1.57	1.20	0.21	0.40	0.17	0.18
	Bazra	0.8	1.15	0.56	0.43	1.30	2.15	0.33	0.19	0.30	0.16
	Sorghum	0.6	1.47	0.38	0.33	0.67	2.04	0.39	0.47	0.34	0.08
Pulses	Pigeon pea	0.48	1.18	0.44	0.39	0.69	2.13	1.04	0.41	0.47	0.18
	Chickpea	0.72	1.87	0.56	1.19	0.82	2.60	0.38	0.58	0.56	0.40
	Blackgram	1.13	1.82	1.04	1.01	1.62	1.94	0.31	0.48	0.50	0.26
	Greengram	0.86	2.00	0.62	0.76	1.63	1.54	0.32	0.36	0.31	0.33
Oilseeds	Mustard	4.54	1.85	1.09	0.54	1.78	1.78	0.33	0.64	0.23	0.19
	Cottonseed	0.59	2.01	0.24	0.32	—	—	0.86	—	0.38	0.02
	Sunflower	1.08	1.08	0.47	0.49	1.31	0.25	0.52	0.11	0.31	0.20
	Soybean	3.14	5.45	0.46	1.17	1.24	1.45	0.49	0.52	0.22	0.07
	Groundnut	4.79	2.05	0.68	0.52	2.72	1.64	0.34	0.43	0.28	0.13

Source: Extracted by authors from report of Indian Council of Agricultural Research (ICAR) on Post-Harvest Loss in 2012 and 2015.

lack of adequate storage facilities, the country faces product loss to the extent of 6.0–10 per cent of total production (Nanda et al. 2012). Tables 10.2 and 10.3 present the percentage loss of selected fruits and vegetables during farm operation and storage.

Table 10.2 *Percentage Loss of Fruits*

	Loss in Farm Operation		Loss in Storage		Total Loss	
Crop	2012	2015	2012	2015	2012	2015
Apple	11.06	9.08	1.20	1.31	12.26	10.39
Banana	4.18	6.04	2.42	1.72	6.60	7.76
Grapes	6.57	6.52	1.73	2.11	8.30	8.63
Guava	13.92	10.90	4.13	3.98	18.05	15.88
Mango	10.64	6.92	2.11	2.24	12.74	9.16
Papaya	5.06	4.12	2.28	2.58	7.34	6.70

Source: Extracted by authors from ICAR report on Post-Harvest Loss in 2012 and 2015.

Table 10.3 *Percentage Loss of Vegetables*

	Loss in Farm Operation		Loss in Storage		Total Loss	
Crop	2012	2015	2012	2015	2012	2015
Cabbage	4.61	6.81	2.33	2.56	6.94	9.37
Cauliflower	4.85	7.55	2.03	2.00	6.88	9.56
Green pea	8.58	5.72	1.70	1.73	10.28	7.45
Mushroom	10.03	7.32	1.51	2.19	12.54	9.51
Onion	5.17	6.05	2.34	2.16	7.51	8.20
Potato	6.73	6.54	2.26	0.78	8.99	7.32
Tomato	9.94	9.41	3.04	3.03	12.98	12.44

Source: Extracted by authors from ICAR report on Post-Harvest Loss in 2012 and 2015.

In view of the substantial post-harvest losses of farm products in India, there is an urgent need to invest in the post-harvest value chain that ensures adequate management facilities of the farm products at various stages right from production to marketing. The public provision of these facilities is not sufficient, which necessitates the private investments in the farm sector. The government of India has now allowed private investments in the post-harvest supply chain of farm output. As a result of such initiatives, the Indian farm sector has been witnessing involvement of the private/corporate sector in the entire post-harvest value chain, particularly in fruits and vegetables. For instance, Field Fresh Foods Private Limited, a joint venture under Bharti Enterprises and Del Monte Pacific Limited, marked its presence in 2004 to connect the Indian farm sector to the world market. Since 2010, it has been rendering services to the farmers through contract farming right from cultivation to marketing of fresh fruits and vegetables in both domestic and international markets. It takes special care in harvesting, handling, transporting, storing, grading, packaging and research so that the products acquire international quality standards. Presently, many large corporations have penetrated in the Indian farm sector, which are at work, to establish a supply chain to bring out farm products from the field to the market. Apart from the Bharti Enterprises, players like Reliance, Aditya Birla Group, Namdhari, ITC, Adani Group and Germany's Metro Cash and Carry have been showing their presence in both wholesale and retail marketing of Indian farm products.

10.4. MARKETING OF FARM OUTPUT IN INDIA AND THE AGRICULTURAL PRODUCE MARKETING COMMITTEES

Problems associated with marketing of farm products have been the long-standing difficulties faced by farmers, particularly marginal and small farmers, in developing countries like India. Markets for farm output in these countries are plagued by various infrastructural lacunae, mostly transportation bottlenecks, access to markets and lack of operational storage facilities, which prevent farmers from directly accessing the markets for selling their products. This provides for the emergence of a number of marketing intermediaries that facilitate a connection between the farmers and the end consumers. With many marketing intermediaries, the supply chain/marketing channels get elongated, reducing the share of farmers in the price paid by the consumers, on the one hand, and increases the time gap from harvesting to marketing causing substantial post-harvest losses, on the other.

The government of India has been taking initiatives from time to time for tackling such problems of marketing of agricultural produce and ensuring remunerative prices to the farmers. As part of such initiatives, the APMCs[5] were formed in different states of the country under the aegis of the Agricultural Produce Marketing Act (APMA). Farmers were allowed to sell their products in the market yards and/or *mandis* designated by the APMCs by paying a fee. Though the step was for improving the farmers' lot by providing them specific market areas, it did not bring them much fruit in reality. It was found that the APMCs started exercising monopoly as farmers had to compulsorily sell through the APMCs. Instead of eliminating intermediaries in the marketing channel, APMCs actually made way for a number of commission agents who charged high commissions from the farmers for bringing the products to the market. In fact, farmers had to pay high fees, cess and commissions that reduced their returns. The required marketing infrastructure was also alleged to be at a dismal level in the APMC market areas. Besides, different markets under different APMCs were not interconnected, restricting farmers to reach out to a national common market for farm products. More importantly, the erstwhile situation did not encourage the involvement of private investments in both production and marketing of farm products, which remained as one of the hindrances in injecting competition in the farm sector of India to become internationally competitive.

---

[5] After independence, many Indian states formed Agricultural Produce Market Committees (APMCs) in every market area for agricultural products, which were constituted under Agricultural Produce Markets Regulation (APMR) Acts enacted by the respective state governments. The prime objective of these APMCs was to formulate rules and regulations for facilitating farm output marketing and safeguarding farmers from the exploitation by market intermediaries.

All these problems called for reforms in the farm sector of India both internally and externally. Internally, reforms were due in the sector to attract both public and private investments for improving pre- and post-harvest amenities and, more specifically, for the betterment of marketing infrastructure and consolidation of agricultural markets. Externally, reforms in the sector were felt as necessary to enhance the competitiveness of Indian agriculture, which has become extremely important in view of the liberalization of trade in agricultural commodities by the World Trade Organization (WTO; Chand 2020).

In order to initiate the process of the much felt reforms in the marketing of farm products, the Government of India enacted the APMC Act, 2003, whose prime objectives were as follows:

1. to facilitate the emergence of an efficient marketing system for agricultural products,
2. to promote the export of agricultural and agro-processed products and
3. to formulate rules and guidelines to set a mechanism for marketing of farm products.

Under this Act, respective state governments may accord permission to individuals, organizations, growers and local authorities to start a new market for agricultural products in an area under the jurisdiction of an APMC. Buyers and sellers are allowed to carry out marketing of farm products such as pulses, cereals, edible oilseed, fruits and vegetables and even goat, sheep, chicken, fish and sugar within the jurisdiction of the APMC area by paying a fee to the APMC. The APMC Act of 2003 seeks to reform the earlier APMC Acts by removing the restriction imposed on farmers to compulsorily sell their produce through the APMCs or intermediaries licensed by the APMCs. Thus, the APMC Act of 2003 reduces the monopoly exercised by the APMCs making the farmers free to choose whether they sell their products through the APMCs or through any other channel. Additionally, this model Act also provides for establishment of consumer–farmer markets where farmers can sell directly to the end consumers and remain free from the exploitation by the commission agents and the marketing intermediaries. As for another measure, instead of collecting various taxes, fees, charges and cess from the traders, the model APMC Act suggests for collecting only a market fee, the proceeds of which are to be used in providing and improving infrastructural amenities such as auction houses, weigh bridges, storehouses, retail shops, canteens, roads, lights, water supply and toilets. Levying only a market fee is expected to further the process of establishing a national common market for farm products (GOI 2015).

The APMC Act of 2003 also aimed at stimulating private investments in provisioning of markets and marketing infrastructures for an improved post-harvest management mechanism of agricultural products in the country. By allowing private parties to enter into the marketing mechanism of agricultural products, the Act actually wanted to achieve twin objectives: first, to add to the public provision of marketing facilities and, second, to reduce the monopoly exercised by the APMCs, thereby reducing farmers' excessive dependence on the APMC intermediaries.

What is noteworthy here is that even after the directives to the state governments to amend their existing agricultural marketing provisions as per the provisions of the model APMC Act, 2003, such provisions are yet to be implemented by some of the states. In states where some modifications have been undertaken in the existing marketing facilities, all the suggested changes by the model APMC Act have not been fully followed. In fact, some stakeholders and vested interest groups involved in the marketing of agri-products are allegedly not in favour of liberalizing markets from the existing APMCs and the *mandi* system. Consequently, the Indian farmers still depend heavily on the APMCs and the *mandis* for disposing of their produces. Apart from the partial implementation of the model APMC Act, 2003, and the consequent inability to make the farmers free from the *mandi*s and the APMCs, the model act remains ineffective in bringing some other required changes in the marketing of agricultural products on several grounds. First, notwithstanding the objective of the model APMC Act to establish a national common market for agricultural commodities, it still has to go a long way to put in place even a state-level common market for such commodities. One of the reasons behind this is that the Act retains the compulsory requirement that the buyers have to pay the APMC charges, irrespective of selling within or outside the APMC area. Though the sellers are not charged directly, the burden of these charges on buyers finally falls on the farmers as the buyers' bids are discounted to the extent of the payments made to the APMC and commission agents.

Second, the provision of the model Act to allow the private sector to establish markets for agricultural commodities has not gone far in infusing competition for the APMCs. This is because the fees collected by the private providers are generally higher as they collect two sets of fees. The first set comprises the market fees collected from the buyers/sellers on behalf of the APMCs, and the second set of fees are collected by the private market owners for providing the marketing amenities and related services.

Thus, the effectiveness of the model APMC Act in setting up a national common market for agricultural products is under question. It is worth mentioning here that the Government of India put in place another effort in 2016 to connect the farmers across states through an electronic platform under the banner of Electronic National Market for Agriculture (eNAM). This electronic platform was expected to connect the farmers with a national market, but in reality, eNAM is yet to be fully operational in facilitating a national market for agriculture. As a result, the absence of an easily accessible national common market has still remained as a factor of farmers' distress in India. As such, there is a need for both the central and respective state governments to act in tandem to design a mechanism, which can ensure hassle-free disposal of farm products even outside the APMC market areas, ensuring remunerative prices to the farmers. The participation of community-based organizations (CBOs) like farmer associations and non-governmental organizations (NGOs) in agricultural marketing may be instrumental in eliminating monopoly of the APMCs and making marketing easy. Such organizations may facilitate marketing through enhancing the capacity of the farmers, farmer groups or farmer communities, establishing links of the traders and related stakeholders with the marketing channel and making farmers aware of modern farming technologies and relevant market information (Kindness and Gordon 2001).

As for the recent move towards bringing in the much-needed changes/reforms in agricultural marketing, the Government of India passed two farm laws and took steps to modify the Essential Commodities Act of 1951 in September 2020. More specifically, these three farm laws were conceived to make changes in the market regulating framework and abolish the restrictions put by the APMC Act in some states. The Farmers' Produce Trade and Commerce (Promotion and Facilitation) Act (FPTC Act), 2020, was intended to allow selling and buying of farm produce anywhere in India within or outside the APMC *mandis*. The Act was supposed to encourage the introduction of electronic platforms to start e-commerce in agricultural products. Thus, this Act was expected to reduce the excessive dependence of farmers on intermediaries and APMCs, on the one hand, and easy marketing of their produce, on the other.

The Farmers' Empowerment and Protection Agreement on Price Assurance and Farm Services (APAFS) Act, 2020, was another newly introduced farm law, which wanted to allow contract farming through agreements between farmers and agribusiness firms with assurance of paying the farmers the price as agreed between them prior to production and providing required services and inputs to the farmers on mutually set terms and conditions. Although private parties would be allowed to penetrate into agricultural activities, their role, under this Act, was perceived to be restricted in buying the produce at the price agreed before production and facilitating required inputs and services.

The third newly introduced Farm Act, that is, the Essential Commodities (Amendment) Act, 2020, was none but a modified version of the erstwhile Essential Commodities Act introduced way back in 1955. Under the old Act, matters related to production, supply and distribution of the enlisted essential commodities are controlled, and no one is allowed to hoard such products and increase prices in situations of shortage and emergencies. Amendment of the earlier Act brought modifications into the coverage of essential commodities, removing foodstuffs such as cereals, pulses, potato, onion, edible oilseeds and oils from the essential commodity list. As per the Act, the central government would regulate the supply of the essential commodities only in situation of emergencies such as war, famine, extraordinary price rise and natural calamities.

However, the introduction of the three farm laws has been vehemently protested by a section of farmers, farmers' associations and stakeholders across states mainly on the ground that the changes are imposed without consulting with the farmers, states and the stakeholders. Leaders of farmer groups, especially in Punjab and Haryana, expressed their concerns that the new Act would withdraw the system of public procurement of farm products through minimum support price (MSP) and would pave the way for big private parties to capture the field. The Essential Commodities (Amendment) Act, 2020, has been criticized that the Act would confer powers to the stockists and market manipulators to control the supply and prices of essential commodities. Amidst year-long apprehensions and farmers' protests, the prime minister of India has announced repealing of the three farm laws on 19 November 2021. Subsequently, the Farm Laws Repeal Bill, 2021, has been passed by the parliament on 29 November 2021. However, after the passing of the Farm Laws Repeal Bill, 2021, protesting farmers and opposition leaders are demanding discussions on farmers' problems in the parliament, specifically about legalization of MSP of farm products.

With the passing of the Farm Laws Repeal Bill, 2021, by the parliament, the process of initiating reforms in the farm sector of India as intended by the three farm laws of 2021 has come to a standstill. Keeping aside the contents of these farm laws, there is no denial of the fact that the farm sector needs urgent changes/reforms in the post-harvest management chain so as to minimize product losses, add value and ensure that the farmers are free from the shackle of the APMCs and commission agents. Moreover, encouraging private investments not only in production but also in post-harvest management is extremely important, which would enable farmers to competitively participate in the international value chain of farm products. Additionally, there is a need to consolidate the existing APMC markets across states, which would follow a common fee structure, thereby giving a step forward to establish a national common market for agricultural commodities. This would definitely pose a challenge before the central and state governments in bringing in the required reforms in the farm sector, satisfying the farmers' greater interests as well as enhancing the sector's capacity to contribute to the economy of the country.

10.5. CONCLUSION

There has been a significant shift in the demand pattern towards processed and high-value food products. Farmers have to keep track with such changes and take measures accordingly to add value to their produce. This is extremely important for increment in farmer's income through enhancing quality and price of their output, on the one hand, and extending the shelf life of agricultural commodities, on the other, which are mostly perishable otherwise. Adding value to the agricultural products requires the act of putting them in a value chain even before harvesting. The value chain starts from choosing the right time and method of harvesting and then going through steps such as harvesting, preliminary processing, storage, final processing and ends with their marketing.

The Indian farmers are yet to take advantage of enhancing quality and value of their produce extensively. A number of factors have been acting as stumbling blocks in post-harvest management of their products. Use of conventional harvesting techniques, limited awareness and ability for primary processing, dearth in storage, especially cold storage facilities, lack of use of modern processing technologies and marketing bottlenecks are some of the factors among a huge set of its kind that are actually restricting Indian farmers from putting their output in an efficient post-harvest management chain.

Although initiatives have been taken at the government level to address the marketing bottlenecks that are faced by Indian farmers through setting up of the APMCs, the functioning of the APMCs are still under doubt. Even today, farmers remain largely dependent on the existing *mandi* system and commission agents for the disposal of their produce, which exerts a negative influence on their income and incentives. The three newly introduced farm laws intended to put in place a few reforms in the existing system of marketing through the markets and agents commissioned by the APMCs, encourage private investors to allow contract farming and redefine the coverage of essential commodities but have been withdrawn amidst farmers' agitations. This has retained the required reforms in the farm sector as the far cry posing a challenge before the country—how to reach the twin objectives of improving the farmers' lot and enhancing the contribution of the sector to the gross domestic product (GDP) of India, making the sector internationally competitive.

REFERENCES

Bhoi, B. K., and C. L. Dadhich. 2019. '*Agrarian Distress in India: Possible Solutions*'. Mumbai: Indira Gandhi Institute of Development Research.

Boss, R., and M. Pradhan. 2020. 'Post-harvest Management and Farm Outcomes'. *Economic & Political Weekly* 55, no. 16. https://www.epw.in/journal/2020/16/commentary/post-harvest-management-and-farm-outcomes.html (accessed on 21 February 2022).

Chand, Ramesh. 2020, November. 'New Farm Acts: Understanding the Implications'. NITI Aayog Working Paper Series 1/2020. Government of India.

Confederation of Indian Industry. 2019. 'Indian Food Processing Sector- Trends and Opportunities'. Food and Agriculture Centre of Excellence. https://face-cii.in/wp-content/uploads/2021/09/food_processing_report_2019.pdf (accessed on 21 February 2022).

Food and Agriculture Organization (FAO). 2011. *Global Food Losses and Food Waste: Extent, Causes and Prevention.* Rome: Food and Agriculture Organization of The United Nations. https://www.fao.org/3/i2697e/i2697e.pdf (accessed on 21 February 2022).

Ganesh, U., M. Shankar, S. Benarji, K. Mahadevan, S. Borthakur, C. Thukral, and S. Yadav. 2016. 'Reducing Post-harvest Losses in India: Key Initiative and Opportunities'. Rockefeller Foundation. Intellcap. http://www.intellecap.com/publications/reducing-post (accessed on 10 May 2021).

Government of India (GOI). 2015. 'Economic Survey 2014–15'. New Delhi: GOI, 117–118.

———. 2020. *All India Report on Agricultural Census 2015–16.* Department of Agriculture, Cooperation and Farmers Welfare, Ministry of Agriculture and Farmers Welfare, Government of India. https://agcensus.nic.in/document/

agcen1516/ac_1516_report_final-220221.pdf (accessed on 21 February 2022).

Hegazy, R. 2013. 'Post-harvest Situation and Losses in India.' https://www.researchgate.net/publication/301770292_Post- harvest_Situation_and_Losses_in_India (accessed 11 May 2021).

Hodges, R. J., J. C. Buzby, and B. Bennet. 2011. 'Postharvest Losses and Waste in Developed and Less Developed Countries: Opportunities to Improve Resource Use'. *Journal of Agricultural Science* 149: 37–45.

Jain, V., S. K. Sharma, B. S., Manvi, and G. Gandhi. 2015. 'Food Grain Storage in India: Problems and Prospects'. Modern Agro-Technologies for Nutritional Security and Health. Solah. https://www.researchgate.net/publication/312383680_Food_Grain_Storage_in_India_Problems_and_Prospects (accessed 21 February 2022).

Jha S. N., R. K. Vishwakarma, T. Ahmed, A. Rai, and A. K. Dixit. 2015. *Report on Assessment of Quantitative Harvest and Post-harvest Losses of Major Crops and Commodities in India*. Ludhiana: All India Coordinated Research Project on Post-Harvest Technology (ICAR CIPHET).

Kader, A. A. 2002. *Postharvest Technology of Horticulture Crops*, 3rd ed. Oakland, CA: University of California Agriculture and Natural Resources.

Kakaty, G. and D. Borah. 2011. 'Impact of Emerging Marketing Channels in Agriculture-Benefit to Producer-Sellers and Marketing Costs and Margins of Orange and Potato in Assam'. Assam Agricultural University Study No. 139. http://www.aau.ac.in/data/reports/Impact_of-EmergingMarketingChannels.pdf (accessed on 21 February 2022).

Kannan, E. 2014. *Assessment of Pre and Post-harvest Losses of Important Crops in India.* Bangalore: Agricultural Development and Rural Transformation Centre and Institute for Social and Economic Change.

Kasso, M., and A. Bekele. 2018. 'Post-harvest Loss and Quality Deterioration of Horticultural Crops in Dire Dawa Region, Ethiopia'. *Journal of the Saudi Society of Agricultural Sciences* 17: 88–96.

Kiaya, V. 2014. 'Post-harvest Losses and Strategies to Reduce Them'. Technical Paper, Scientific and Technical Department, Action Contre la Faim (ACF). https://www.actioncontrelafaim.org/wp-content/uploads/2018/01/technical_paper_phl__.pdf (accessed 21 February 2022).

Kindness, H., and A. Gordon. 2001, February. 'Agricultural Marketing in Developing Countries: The Role of NGOS and CBOS.' Natural Resources Institute. https://assets.publishing.service.gov.uk/media/57a08d2d40f0b652dd0017e4/R7941002.pdf (accessed on 21 February 2022).

Kumar, Praduman.1998. 'Food Demand and Supply Projections for India'. Agricultural Economics Policy Paper 98-01, New Delhi: Indian Agricultural Research Institute.

Meenakshi, J. V. 1996, 14 December. 'How Important Are Changes in Taste: A State-level Analysis of Food Demand'. *Economic & Political Weekly*, 3265–3269. https://www.jstor.org/stable/4404884 (accessed on 21 February 2022).

Murthy, K. N. 2000. 'Changes in Taste and Demand Pattern for Cereals'. *Agricultural Economics Research Review* 13, no. 1: 26–53.

Nanda, S. K., R. K. Viswakarma, H. V. L. Bathla, A. Rai, and P. Chandra. 2012. *Harvest and Post Harvest Losses of Major Crops and Livestock Produce in India*. Ludhiana: All India Coordinated Research Project on Post Harvest Technology, Indian Council of Agricultural Research (ICAR).

Radhakrishna, R., and C. Ravi. 1992. 'Effects of Growth, Relative Price and Preferences of Food and Nutrition'. *Indian Economic Review* 27: 303–323.

Rao, C. H. Hanumantha. 2000, 22 January. 'Declining Demand for Foodgrains in Rural India: Causes and Implications'. *Economic & Political Weekly*: 201–206. https://www.jstor.org/stable/4408846 (accessed on 21 February 2022).

Chapter 11

Picking up the Threads

Madhurjya Prasad Bezbaruah

What markets essentially do is to correct the imbalances in the endowments in the hands of the economic agents. Had each agent, be it an individual, a household, a firm or a government, possessed different resources in the proportion it wanted the resources to be in, there would be no need to exchange anything for something else and, hence, there would be no role for markets to play. However, in reality, agents often possess some commodities in excess of their requirements but other commodities in less than the optimal quantities. Markets give agents the platform to exchange commodities possessed in excess of requirements for commodities, which are possessed in less than required quantities. Under ideal circumstances, a system of competitive markets, in which prices are determined through competitive bargaining among buyers and sellers, allocates resources of the economy among their users in an efficient manner.

In this volume, we have seen that markets of factors used in agricultural production in India have been evolving and also growing in numbers. This in itself is a positive development, because as factors of production are traded among farmers and owners of the factors, their allocations get more optimally distributed among farms. The emergence of a new factor market means new opportunities for reducing resource imbalances across farm households. On the other hand, deepening of an existing market, in the sense of having more transactions in it both in numbers and in volumes, makes its price a better reflector of the relative scarcity or abundance of the resource. Having acknowledged the opportunities created by broadening and deepening of the market network, it is, however, necessary to admit that most markets related to agriculture, especially those of its factors of production, are often prone to distortions or imperfections, which limit their ability to return the most efficient outcomes. Such distortions and imperfections in different agricultural factor markets and the markets of key supporting services to agriculture in India, and the possible policy interventions to mitigate the imperfections, have been specifically discussed in the individual chapters of this volume. This concluding chapter is an attempt to gather the policy approaches for improving the market outcomes of different agricultural factor markets as parts of a holistic package.

Traditionally, the two most significant factor markets in agriculture have been the market for agricultural land and the market for agricultural labour. Land being the primary input in agriculture, let us begin by summarizing our findings regarding the land markets. Agricultural land has two types of markets. One is the short-term land-lease markets or land rental markets. The other one is the market for land sale, where the ownership of agricultural land is transacted.

The more active of the two types of land markets is the land rental market. In post-independence India, the land rental market has been subjected to many restrictions. As a result, the market has not been able to function freely. When India attained independence, it was predominantly a rural economy with widespread poverty and inequality. In that rural setting, land used to be, as it still significantly is, a very important asset. But most of the village land used to be held by a few landlords. The consequent agrarian structure was generally non-conducive for either efficient or equitable use of land. So, the federal and state governments in independent India soon initiated land reforms, which were aimed at eliminating the inefficiencies and securing more equitable order in rural societies. Since tenant farmers were seen as victims of exploitation, the tenancy reforms adopted by different states were targeted at protecting the interest of the sharecroppers and other tenant farmers. While some states limited themselves to putting an upper limit on the land rent, some others went to the extent of completely prohibiting sharecropping and tenancy. However, tenancy survived as it had been of use for farmers at both ends of the distribution of village land. While small and marginal farmers need to add more land to their smallholdings for fuller utilization of their family labour, the bigger landowners needed to lease out the land they could not cultivate themselves. The policymakers, well-meaning as they were, were either oblivious or chose to overlook this practical role of leasing in and leasing out of land. Consequently, restrictions imposed on leasing actually drove tenancy underground and informal. This in turn meant that the tenant farmers were unable to take the advantage of the protection the law intended to provide them. Meanwhile, land rental markets continued to survive and even thrive albeit with inefficiencies traceable to the tenancy laws. The policymakers and researchers are now talking about the need for reforms to liberate the land-lease market from the anachronistic restrictions, so that the more efficient and sustainable outcomes both in the short and in the long run can be achieved.

The markets for outright transfer of ownership of agricultural land have generally been thinner in the sense that transactions in these markets are rather infrequent. The thinness of these markets and other imperfections that vitiate these markets render the prices recorded in land transfer transactions poor reflectors of the true value of land parcels. The inefficacy of the prices thrown up in land sale markets severely limits their usefulness in designing compensation packages for land acquisition for infrastructure and industrial projects. Recent legislative attempts to amend the situation have not yielded a practicable solution. In view of the impasse, solutions based on auction process or long-term leasing suggested by some researchers have been advocated for experimental trials. Such trials can be followed up with refinements for innovating more satisfactory and practical land acquisition procedures.

The markets for agricultural labour have fewer a priori reasons for imperfections as there usually are many suppliers and reasonably good number of demanders meeting the basic requirements of competitive market structures. Yet, several imperfections can be seen in the market for labour in rural India. Landless agricultural workers constitute the poorest sections of India's rural societies, and they are often trapped in the intersectionality of the land, labour and credit markets of India's rural set-up. As a result of the interlocked nature of these markets, many workers do not enjoy the voluntary choice of participation and/or the bargaining power in the labour market. Notwithstanding some short spans of rise in real wages of agricultural workers, these wages have generally tended to stagnate. Moreover, social hierarchies along caste and gender lines prevalent in Indian society also spill over to these markets. The quickened pace of structural transformation of the Indian economy post-2000 might have eased the stranglehold on agricultural workers to some extent by broadening their options for some horizontal, if not vertical, mobility. Given that some of the distortions of the markets for agricultural labour arise from the interlocked nature of the rural market systems, reforms for better functioning of the agricultural labour markets in India will have to be concomitantly pursued with reforms in related markets of rural credit and land rental. Hence, reforms of the rural and agricultural factor markets need to be viewed as a comprehensive single undertaking with interventions introduced in one market complementing interventions in other markets. The other distortions arising from more stubborn social divisions will take more time to correct. But the ongoing migration from farm to non-farm sectors can eventually create the conditions for markets to function in a less distorted manner.

The two sets of markets, which have emerged more recently or perhaps become more visible in recent times, are the water markets and rental markets for farm machineries and equipment. With India moving to a market-oriented economic system since the early 1990s, the economic environment became conducive for different market structures to emerge and expand. In the domain of factor markets in agriculture, we have seen the emergence of water markets and rental markets of farm machineries. Both the sets of markets have been contributing to the better utilization of agricultural technologies by both large and small firms. Small farmers, who otherwise are not able to make the necessary investment to mechanize their farming operations, are able to use the advance technology by buying irrigation water from farmers with excess water availability and hiring farm machinery in the rental markets. The bigger farmers are also benefitted from extra earnings from selling the spare water from their irrigation systems and renting out of the excess capacity of the farm machinery at their disposal. Water markets have, however, demonstrated some negative environmental externalities, especially in regions where the groundwater resources are less abundant, and/or aquifer replenishment is insufficient. In such regions, it is necessary to put appropriate regulations in place to ensure sustainability of water extraction and use. A free run of water markets in such regions can have disastrous environmental consequences. But in those parts of the country where the monsoon precipitations are plentiful and emptied aquifers are quickly replenished, environmental externalities are less severe and often negligible. Accordingly, the need to regulate the markets is less compulsive. The rental markets of farm machineries are generally free from major market failures. Though these markets have not been extensively studied as yet, the available evidence suggests that these markets have been functioning fairly effectively and efficiently.

Unlike the rental markets of firm machineries or the water markets, the market of the very important supporting service to farmers, namely extension service, did not emerge spontaneously in India. In the absence of a market for this critical service for technology transfer from laboratories and experimental centres to farmers' fields, governments in India did well by coming forward to strengthen the extension service wings under their agricultural departments. Government-run extension services in tandem with the agricultural universities played a pivotal role in making the Green Revolution in India a resounding success. It may be recalled that the revolution transformed India from a country of chronic food shortage to one that was self-sufficient in key cereals of mass consumption in a matter of just a decade from the late 1960s to the late 1970s. As a conduit between research and experiment for adaptation, the new farm technology for the Indian farming conditions and application of the technology in farmers' fields, the public sector extension service played a crucial role in the country's drive towards food security. Following India embarking upon a market-oriented economic reform agenda in 1991, there was reorientation of the role of the state in its economy. As fiscal profligacy of the governments was seen as a main cause of the economic crisis preceding these reforms, rationalization of public expenditure and better targeting of government subsidies were introduced in the reform programme as an important component. Unfortunately, this component of reforms hit the extension service, as allocation for this important activity ceased to be as liberal as before. Independent markets for providing agricultural extension service did not emerge to fill the void created by reduced intensity of government-provided exertion service. As a result, farmers started to depend on input suppliers for their farming advice. The resulting conflict of interest arising from input suppliers doubling up as extension service providers can breed the hazard of farmers succumbing to excessive input use and adopting unsustainable practices. Before this potential danger manifests with disastrous consequences, it has become imperative to revive the state-provided extension service and also facilitate the development of independent markets supplying the service. As a new generation of technological breakthrough waits round the corner to be ushered in, strengthening of extension service network has assumed greater urgency.

Two other markets of India's rural economy, which have a significant impact on farm outcome and farmers' lives are the rural credit market and the agricultural insurance market. Markets for credit and insurance are, in general, notorious for distortions, originating from asymmetric information and hidden action. In India's rural set-up, imperfections of these markets are further compounded due to the interlocked nature of the rural factor markets.

For insurance, there is the additional problem arising from the fact that production risks of farmers in a locality are typically interrelated across farms. Because of this special problem in insuring agricultural production, the market is unlikely to provide much supply at affordable premium. It is, hence, necessary for the state to come forward to subsidize the insurance premiums. While the Government of India has floated successive schemes for crop insurance, insurance penetration into India's farm sector has remained shallow. As discussed in detail in Chapter 9 of this volume, the problem of insurance market for farmers is not limited to only insufficient supply offers. However, demand for insurance has not been an issue because of communication gaps and lack of awareness about the nature of the insurance business, and individual farmers' requirements for crop insurance covers do not get adequately translated into market demand for insurance. This phenomenon is sometimes mistaken as a lack of demand for crop insurance among farmers.

The structure of insurance business in India is oligopolistic in nature with a few large firms controlling practically the entire volume. It is natural for these large operators to find insuring myriads of small landholders inconvenient and transaction cost intensive. So apart from government support in the form of premium subsidization, there is a need for innovations of delivery of the insurance service at the grassroots. Here, the insurance market can take a leaf out of institutional innovation in the credit markets to reach out to the micro and tiny operators. It is well known that banks, instead of dealing directly with the large number of small borrowers, lend in lumpy amounts to microfinance institutions and self-help groups, who in turn reach out to the small and micro-clients. Despite microfinance operations having their own set of issues in the field from time to time, a parallel micro-insurance model is worth experimenting with.

Coming back to the rural credit market in India, it is worth noting that the market has seen many government-initiated and spontaneously emerging institutional developments over the years. Nationalization of major commercial banks way back in 1969, innovating regional rural banks and extending their network nationally and imposition of minimum quota for priority sector lending are some notable state-induced initiatives for percolation of institutional credit to agriculture and other rural sectors. Arrival of microfinance and self-help groups added a semiformal arm to the banking sector of the country to reach out to the micro- and tiny units in both rural and urban areas. Given the challenges of ensuring credit and insurance services to the farmers at the grassroots, further institutional fine-tuning will be required for making delivery of these services more reliable for farmers and financially sustainable for the providers. Unfortunately, positive developments in the rural credit markets have been periodically distorted by populist political interferences. The promise of loan waiver by political parties made from time to time, primarily for attracting votes in elections, are generally detrimental to repayment discipline and hence obstructive for healthy growth of the rural credit markets. It is time to free these markets from politically motivated distortions and allow them to evolve and expand further with proper checks and balances for guarding against the usual moral hazards and adverse selections.

Apart from discussing these factor markets, a chapter in the volume has been devoted to discussions on the supporting services of the post-harvest value chain for agricultural products. These services have assumed greater importance than ever before as a result of the compositional change in Indian agriculture and also a compositional change in the preference of the consumers in the country. Since consumers' preferences have shifted away from cereals towards less storable or more perishable horticultural and livestock products such as fruits, vegetables, milk, egg, fish and meat, the post-harvest value chain has become extremely important. Right from harvesting, processing and further value addition to reaching out to the ultimate consumer, the value chain has many links that need to be developed and/or strengthened further. There have been state-induced and independently emerging arrangements for meeting the needs of the post-harvest disposal of different types of farm products. Co-operatives, farmer producer companies and contract farming systems have had successes and failures from situations to situations. It is necessary to learn from the experience of these institutions and replicated them with suitable local contextualization.

The land and labour markets, the most basic of the agricultural factor markets, have had a considerable amount of inherited issues in India. These issues deserve urgent attention in view of the quickened pace of structural transformation of the Indian economy in the first two decades of the 21st century. As India started to shift to a market-oriented economic system in the last decade of the 20th century, new factor markets quietly emerged in rural areas, which have been contributing to the growth and resilience of agriculture in the country by enabling greater participation of even the smaller farmers in technological transformation of the sector. Now, similar developments are needed in the field of extension services also. The country waits for the emergence of independent suppliers of extension services, which can play a very crucial role in ushering in both evolutionary and revolutionary technological innovations, which are emerging in response to challenges of resource scarcity, productivity stagnancy and climate change. Reforms of the credit and insurance markets to increase their penetrations and effectiveness are also needed. The post-harvest value chain, which has several weak links, need to be further strengthened, so that the Indian agriculture can move ahead in performing its due role in the increasingly dynamic economy of the country.

About the Editors and Contributors

EDITORS

Anup Kumar Das is Assistant Professor in the Department of Economics, Rajiv Gandhi University (RGU), Arunachal Pradesh, since 2012. Before joining RGU, he served as an assistant professor in Rangia College, Assam, for a period of four years. He completed both MA and PhD from Gauhati University, Assam. The areas of his research interest are agricultural economics and rural development. He has published research papers in journals such as *India Journal of Agricultural Economics*, *Bangladesh Development Studies*, *Indian Journal of Human Development*, *Agricultural Economics Research Review*, and *Journal of Land and Rural Studies,* besides contributing some chapters to edited books.

Binoy Goswami is currently Senior Assistant Professor in the Faculty of Economics, South Asian University (SAU), New Delhi. His teaching and research interests include agricultural economics, environmental economics, international trade and macroeconomics. His publications include one authored book on Assam's agriculture titled *Economic Analysis of Agrarian Institutions: The Case of Tenancy* (2017) and one edited book titled *Indian Agriculture after the Green Revolution: Changes and Challenges* (2018). He has also published several research papers in peer-reviewed national and international journals.

Madhurjya Prasad Bezbaruah is Professor of Economics in Gauhati University, Assam. He primarily teaches econometrics, microeconomics, environmental economics and macroeconomics. He has successfully supervised works of 31 doctoral scholars. His areas of research are primarily agricultural economics, environmental economics and issues of regional development. He has conducted individual and group research funded by UGC, ICSSR, UNDP, Planning Commission, the 13th Finance Commission and UNICEF, and he has also conducted environmental impact assessments for Oil India Ltd, IOCL and ONGC. He is currently a member of the ICSSR, vice-president of the Indian Econometric Society and a member of the Research Programs Committee of the Indian Society of Agricultural Economics. He has served as a member in boards/committees of the Government of Assam and RBI, and academic councils of several universities/institutes.

CONTRIBUTORS

Prasenjit Bujar Baruah is Assistant Professor in the Department of Economics, RGU, Itanagar, Arunachal Pradesh, India.

Mrinal Kanti Dutta is Professor in the Department of Humanities and Social Sciences, Indian Institute of Technology, Guwahati, Assam, India.

Sumit Ghosh is Assistant Professor in the Department of Economics, BHB College, Sarupeta, Assam, India.

Maheshwar Giri is a PhD scholar at the Faculty of Economics, SAU, New Delhi, India.

Binod Goswami is Assistant Professor in the Department of Economics, Nowgong Girls' College, Nagaon, Assam, India.

Faridus Mamun Khan is a PhD scholar at the Department of Economics, Gauhati University, Guwahati, Assam, India.

Raju Mandal is Associate Professor in the Department of Economics, Assam University, Silchar, Assam, India.

Amiya Sarma is Assistant Professor in the Department of Economics, Gauhati University, Guwahati, Assam, India.

Abhijit Sharma is Associate Professor in the Indian Institute of Bank Management, Guwahati, Assam, India.

Jitu Tamuli is Assistant Professor in the Department of Economics, THB College, Jamugurihat, Assam, India.

Index